Bold Women
in
Montana History

BETH JUDY

D0877560

2017
Mountain Press Publishing Company
Missoula, Montana

Library of Congress Cataloging-in-Publication Data

Names: Judy, Beth, 1961- author.
Title: Bold women in Montana history / Beth Judy.
Description: Missoula, Montana : Mountain Press Publishing Company, 2017. |
  Includes index.
Identifiers: LCCN 2016059265 | ISBN 9780878426768 (pbk. : alk. paper)
Subjects: LCSH: Women—Montana—Biography. | Women—Montana—History. |
  Montana—Biography.
Classification: LCC CT3262.M9 J83 2017 | DDC 920.7209786—dc23
LC record available at https://lccn.loc.gov/2016059265

PRINTED IN THE UNITED STATES

MP Mountain Press
PUBLISHING COMPANY
P.O. Box 2399 • Missoula, MT 59806 • 406-728-1900
800-234-5308 • info@mtnpress.com
www.mountain-press.com

What a gift! With clear, concise language and impeccable research, Beth Judy offers unforgettable portraits of eleven remarkable women in Bold Women of Montana History. *This wonderful collection covers a diverse array of women warriors: politicians and poets, artists and rodeo riders. Meet Jeanette Rankin, the first woman elected to the U.S. Congress in 1916; Alma Smith Jacobs, Montana's first African American state librarian; Elouise Cobell, the Blackfeet accountant who successfully sued the BIA for misuse of millions of dollars in Indian trust funds. Judy's book is entertaining and inspiring, a testament to women whose visions are as expansive as our big sky.*

—CAROLINE PATTERSON
Editor of *Montana Women Writers: A Geography of the Heart*
and author of *Ballet at the Moose Lodge*

———•••———

In these engaging stories, Beth Judy brings to life some of Montana's boldest characters. She conveys in rich detail the ways in which ordinary women turned their curiosity, passion, and grit into extraordinary accomplishments that profoundly changed the face of Montana. Pleasure and inspiration abound in this book.

—MARY MURPHY
Distinguished Professor of History, Montana State University

———•••———

This valuable historical resource fills a role in educating Montana's youth about their state's history and women's contributions to it, passing these important stories down to future generations. In this book, Beth Judy makes history accessible and relatable, creating a great addition to any Montana history curriculum.

—PENNY REDLI
Executive Director,
Museum of the Beartooths

Bold women I am especially grateful to:

Mary Ann, my mother
Mary and Margaret (Peg), my grandmothers
Cindy, another mother
Carol, who I hitchhiked with
Hannah, who brought me books
Sanni, maker of hats and glogg

This is for you.

Contents

Acknowledgments

For help with writing and research, I am deeply grateful to: the Montana Historical Society, especially Ellen Baumler; the Missoula Public Library; the Mansfield Library, especially Archives and Special Collections; Margaret Kingsland; Mary Murphy; Alexei Carlisle; Dona Rutherford; Darnell and Smokey Rides at the Door; Cynthia Kipp; Gwen Florio; Thedis Crowe; Sally Thompson; George Price; Aaron LaFramboise; Jesse DesRosier; Judy Myllymaki; John Fitzgerald; Ernie Heavy Runner; Milo McLeod and Janene Caywood; Riley Auge; Cindy Stalcup; Deirdre Black; Sydney Bacon; Dee Garceau; Pat McDonald; Steve Neal; Kermit Edmonds; Museum of Military History (Missoula); Gene Felsman; Granite County Museum; Rick McGill; TJ Vietor; Kirby Mathew; Timothy McCleary; Bill and Karen Snell; Robyn Klein; Quita and Cony Pownall; Kaneeta Red Star; Tom Elpel; Jeannette Rankin Peace Center and Betsy Mulligan-Dague; the staff at Grant Creek Ranch; Cyndy Hull; Washington Corporation; Sue Lawrence and the Jeannette Rankin Foundation; Jo Jakupcak; Vivian Brooke; Lucille Knight; Ellen Crain and the Butte–Silver Bow Archives staff; Marilyn Maney Ross; Whitney Williams; Janet Finn; Bill Antonioli; Dave Emmons; John Truzzolino; Dick Gibson; Noorjahan Parwana; Mark Anderlik; Barbara Larsen; Cindi Shaw; Jill Gerdrum; Betsy Griffing; Clark Grant; George Everett; Susan Leaphart; Arnie Malina; Alexandra Swaney; Rick Newby; Leora Bar-El; Gene Fischer; Penny Redli and the Museum of the Beartooths; Laura Millin; Donna Forbes; Gordon McConnell; Sandra Dal Poggetto; Joe and Johanna Kern; Bill and Betty Hart; Jack Ross; Ted Waddell; Roxanne and Lee Dunn; the Montana Arts Council; Dan Aadland; Liz Harding; Ross Keogh; Caroline Patterson; Debbi and Albert Brown; Guynema Terry; Jay and Sandy Cahill; the Carbon County Museum; Doris Loeser;

Mary Lou LeCompte; Chuck and Nancy Henson; Jim Bainbridge; Kay Whitlock; Randi Rognlie; Mary Ann Judy; Virginia Griffing; Alan Thompson; Ruth Parker McClendon; Ken Robison; Patricia McNamer; the Great Falls History Center staff; Kathy Mora; Darlene Staffeldt; Maisha Winn; Candace Atwood; Joy Hamlett; Zita Bremner; Turk Cobell; Julene Kennerly; Jim Scott; Leslie Jensen; David Dragonfly; John McGill; Melissa Janko; Stone School Inn; Steve Smith; Germaine White; Thompson Smith; Kim Ericsson; and many more. Special thanks to editor Gwen McKenna, who invited me to do this book and vastly improved it; Jeannie Painter, Jennifer Carey, John Rimel, and everyone at Mountain Press; the Matthew Hansen Endowment for support; Stephanie Frostad for the beautiful, heartfelt cover art; and to my family and friends.

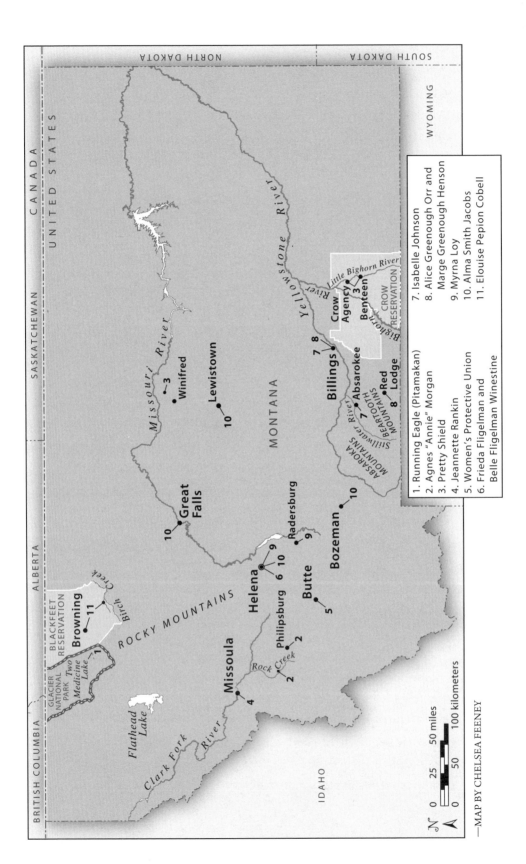

—MAP BY CHELSEA FEENEY

1. Running Eagle (Pitamakan)
2. Agnes "Annie" Morgan
3. Pretty Shield
4. Jeannette Rankin
5. Women's Protective Union
6. Frieda Fligelman and
   Belle Fligelman Winestine
7. Isabelle Johnson
8. Alice Greenough Orr and
   Marge Greenough Henson
9. Myrna Loy
10. Alma Smith Jacobs
11. Elouise Pepion Cobell

Introduction

My understanding of the word *bold* comes from my Irish grandmother, Margaret Hickey. She used it to describe anyone audacious and brave enough to do something out of the ordinary. Boldness usually requires strength—sometimes outer, physical strength, but always the inner kind, mental, emotional, and moral. It involves thinking for yourself and taking action, even if that action is a decision to wait or the nurturing of a dream. Boldness is not determined by its results, which can be praise—or disgrace. Though often associated with the public sphere, boldness can be just as challenging in private—say, in a relationship with a friend or loved one.

I tapped into some of my own boldness in writing this book. While the job was a dream come true, since I love Montana, Montana history, and women's history, there was a surprising lack of information about some of my subjects, so I had to dig extra deep while doing research, sometimes even traveling to where they had lived and talking with people who had known them. As a result, this book contains some new findings, from fresh clues to black homesteader Annie Morgan's background to details of Isabelle Johnson's childhood roots in art to the most complete biographies of Lena Mattausch and Bridget Shea to date. During the course of this research, I fell in love with each of my subjects. I felt honored to meet their descendants, step inside their former homes, or stand before their graves. Often it wasn't so much the women's achievements that moved me, but rather their courage in the face of hardship or even failure.

Every now and then in my research, I got a thrill when two of my subjects' lives touched. In Alma Snell's account of growing up with her grandmother, Pretty Shield, she describes her older sister Cerise laboring in front of the mirror, making herself up to look like Myrna

Loy. The government agency for the Crow Reservation, where Pretty Shield and Alma lived, was very near what would become, in less than five years, Isabelle Johnson's family ranch. Isabelle once noted, in her personal writing, Jeannette Rankin's run for office. Jeannette had a direct relationship with Belle Fligelman, who served as the congresswoman's secretary. Truly we are all connected—especially in Montana.

I hope that by reading this book, the courageous and creative decision-making of these Montana foremothers will rub off on you. May their stories inspire you to call forth, again and again, the boldness that is inside every one of us.

RUNNING EAGLE
(Pitamakan)

When winter comes in Montana and snow lies on the ground, it is time, among some Native Americans, to tell stories. Among the Amskapi Pikuni ("ahm-SKOP-ee bee-GUNN-ee), or Pikuni, also called the Blackfeet, of north-central Montana, some of those stories are about Pitamakan (bee-duh-maw-KHAWN), or Running Eagle, the famed woman warrior of their tribe. These tales of long ago tell how the girl born Brown Weasel Woman came to be the warrior called Running Eagle, and the storytellers, the oral historians of their people, recount some of her exploits and battles in great detail. She has been described as a tall and handsome young woman with fine war clothes of white buckskin decorated with dyed porcupine quills and a war bonnet of eagle feathers.

Running Eagle's story sounds like a legend, yet she was a real woman who lived at least two centuries ago. No one knows for sure the year she was born or what she looked like, and different sources disagree about the specifics of her life. A major source used for this chapter was *The Ways of My Grandmothers,* a 1980 book by Canadian Blackfoot tribal member Beverly Hungry Wolf. Her book, about women of the Blackfoot Confederacy, includes the tale of Running Eagle. Another important

Pitamakan Falls (also called Trick Falls), Glacier National Park —Photo by Rollin H. McKay (July 1939)

source was the historical marker at Pitamakan Falls, the waterfall in Glacier National Park that was named after Running Eagle. The story on the marker was composed by a team that included park officials, Blackfeet historians, and at least one of Running Eagle's descendants.

An older source is a book called *Running Eagle: The Warrior Girl* by James Willard Schultz, published in 1919. Schultz, a white man, lived for years among the Pikuni and based his book on stories he had heard from them. Such stories, passed down orally through generations, can, despite some uncertainties, be quite accurate.

Running Eagle was different from the other girls and women in her culture. From the time she was a child, the warrior life called to her strongly. Many of her people disapproved of her desire to hunt and fight battles, occupations that only men were supposed to embrace, and they discouraged her from pursuing her aspiration. Yet deep down, Running Eagle committed herself fully to her own path, never marrying or having kids as was expected of most Pikuni women. Eventually, because of her persistence, her people came to understand and accept her unusual choice, and they supported her as a warrior from then on. Her people still honor her today.

———•••———

The warrior known as Running Eagle was born Brown Weasel Woman, or Otaki (oo-daw-KEE). She is believed to have been the eldest of five children, three girls and two boys. According to James Willard Schultz's book, her father's name was Morning Plume, but this is not known for certain, and her mother's name is unknown.

Otaki and her family belonged to the Small Robes, a smaller division, or band, of Pikuni people who followed a leader named Lone Walker. Their home was the plains east of the Rocky Mountains in what is now north-central Montana. To the Pikuni, the Rockies were the Shining Mountains, the backbone of Mother Earth.

The Pikuni, or Blackfeet, also known as the Southern Piegan (pay-GANN), are the southernmost tribal nation in the Blackfoot Confederacy, an alliance of four related Indian groups. The three others, all located in Canada, are the Kainai (KYE-uh-nye), also called the Blood; the Siksika (seek-seek-AH), or Blackfoot; and the Ahpatsi Pikuni ("ah-pot-see bee-GUNN-ee"), or Northern Piegan. The four nations of the confederacy all share a common language and culture, though with some differences.

Some believe Running Eagle was born in the early 1700s, before non-Indian people had even ventured into the land now known as Montana. Others pinpoint her birth at around 1820, a date supported by certain details of her life story. For one thing, many accounts of her life say she was as skilled with a rifle as she was with a bow. Yet guns did not become widespread among the Pikuni until the late 1700s, suggesting she was born after that time.

In addition, according to the stories told about her, Running Eagle engaged in raids and battles against the peoples of the Flathead Valley to the west—the Salish, or Flathead; the Pend d'Oreille ("pon-dor-AYE"), or Kalispel; and allied tribes. For most of the 1700s, however, the main westerly enemy of the Pikuni had been the Shoshone, who blocked their access to the Rocky Mountains. By the early 1800s, the Pikuni had driven the Shoshone away, opening their paths through the mountains and into the Flathead Valley. So if Running Eagle fought in the Flathead region, it's more likely that she lived in the nineteenth century than the eighteenth.

Because so many details of Running Eagle's life are unknown, we must use our knowledge of the traditional ways of Blackfeet women, men, and children—ways that remained much the same over generations—to suppose how her daily life might have been. Like other Pikuni bands, the Small Robes did most everything together, helping one another as a community. When they set up camp, they arranged their tipis, or lodges, in a large circle.

Inside, the lodge of Otaki's family was no doubt arranged in the same way as everyone else's. In the middle of the round space was the fire and cooking area, vented through a hole in the top of the lodge. Simple mattresses, called couches, lay near the perimeter, with the women and girls sleeping on the south side and men and boys on the north. The people slept under furry animal hides, or robes, for warmth. During the day, willow backrests were used on the couches for back support, like the backs of chairs. The lodge's doorway always faced east. To the west, at the back of the lodge, was a cleared space and a sort of altar used for spiritual practices. Important sacred objects were kept in that space.

At sunrise, Pikuni women like Otaki's mother prepared incense at the altar, carrying coals from the fire with a forked stick and sprinkling them with fragrant sweetgrass or balsam-fir needles. When the rest of the family got up, they rubbed the sweet-smelling smoke over their bodies to cleanse their minds and hearts. Daily life was full of such ceremonies. The tribe's relationship with the world around them, including the spirit world, demanded constant attention and care.

As Otaki grew up, she would have played with her siblings, cousins, and friends in the camp, participating in a variety of activities. Training and riding horses was an exciting pastime for Pikuni kids, as was hunting and trapping small animals. In winter, children laid out large animal hides to freeze until stiff, then climbed aboard them to slide down snowy hills. Frozen rivers were ice rinks on which to bat rocks around with sticks. All year long, Pikuni kids played with wooden tops, stuffed leather balls, and handmade dolls and toy animals. Some of these toys were meant only for boys, such as small bows and arrows, others for girls, such as dolls and play tipis. As we will learn, Otaki preferred boys' toys and games.

Of course, Otaki did not spend all her time playing. Her mother began teaching her, at a young age, the skills she would need as a woman. There was so much to know about taking care of a family, a lodge, and a community. Food preparation and cooking were essential skills. Pikuni women and girls harvested wild plant foods, such as berries, seeds, bulbs, and herbs, as each plant came into season. Other plants were gathered for medicine and for ceremonies. Meat brought in by the men was butchered and cooked or dried by the women. To cook, women sat or knelt before pots hung on a tripod over a fire. Besides daily meals, women prepared food for the winter, roasting, drying, and carefully storing meat and roots and mixing berries with animal fat for pemmican.

In addition to food preparation, Pikuni women were responsible for making clothing, lodge covers, and many household items from animal hides, especially those of bison, or buffalo. This work was labor-intensive. They scraped the tough hides clean and processed them into leather, rawhide, or buckskin, depending on what they were going to be used for—for example, rope, storage bags, dresses, moccasins, or something else.

Like many Native Americans of the plains, the Pikuni did not stay in one place and farm. Instead, they moved around, following their sources of food—mainly the vast herds of buffalo that roamed across their land. Moving camp, therefore, was a basic part of life. Women did most of the work required before, during, and after the moves. Pikuni mothers taught their daughters how to break down the lodges, pack everything efficiently onto horses, and quickly set up camp in the new location.

Pikuni women also devoted much of their attention to spiritual practices, in which they played a special role. In addition to preparing incense for her family's morning cleansing, a mother had many obligations to keep, both to living people and to the spirits. As part of this, many everyday tasks had to be performed in certain ways, which mothers carefully taught to their daughters. Girls also learned how to heal sick family members with medicine and prayer, and they were taught the special songs women sang and women's roles during different ceremonies. Everything that girls learned, they were expected to pass on one day to their own daughters.

Otaki and other girls were encouraged to practice all these skills while playing with their dolls. For example, they sewed clothes for their dolls, tiny versions of the dresses, shawls, and moccasins their mothers made for them. From scraps of leather, they fashioned small lodges for their doll families to live in.

For Otaki, however, dolls held no interest. Although she obediently helped her mother and learned everything she was taught, her heart was not in the work of the lodge. She envied the boys with their bow-and-arrow games and their pretend hunts and battles. Whenever she had the chance, she spent time with her father. One day, in fact, she asked him to teach her to hunt. Seeing no harm in teaching her a little, he showed her how to use his bow. She learned quickly and became good at it. Soon, Otaki was begging for her own bow and arrows. Her mother disapproved, but again, thinking it wouldn't hurt, her father made her a set from strong, flexible wood.

When the people in the camp heard that Otaki was learning to hunt, they weren't sure it was a good idea. Normally, Pikuni women hunted only when they had to, because providing fresh meat was a job for men, as was protecting the community and its hunting grounds by driving enemies away. Once in a while, the elders told stories of women who had adventures and fought like men, but those were legends from long ago. True, Pikuni women did occasionally ride with their husbands or male relatives on raids or into battle for moral support or just for excitement, but they rarely took part in the fighting. Allowing women to hunt and fight like men simply wouldn't work. What if all girls decided to hunt and fight? Who would do all the hard work that their families and communities required of them?

Despite what people said, Otaki kept honing her hunting skills. As she grew into a teenager, the time when most girls became interested in romance and often married, she remained reluctant to become a wife and mother. Meanwhile, at this age, boys began assisting on buffalo hunts and working their way up through the all-male warrior societies. Younger boys started in lower-level societies—the Pigeons or the Mosquitoes. Upon proving their skill and courage, they could move up to a higher society. The most elite warrior society among the Pikuni was the Crazy Dogs. Society members supported one another like brothers during hunts, raids, and war.

Otaki longed to chase bison and practice war games like the boys. When the men of the camp recounted tales of their daring on the war trail, she listened closely, imagining herself in their place. When they brought in meat, she wished she could have been with them on the hunt.

Finally, unable to stand it any longer, Otaki approached her father about going on a buffalo hunt. Buffalo were massive and dangerous animals, but Otaki's father, knowing how tough and fearless she was, gave in to his persistent child and agreed to teach her to shoot his rifle.

Otaki's first buffalo kill was thrilling. Afterward, she learned how to cut up the meat and pack it onto the horses.

On one of their next buffalo hunts, Otaki and her father were tying the last load of meat onto the backs of their horses when they saw enemy warriors riding at them at full speed across the field. They leapt on their horses and kicked them to a gallop. Then Otaki heard shots and looked back to see her father's horse roll out from under him. He hit the ground, grimacing in pain. Otaki turned her mount and galloped back. To make room on the horse, she reached back with one hand to loosen the ropes holding the meat, which fell as the horse galloped. When she reached her father, he clambered on behind her, injured but okay. Bullets whizzed around them, but none hit. As Otaki and her father sped toward camp, they passed their own warriors galloping out to drive off the raiders.

The camp buzzed with the story: Otaki had saved her father! Everyone praised the brave girl. But later, a few grumbled about it. Sure, it had turned out all right, but what was a girl doing in such a perilous situation in the first place? Such reckless behavior, they asserted, should not be encouraged in a female. Women were meant to take care of the camp and the children, not ride off into dangerous situations.

Unfortunately for Otaki, the critics soon got their way. Shortly after her triumph, her mother became ill, and before long, the sick woman was unable to get out of bed. As the eldest daughter, it was Otaki's responsibility to step in and care for the family. She searched her heart. No matter how strongly she wished to continue hunting, she knew her duty to her family must come first.

And so it was with great sadness that Otaki put her hunting ways behind her and accepted the work of the lodge. She worked hard to master the skills her mother had taught her, making her family's meals, clothes, and shelter; preparing medicine for her mother; and tending to spiritual responsibilities. To her credit, Otaki performed all of her domestic duties very well. This is not to say that she enjoyed them. She still watched longingly as her father and the other men came and went on hunts and raids. As soon as her mother was well, she vowed to herself, she would return to the life she loved. Not only would she hunt, she would fight, too. Her true calling, she knew, was to become a warrior.

One day, a party of warriors returned with terrible news. Otaki's father had been killed on the war trail. The family went into mourning. Shortly after her husband's death, Otaki's frail mother died—of grief, it was said. Now, it seemed, Otaki would never realize her dreams. Tradition demanded that she be both mother and father to her younger siblings and fulfill the family's obligations within the community.

Yet Otaki was determined to somehow keep the vow she had made to herself. Then she had an idea. She went to the lodge of a poor widow she knew and made the woman an offer: if the widow would live with Otaki's family and take care of her siblings, Otaki would provide food for her as well as protection and anything else she needed. The widow agreed.

One day, Otaki learned that a war party was about to leave to recapture some horses that had been taken by Crow warriors. Capturing horses from other tribes on raids was a form of war that did not require killing the enemy. Raiding was still very dangerous since, if the raiders were caught, shots might be fired. Scouting a rival camp, getting close enough to cut the horses loose, and leading them away without alerting the enemy took both skill and courage.

Raiding enemy camps for horses was common because, among the Pikuni and other Plains tribes, horses were a main source of wealth and power. These animals were valuable in many ways. Clearly they were useful for transportation and packing heavy items. But more than that, acquiring horses gave people greater might against their enemies. Capturing a rival tribe's horses left the victims weaker and the raiders stronger. It also earned the raiding party great respect and prestige in their community. But successful raids often led to retaliation from the victims, usually in the form of an opposing raid, as was the case that day.

Otaki watched as the war party prepared to depart. Before the men headed off, they donned their finest clothes for a ceremony called the Riding Big dance. Its purpose was to hearten everyone: the warriors, who faced trials and challenges ahead, as well as those left behind, who would have to endure without them. The warriors' faces were painted with special designs, and they painted the bodies of their horses, too, with pictures of their past brave deeds.

After much dancing, singing, honoring, and farewell, the warriors changed back into plain clothes and grabbed their war sacks, packed with pemmican and other necessities. One of the warriors that day was Otaki's favorite cousin, considered her brother in Blackfeet tradition. In Schultz's book, his name was White Weasel, later called Tail Feathers Coming Over the Hill. Otaki watched as the men left the camp on foot, running; they expected to be on horseback when they returned.

Somewhere along the trail, a member of the war party noticed they were being followed. The men circled back and confronted the person. It was Otaki! Dressed in a long shirt and leggings, she carried her father's gun. The war chief ordered her to go back. If she didn't, he said, they would all have to return. Otaki simply laughed. She told him that they could go back if they wanted, but she was going on regardless. Her cousin stepped forward and promised to look after her. And so Otaki was allowed to stay.

For several days, the party followed the trail of the raiders and their stolen horses. Finally, they located the Crow camp. As their enemies were sleeping, Otaki and her cousin crept into the camp and stole many fine horses from in front of the lodges. Otaki took eleven of them by herself. Soon she and her tribesmen were riding toward home, driving a herd before them. For a time, the Crow gave chase, but by switching to fresh horses as needed, the Pikuni got away.

Many hours later, the party stopped to camp. After eating, they relaxed, swapping stories of their adventure. But Otaki couldn't relax. Taking her gun, she climbed a nearby butte and studied the unfamiliar landscape below. That's when she saw them—two Crow men circling the horses, preparing to steal them back.

Alerting her companions would also alert the intruders. Instead, Otaki sprinted down the butte straight to the herd's lead horse and grabbed its rope, which kept the rest of the herd from running. The two Crow men spotted her then, and they started for her. One had a rifle. Otaki

An artist's conception of Running Eagle in the incident with the Crow.
—From *Running Eagle: The Warrior Girl* by James Willard Schultz (1919)

lifted her rifle and shot him dead. The other man veered away. Instead of taking the time to reload, Otaki grabbed the dead man's rifle and fired at the other Crow warrior. She missed him, but by now her companions, having heard the shots, were arriving. They followed the second Crow man and killed him.

In Blackfeet tradition, war deeds are ranked; some bring warriors more honor than others. Otaki's companions were very impressed that on her first raid, she had accomplished some of the highest-ranking deeds of war: capturing an enemy gun, killing an enemy, acquiring many horses, and preventing their recapture. When the war party returned home, everyone in camp celebrated, many heaping praise on Otaki. But some still questioned: Wasn't it wrong for a woman to go to war? Why weren't their leaders stopping her?

The elders who were sympathetic to Otaki suggested that she do something that could settle the question of her status once and for all. She should go on a quest for spiritual guidance. According to Pikuni custom, tribal members—usually male—would go out at crucial times in their lives to seek guidance from their spirit helpers. They went alone, with little or no food or water, to a quiet place to meditate and pray. Sleeping only a little and eating next to nothing, depriving their bodies of all comfort, they stayed for several days. If they were fortunate, their suffering would be rewarded with a visit from a spirit being—an eagle, a stone, a star—in a dream or vision. This spirit guide would tell the seeker what he or she needed to do—for example, make a sacrifice or perform a ritual. The spirit might teach the person a certain song or dance, which they must commit to practice and learn, sometimes over many years.

Following this tradition, Otaki went to a beautiful place in the mountains near Two Medicine Lake, in what is now Glacier National Park. It was a place she had visited often to collect medicinal plants. At one special waterfall there, the water flowed out of a hole in the rock. Nearby, Otaki sat and fasted, suffering for four days and nights. Finally—and wonderfully—she received a visit from a powerful spirit helper. In some accounts, Otaki's medicine, as a person's spirit helper and the power it bestows are called, was the Sun itself. When Otaki returned to the camp and recounted her experience, her people agreed that she had been given special powers. They could not question it. Her choice of paths had been affirmed. She was indeed a warrior.

Otaki's embrace of the warrior's path was unusual for a girl, but female warriors were not unknown among Native Americans. In Montana alone, there have been several who stood out. A war leader called Woman Chief, born Gros Ventre (GROW-von) but raised among the Crow, lived during the same time as Running Eagle. Several other Crow women of that time also became warriors. Other tribes had female fighters, too. In the 1876 Battle of the Rosebud, Buffalo Calf Road Woman, a Cheyenne, rode onto the battlefield to save her fallen brother. Her courage inspired the retreating Cheyenne warriors. Only a week later, she fought at the Battle of the Little Bighorn, where she was said to have struck General

George Armstrong Custer from his horse before he died. Around the turn of the twentieth century, an Indian woman named Elk Hollering in the Water, who was Pikuni like Running Eagle, became known for the daring she showed on raids. These are a few examples, but there were others.

On her next adventure, Otaki and her party crossed west over the mountains through Bear (Marias) Pass into the Flathead Valley, where she did her part in capturing over six hundred horses. The Pikuni raiders were discovered, however, and a fight broke out. Otaki fought not just with her rifle and bow, but also with her knife and club. Twice, arrows almost hit her, but she deflected them with her strong rawhide shield.

Soon after that, it was time for the Okan (OH-kawn), sometimes called "Going Home Week," the annual summer gathering of families from throughout the Blackfoot Confederacy. It was the biggest event of the year, where the different bands reconnected to share news, tell stories, and celebrate life. The Okan was also a time to perform important spiritual rituals and ceremonies.

One special Okan ceremony was a storytelling session where certain warriors were invited to recount their feats on the war trail. At this one, Otaki was honored with an invitation to describe her recent war deeds. When she finished, the people cheered and beat on drums in appreciation.

At the end of Otaki's story, the head chief of the Small Robes band, Lone Walker, announced that, in light of Otaki's bravery, he was giving her a new name. Some Pikuni warriors received many names during their lives, based on their deeds, but it is said that Otaki was the first woman to receive a new name in this way. Lone Walker chose the name Pitamakan, or Running Eagle, which had belonged to several well-respected warriors before her. Afterward, the prestigious Crazy Dogs Society of warriors asked Running Eagle to join their group.

For the rest of her days, Running Eagle led a warrior's life. Quickly proving her skill and judgment, she soon became a war chief, sometimes leading hundreds of men. While many details of her raids, the horses she acquired, and her extraordinary deeds are lost, numerous stories about this remarkable Pikuni woman warrior are still recounted. Some say that several men were desperate to marry Running Eagle, but she always told them that she had committed herself to her medicine, the Sun, and could not marry. If she broke that vow, she said, she would die.

Around 1850, when Running Eagle was about thirty, she headed out with a large party of warriors toward a Salish camp on a mission to avenge the murder of some Pikuni hunters and their women. After reaching the enemy camp, Running Eagle's party took many Salish horses during the night. Then, just before dawn, they attacked. After an initial fight with guns and arrows, the battle came down to hand-to-hand combat with clubs and knives. At one point, a Salish warrior came at Running Eagle with a club, but she fought him off and killed him. Behind her, however, another enemy sneaked up with his club and brought the weapon down forcefully on her head. One of her brother warriors soon dispatched the man, but Running Eagle was dead. The Pikuni won the battle, though at the cost of their beloved and respected war chief.

Sorrowfully, Running Eagle's warriors put her body on a horse and carried it back across the mountains to the Small Robes camp. It was customary to take the bodies of fallen warriors to a place that had been special to them. For Running Eagle, the special place was the area around Two Medicine Lake and the waterfall where her warrior way had been affirmed. Her body was probably placed, in Pikuni tradition, on a scaffold built high in a tree, surrounded by her finest possessions.

Today the waterfall Running Eagle loved, in Glacier National Park, is called Pitamakan (Running Eagle) Falls. In addition, the mountain pass that she frequently crossed on her raids, labeled Marias Pass on maps, is still known by some locals as Running Eagle Pass. Most meaningfully, among the Pikuni, a number of girls and women have been given, over the generations, the name Otaki, Brown Weasel Woman, or Pitamakan, Running Eagle.

For all these tributes, Running Eagle's greatest legacy is her story. Ever since her death, her people have told and retold, thousands of times, tales of her amazing life. Versions of her story have also appeared in books and articles. Generations of Blackfeet people and others have been moved and inspired by the story of this exceptional Pikuni warrior girl.

"Who am I?" is a question almost everyone asks once, if not many times, during their lifetime. Even though it made her life difficult at times, Running Eagle was determined to discover who she really was and follow the answer wherever it led. This might be why her story still seems fresh even today.

Perhaps more impressive than her courage in seeking her true path, even more than her valor in battle, was the fact that Running Eagle never lost sight of her responsibilities to her family and community. For this, Pitamakan, Running Eagle, won the respect and admiration of her people not only in her own time, but to this day.

This is the only known photograph of Annie Morgan, pictured in front of her cabin. The date of the picture and the identity of the visitor are unknown. —Courtesy Granite County Museum

ANNIE MORGAN

COOKING UP A NEW LIFE IN THE WEST

From its headwaters southwest of Philipsburg, Montana, Rock Creek runs north for fifty-two miles, passing through a narrow and secluded valley just east of the Sapphire Mountains to join the Clark Fork River about twenty miles east of Missoula. In the middle section of the valley, within today's Lolo National Forest, a small ranch sits in grassy fields between the creek and a steep hillside. There stands a cabin now owned by the U.S. Forest Service. For many years the cabin was empty and falling down, but in 1999, Forest Service workers and volunteers began to restore the building so it could be rented out to the public.

Eight years later, in 2007, as work on the cabin continued, carpenter Kirby Mathew was enlarging the cabin's back door for wheelchair access when his fingers brushed something odd behind the trim. He pulled out a rolled-up cloth bag. Inside was a curious collection of items, including a folded soap wrapper; a carved wooden spatula about the size of a pen; bits of string, tape, and cloth; and a handwritten grocery receipt from the nearby town of Philipsburg. The receipt, at least, made sense. It was written to the cabin's first owner, an African American woman named Agnes, or "Annie," Morgan, an early homesteader and former army cook.

The cloth bag wasn't some random object. Archaeologists recognized the bag and its contents as a "bag charm," an item used in the ancestral

African American spiritual tradition known as hoodoo. Hoodoo practitioners used such items in calling upon supernatural forces, including the spirits of the dead, to change the course of people's lives—for example, to heal a sick person or change someone's luck. Hoodoo could be used for good—to help others—or for ill, to harm them. Hoodoo healers, who employed herbal preparations, rituals, and magic to treat the sick and injured, used the practice for good.

In America, bag charms are usually found in the South, where the slaves who brought hoodoo traditions from Africa introduced them, so the discovery of such a charm in distant Montana was special and exciting. The cloth bag shed new light on Annie, who had a reputation as a healer. It suggested that, privately, she may have drawn at least in part on hoodoo methods. Publicly, Annie was probably best known for her claim that, early in her life, she cooked for Custer—the famous army general who died, along with almost all his men, in the 1876 Battle of the Little Bighorn. From a modern perspective, we can also appreciate Annie as an adventurer who pursued independence and new experiences in the West. She was a savvy woman who, despite few resources, pulled herself out of poverty and made herself a home.

The discovery in the cabin doorway offered some information about who Annie Morgan was, but facts about her, particularly from her early years, are hard to find. For example, as far as we know, the Annie Morgan we are looking for appears in only two U.S. government censuses (an accounting of all citizens that takes place every ten years), in 1880 and 1910. During her lifetime, the government kept few records on poor women, especially African American women. Also, information we do have about Annie was written mostly by white observers, so it may be tainted with the prejudices of the day. Finally, as one of only a few people of color in her area, in an era when white culture dominated and racial discrimination and even violence were normal, Annie may have been reluctant to expose herself to prejudiced judgments and gossip by sharing personal information.

———— • • • ————

When Annie arrived in Rock Creek around 1892, she was in her fifties or sixties. Her exact age is unknown—even Annie herself may not have known her own date of birth. It appears differently in different records. For example, at the time of her death in 1914, her age was recorded on the death certificate as "about eighty," which would mean she was born around 1834, but her gravestone states that she was seventy.

We also don't know Annie's last name at birth or her parents' names—Morgan was probably her married name. We do know that she was born in Baltimore, Maryland, during the time of slavery, but it is not certain whether she and her parents were slaves. Mid-nineteenth-century Baltimore had many free African American citizens. Even if Annie and her parents were free, however, life in Maryland and other slave states offered little opportunity, dignity, or even personal safety for African Americans.

According to her obituary, Annie worked as a domestic servant—probably cooking and/or housekeeping—in a Baltimore household before leaving the city for good, which was probably after 1865, the end of the Civil War. Annie would have been in her twenties or thirties when she headed west. We don't know why she left, but at this time in history, if women longed for greater independence and opportunity or wished to leave difficult circumstances behind, going west was an appealing option. Apparently Annie started her journey by hiring on as a cook on a steamboat going up the Mississippi River. Sometime after that, she found work as a cook with the army on the western frontier.

Across the West, a few women lived at most forts, which were predominantly male. Besides the wives and daughters of officers and enlisted men, there were female workers, including cooks, house servants, laundresses, and others. Such army jobs were good opportunities for poor women. More than that, though, the frontier West promised independent-minded women a degree of adventure as well as freedom from the rigid rules of eastern society. Many western territories had not become states yet, so laws were loose and living was informal. Even the landscape was a novelty. Compared to the greener and more developed lands of the eastern United States, the West's vast, arid openness was dramatically different. The army itself was a mixing pot in which people from diverse backgrounds lived and worked together.

Western army life centered around the fort. Most frontier forts had been built to protect white travelers and settlers from Indian attacks. At this time, a major war over land and way of life was unfolding between the army and Indian tribes west of the Mississippi. Some army posts were isolated, while others were near towns or settlements. Regardless of location, western forts were beehives of activity. In between preparations for and returns from campaigns out in the field, soldiers practiced marching, riding, and shooting. They were responsible for keeping themselves, their weapons, and their quarters clean. If they were cavalrymen, they also had horses to take care of. For everyone at the fort, daily life followed regular schedules and strict rules.

Female cooks and house servants at army posts were usually hired and paid directly by an officer or his wife out of their personal funds. In some eras, laundresses were actual employees of the army; at other times, soldiers had to pay laundresses with their own money. Women at forts also earned income on the side by mending soldiers' clothes and giving haircuts. Some women baked delicious treats to sell to the soldiers.

We know that Annie worked as a cook for at least one army officer's family in Dakota Territory (now South Dakota). Historical diaries of frontier army wives shed light on the life she probably led in that role. Officers' personal cooks usually lived in their employers' homes and prepared all the meals. In addition to serving family members, cooks were often called upon to whip up meals for unexpected dinner guests, sometimes many of them, in keeping with the tradition of army hospitality.

In addition to these impromptu gatherings, officers and their families planned elaborate dinners, parties, and holiday celebrations to break up the monotony of fort life. Such events kept their servants busy. Cooks worked with their employers to plan menus and acquire necessary ingredients, then they prepared the food. If other households were involved in planning an event, their cooks might collaborate. Female cooks and domestic servants, nicknamed "Abigails," were vital to officers and their families. A good Abigail didn't have to worry about unemployment. If one household moved away, another would undoubtedly have cooking, cleaning, or child care for her to do.

The foods army cooks prepared depended on what was available at or near the fort. Cooks generally had access to staples such as flour, beans, sugar, and such. Soldier hunters brought in fresh meat, and many posts had vegetable gardens. Still, choices of ingredients were limited. To vary the menu, enterprising cooks gathered wild greens and nuts and concocted sauces and jam from wild berries.

Sometimes cooks and other servants traveled with their employers. For example, they went along on pleasure outings, such as picnics or hunting trips, to serve baskets of food or cook outside on campouts. A cook might also travel with her employers when they moved between posts or even, if there was no chance of fighting, out into the field with the troops. At such times, a kitchen tent was set up with a stove inside. On blustery days, strong winds snatched at the cook's utensils and deposited debris in the food. In winter, cold stiffened her fingers as she cut meat and stirred pots. In hot weather, with no refrigeration or coolers, keeping food from spoiling was a challenge.

In a book published in 1890, Libbie Custer, the general's wife, wrote, "Our friend's cook had lived long on the frontier, for she was a soldier's wife, and being out at service with the officers, she was accustomed to husband[ing] all supplies most carefully, not knowing when they would be replaced." Cooks who managed provisions with care and unflappably produced satisfying meals in all kinds of conditions earned their employers' respect.

The exact details of Annie's career as an army cook, however, are foggy. Her obituary said she cooked "in the officers' mess [dining area] of General George Custer's command in the campaign against the Indians," but there is no definite evidence to support this claim. Historians have identified Custer's regular household cooks, and Annie Morgan was not one of them. Some even assert that Annie was with Custer when he was killed at the Little Bighorn, but experts say women never accompanied troops on military campaigns.

However, in 1880, according to census records, Annie was working at Fort Meade, in what is now South Dakota, at the home of Myles Moylan, an officer in the Seventh Cavalry—Custer's regiment—and a relative of Custer. Custer had been dead for four years by then, but we don't know how long Annie had been with Moylan or the Seventh Cavalry; if she was with Moylan before Custer died, perhaps she filled in for the general's regular cook on occasion or served him meals as a guest in her employer's home. Annie's tombstone repeats the claim that she cooked for Custer, adding that it was "in the early days." Perhaps "the early days" refers to an earlier time in Custer's career, when he was in the Black Hills or in Oklahoma, and Annie cooked for him under circumstances too informal to be recorded.

The 1880 census also lists Annie, then in her 40s or 50s, as married, though no husband is listed with her. Who was Annie's husband? No marriage license or other records have been found to establish his identity. He may have been someone she left behind in Maryland or along the way. If he was black, perhaps he was a "buffalo soldier," as African American troops were called. Congress established black infantry and cavalry units in 1866, and buffalo soldiers crossed paths with the Seventh Cavalry several times over the course of the Indian Wars in the West. One of these times was in Oklahoma in 1868. Perhaps Annie, traveling with an enlisted husband, parted from him at this time to cook with the Seventh.

Another possibility is that Annie met and married a buffalo soldier at one of the posts. In 1880, the year the census was taken, the African American 25th Infantry was stationed at Fort Meade, so it's conceivable that she met her husband there. It's also possible that Annie's husband was white. Interracial marriages, seldom accepted in the civilian world, were tolerated in the army. Furthermore, he may not even have been a soldier. The army employed a few civilian (non-military) men, such as storekeepers and freight packers, at frontier forts. Unfortunately, this is all guesswork—old military records, which are often incomplete for individuals, have yielded few other clues. An 1887 post report from Fort Meade does list a Frank Morgan as a "casually assigned recruit," with no information as to race or age. Was he Annie's husband? Morgan is a common surname, so it is probably a coincidence. Anyway, around that time, Annie seems to have left Fort Meade, journeying on into the next episode of her life.

"About 1887," according to her obituary, Annie arrived in Philipsburg, Montana. Evidence from a few years later suggests that when she arrived in the silver-mining boomtown, either she was without her husband or he was with her but died soon after. The 1910 census listed Annie as a widow, so presumably her husband died sometime between 1880 and 1910. In 1890, Annie was arrested in Philipsburg for vagrancy. The offense of "vagrancy" can refer to a number of conditions and behaviors, but chief among them are joblessness and homelessness (at that time the line between crime and poverty was razor thin). The arrest suggests that Annie was on her own, possibly in an unstable condition, with no spouse looking out for her. Annie's obituary stated that she was "addicted to drink." Public drunkenness is another factor in vagrancy. Whatever the specifics were, it appears that Annie's early years in Philipsburg may have been a low point in her life.

Despite her troubles, by 1892, at least, Annie was not alone and friendless in Philipsburg. That year, a young lawyer named David Durfee offered her a job. Durfee and his wife, Emelie, had moved to Philipsburg from Maryland, where Emelie had a connection to Annie: the Baltimore household that Annie worked in before she came west belonged to Emelie's uncle. At the time, Emelie, born around 1862, was a child, but if she was close to her uncle, she may well have known his servant. Did Annie realize that Emelie was living in Philipsburg before she moved there? If so, that could have been the reason she went there in the first place. Although it could have been just a coincidence, it seems likely that Annie and Emelie were at least aware of each other's presence in Philipsburg. Perhaps David hired Annie to help his wife's old acquaintance out of difficult times.

The job that David hired Annie for involved nursing an elderly alcoholic man, probably his own uncle, back to health. He set the two of them up in a cabin in the middle of the Rock Creek Valley, three hours from

Philipsburg by wagon. David may have chosen the isolated location to be sure the old man was far from town gossip as well as from easy access to alcohol—probably a good thing for both Annie and her patient.

Within a year or two, Annie's elderly patient was gone—it's unclear whether he recovered or died. Possibly as payment for Annie's services, a nearby tract of homestead land became hers, but for a while she stayed on at the same cabin by herself, settling into an independent life.

Life in Rock Creek seemed to suit Annie. Some women might have felt unsafe living on their own in that remote valley. After the silver mines suddenly closed in 1893, thousands of unemployed miners left the Philipsburg area, some of them migrating through Rock Creek. Jobless, possibly hungry and desperate, the miners might have posed a threat to a woman alone with no close neighbors. In fact, until sheriffs killed him in 1904, a well-known outlaw named Frank Brady, known to prey on ranchers and farmers, lived just down the valley from Annie.

As a woman on her own, Annie had to be careful, but as a person of color, she walked on even thinner ice. In those days, while many white Americans accepted people of other races, most still considered them "inferior" to whites. As a result, what happened to minority people was seen as less important, and violence against them was not taken as seriously. In 1896, for example, down the creek from Annie in a boomtown called Quigley, a Chinese man named Wong Ying, who had lived in the Philipsburg area for twenty-six years and went by the nickname "Yank," was murdered after refusing to sell land to a white man. The crime was never investigated, much less punished. Nevertheless, Annie took her chances, choosing to live on her own. Perhaps her years with the army had toughened her and sharpened her skills for dealing with all sorts of people and problems. It's even possible that she felt safer away from town, where she had been arrested. Whatever the case, as it turned out, she soon had company.

One day in 1894, while walking along Rock Creek, Annie came upon a white man collapsed on the bank, terribly sick. He was suffering from typhoid, a common illness back then that was often fatal. Annie was a small woman, but she somehow managed to get the man to the cabin and put him to bed. Over time, she nursed him back to health. When he was able to speak, she learned that his name was Joseph Case. He was a Union army veteran who had worked as a teamster in Philipsburg after the Civil War. Now he made his living by fishing in Rock Creek and selling his catch in town, an occupation that earned him the nickname "Fisher Jack."

Under Annie's care, Joseph recovered. She had saved his life. In gratitude, as soon as he was strong enough, Joseph offered to do some work on Annie's homestead down the road. She asked him to build a fence around the property, and so he set to work. By the time he was done, he and Annie realized that they worked well together and enjoyed each other's company. Annie offered Joseph a deal. If he helped her improve the homestead—something the government required for a settler to gain full possession of the land—she would give him half ownership. Joseph accepted. In all likelihood, it was Joseph who built the first ranch buildings on the property, including the modest cabin where he and Annie lived until her death.

Annie's homestead, as seen from the mountain behind it. Her cabin is in the foreground. Its middle section was built first; the section to the right was joined to the main part later; the section to the left, with porch, was added after Joseph sold it, so this picture was taken after 1924. The small bunkhouse at the rear hosted paying guests.
—Courtesy USDA Forest Service

Although Annie and Joseph appeared to be a couple, no one knows for sure. Evidently they never married, although they could have. At the time they began living together, interracial marriage wasn't against the law in Montana (though it was outlawed later, from 1909 to 1953). Even so, they may have feared the community's negative reaction. It's also possible that they were not lovers at all, but merely friends and business partners— "partner" was the term used in Annie's obituary. Historical photographs show that the cabin Annie and Joseph lived in was once two cabins, side by side, later joined into one building. This suggests that Annie and Joseph may have lived separately for a time and combined their households later. Whatever Annie and Joseph's relationship was, they lived together on the homestead in apparent affection and respect for twenty years.

After settling into their new home, Annie and Joseph started farming the property. They tended a large vegetable garden and grew hay for their several cows and horses. In addition, Annie sold homegrown strawberries and freshly baked pies to her neighbors and in Philipsburg. Up on the steep hillside behind their cabin, Annie and Joseph dabbled in mining. Later, Joseph built a bunkhouse to accommodate paying guests who came to Rock Creek to fish and hunt. During the summer, some guests pitched tents in the Ponderosa pine grove between Annie and Joseph's cabin and the creek. Some of these visitors stayed for weeks. Reportedly, Annie's hospitality—and her pies—made her a beloved figure in the Rock Creek Valley.

In March 1914, sensing that her end was near, Annie traveled to Philipsburg to arrange for her burial and for Joseph to inherit the ranch. She died a few weeks later, on April 8, and was buried in the Catholic section of the Philipsburg cemetery. Her gravestone, a white pillar inscribed "Mrs. Agnes Morgan," says she was "very neighborly and well liked by all who knew her." Joseph lived at the ranch for ten more years, then sold it and moved to a veterans' home in Columbia Falls, where he died in 1930. He is also buried in the Philipsburg cemetery, though not near Annie.

For almost a century, the cloth bag in Annie's cabin lay in darkness, stuffed behind the door trim. Brought to light, what did it reveal? Annie's reputation as a healer is part of her legend. We know that she nursed

Joseph Case, aka Fisher Jack, in 1921, after Annie's death, standing between two forest rangers in the doorway of his and Annie's cabin —Courtesy USDA Forest Service

one ailing man and saved another from typhoid. As noted earlier, the bag shows that she probably drew on African American hoodoo healing methods. Hoodoo was based on spiritual traditions that African captives brought to North America during the slave trade. Eventually, these West and Central African belief systems mixed with the European Christianity that was already established in the New World. One result was hoodoo.

In addition, some hoodoo traditions migrated to America from the Caribbean, where a similar tradition, called voodoo, was practiced. Emelie Durfee was descended, on her mother's side, from French people who colonized the Caribbean nation of Haiti, then known as Santo Domingo, in the eighteenth century. In other words, Emelie's ancestors were slave owners. In the 1790s, Haiti saw a major slave revolt, compelling Emelie's ancestors to flee for their lives. They immigrated to Baltimore, bringing some of their slaves and servants with them. Records suggest that the man Annie Morgan worked for in Baltimore, Emelie's uncle, was on the French side of Emelie's family, so it's possible that Annie's ancestors were among the servants or slaves who came to America with Emelie's ancestors. If so, and if Annie learned hoodoo practices from her family, her methods may have been influenced by Afro-Caribbean beliefs and traditions.

There were two main types of hoodoo. One was root-doctoring, a method of healing sick and injured people. In addition to making medicines from plant parts, including roots, root-doctors used charms and rituals to summon the spirit world for help in healing the patient. The other type of hoodoo, called conjuring, invoked the same forces but used them for harm—to inflict revenge, for example, or punishment.

Did Annie use hoodoo for good or for ill—for root-doctoring or conjuring? The items in Annie's bag charm relate to healing and suggest that she was a root-doctor. The wooden spatula was an essential tool for crushing and mixing plant material for medicine. String and tape have to do with binding and mending—important concepts in healing. Soap relates to purification. Color is important in hoodoo, and the soap wrapper was printed with vibrant red, the color of life's blood, and blue, the color of water, which was considered an important boundary between the spirit and living worlds. One scrap of cloth in the bag appears to have come from the bodice of a camisole or nightgown—personal clothing worn close to the skin and heart, perhaps symbolizing Annie's most intimate and truest self. The receipt with her name on it was also meaningful. In hoodoo, someone's written name represented that person as if she were physically present, identifying her to the spirits.

Like the bag charm in Annie's cabin, objects used in hoodoo were often hidden in dark places or buried in the ground. Darkness was considered the realm of the spirits. Root-doctors often placed their charms in or around a home's threshold to act as a sort of calling card for spirits, informing them about who lived inside the dwelling and what powers that person had. Charms like Annie's cloth bag also served as a warning, or barrier, to keep unfriendly spirits outside. Hoodoo practitioners were not afraid of spirits and ghosts—on the contrary, they had the ability to control and communicate with them, tapping into their otherworldly energy and directing it toward their own aims. In the American South,

The soap wrapper (unfolded) found in Annie Morgan's bag charm —Courtesy USDA Forest Service

this power made hoodoo practitioners respected and often wealthy members of black communities.

Annie's root-doctoring bag was the first such hoodoo artifact discovered in the Pacific Northwest. It's an important part of Annie's legacy, as is her cabin, though changes have been made to the structure since her time. The U.S. Forest Service now rents the cabin out to the public—continuing, in a way, Annie's tradition of hospitality. Her ranch is also listed on the National Register of Historic Places as an example of how Montanans on small homesteads scratched out a living in rugged places. In 2013, Annie Morgan was inducted into the Montana Cowboy Hall of Fame.

Annie's story remains incomplete, but hopefully historians will keep working to piece together a fuller picture. Even in its unfinished form, her story manages to inspire. From Maryland to Montana, Annie's independent life was unusual not just for an African American woman at that time, but for an American woman of any race. Annie's long and eventful journey ended at Rock Creek, where, like a good cook, she set about gathering the ingredients for her own contentment—a home, a capable partner, meaningful work, rich spiritual traditions, and community respect. Mixing them together, she created for herself a happy and satisfying life.

Pretty Shield with firewood. Photographed here between 1937 and 1941, she is in her eighties. Photo by Harrison R. Crandall. —Courtesy Quita Pownall

PRETTY SHIELD

GUARDIAN OF CROW CULTURE

Pretty Shield, born in March of 1856 in what is now north-central Montana, a few miles northeast of today's Winifred, grew up like generations of Apsaalooke (ab-ZAHL-uh-guh), or Crow, women before her. Her people roamed a vast area that encompassed much of today's Montana and Wyoming, moving with the seasons to wherever their major foods could be found. Their beautiful home territory teemed with bison (also called buffalo), which was their main source of food, as well as other game and edible and medicinal plants.

When Pretty Shield was a child, explorers and fur traders from the populated eastern side of the continent sometimes passed through Crow country, but otherwise, Euro-American culture was far away and largely unknown. By the time Pretty Shield was a grown woman, however, Crow life was changing rapidly. Confined to a reservation, or *Annuukaaxuwua* ("Living Within a Line Drawn on the Ground"), the Crow suffered hunger, poverty, and disease. Life became more terrible than Pretty Shield could have imagined, but she never gave up. She kept fighting for her family and community and took bold steps to preserve her threatened culture.

Later in her life, wanting to preserve some of her people's history, Pretty Shield told her story to a writer who published it in a book. She also intensively schooled one of her granddaughters, Alma Hogan, in traditional Crow knowledge. As a grown-up, Alma Hogan Snell shared her grandmother's teachings about medicinal plants and healing, tribal stories, and Crow traditions with other people, Indian and non-Indian alike.

———•••———

Born about twelve years before the U.S. government moved the Crow tribe onto a reservation, Pretty Shield was the fourth of eleven children born to Kills in the Night, her mother, and Crazy Sister-in-Law, her father. When Pretty Shield was four days old, her paternal grandfather named her in honor of his handsome and sacred war shield.

Pretty Shield's clan, or family group, was called the Sore Lips. According to Crow lore, the clan was so named because its people were great hunters who loved to be outdoors, no matter what the weather. As a result, their lips were always chapped. During Pretty Shield's youth, the Crow lived and worked well together and always had plenty to eat. Life was good, but that doesn't mean there was no sadness or fear. The Crow fought constantly with their enemies, the tribes who used the same hunting grounds—the Lakota, Cheyenne, Arapaho, and Blackfeet—who, together, outnumbered the Crow. In these wars, men, women, and children could be killed or taken as slaves at any time, so Crow scouts, known as wolves, kept vigilant watch over their people at all times.

When Pretty Shield was not yet three, her aunt lost her husband and two daughters to Lakota warriors in one of these frequent attacks. To "heal her heart," Pretty Shield's parents gave their little girl to the grieving woman. The Crow often shared their children with others, such as childless relatives or elderly folks who needed a hand. Similarly, when she was grown, Pretty Shield would help raise several children who weren't her own.

Pretty Shield's aunt, Strikes with an Axe, was kind, and Pretty Shield loved her, but she lived in a different camp from Kills in the Night and Crazy Sister-in-Law, so sometimes Pretty Shield was homesick and missed her family. Fortunately, she often stayed with her parents and siblings, especially during the summer. In this way, Pretty Shield was like many children today, moving between two homes. Overall, Pretty Shield remembered her childhood as a happy one.

Growing up, Pretty Shield had many playmates among her siblings, cousins, and friends. They enjoyed racing each other on horses. In the winter, they made sleds from buffalo ribs to ride down snowy hills. Pretty Shield had pets, too—a baby bear and a baby buffalo, among others. When these pets grew big, they were let loose. Sometimes Pretty Shield wanted even more wild pets, but her parents said no.

As a child, Pretty Shield had a small tipi, or lodge, which she erected beside her aunt's large one. Every year, as she grew older, Pretty Shield cut and sewed a new, larger play tipi. Even after she was married, she continued setting up her own smaller tipi beside her lodge. Young Pretty Shield also had two prized childhood possessions: a doll her mother had given her and a ball that one of her sisters had made from the thin lining around a bison heart stuffed with antelope hair. During a Lakota attack on her camp, Pretty Shield's main fear was that the invaders would get her doll and ball. As arrows flew, she ran to her lodge, snatched up her toys, and took off running. Fortunately, a woman grabbed her and pulled her into her lodge until the fighting was over.

Enemies were one source of danger in Pretty Shield's world. Wild animals were another. Once, when her camp was moving, Pretty Shield and another girl fell behind to help a younger girl. Just as they caught up enough to see their families ahead, they also spotted a vast herd of running buffalo that would soon cut them off. Pretty Shield's friend spurred her fast horse and beat the herd across, but Pretty Shield's old mare couldn't make it. A sea of massive, thundering creatures overtook Pretty Shield and the mare. To survive, the horse turned and ran with the bison herd.

In the thick, blinding dust, deafened by the roar of pounding hooves, Pretty Shield held on for dear life. If the old horse stumbled or fell, Pretty Shield remembered later, "we should both be trampled into bits too small for even a magpie to notice." Just as the girl felt her saddle slipping, she looked up and saw her father. He had ridden into the herd and worked her mare to the side, where another man roped it. Pretty Shield was safe.

Another encounter with a buffalo left Pretty Shield with a permanent scar. When she was about seven, she was out with other girls and women gathering prairie turnips, also called Indian bread root, a plant in the pea family whose bulbous roots were an important food source for the Crow. Crow women unearthed them using root-diggers, sharpened sticks with handles. The day was hot, and suddenly the group looked up to see an old bison bull, maddened by the heat, charging them. They all took off running, but Pretty Shield's moccasin string caught on a bush and she fell. Her root-digger stabbed into her forehead, its tip lodging at the corner of her eye.

Men from the camp killed the bison and rescued Pretty Shield. But when a boy tried to pull the root-digger from Pretty Shield's forehead, her eye started to come out with it. Her mother ordered the boy to stop and sent for a healer. When the healer arrived, Pretty Shield's father gave him his finest warhorse and her brother added his best leggings and shirt as payment for his services. With four pulling motions, and without even touching the girl or the digger, the healer removed the tool, saving Pretty Shield's eye. She recovered, but bore a scar on her forehead for the rest of her life.

Most days passed with less drama, though Pretty Shield was never one to feel bored. One regular part of Crow life that Pretty Shield loved was moving camp. On moving days, the women directed and did much of the work, breaking down the lodges, packing and loading them, and at the new site, quickly erecting the lodges and remaking their homes. Traveling between places, women and girls often rode together, enjoying the chance to relax and chat. In the warmer months, the moves were more frequent as the people intensively hunted game and gathered wild plants. In the winter, they set up longer-term camps in sheltered spots offering protection from the weather.

In 1868, all the Crow moved onto a newly established reservation around the Bighorn River, southeast of Billings. Pretty Shield was twelve. After the move, her people continued to hunt, move camp, and follow their age-old traditions, though they were told to stay within the reservation boundaries.

When Pretty Shield was thirteen, her parents arranged her engagement to a young man named Goes Ahead. Crow parents typically arranged marriages, according to custom. "Young women did not then fall in love and get married to please themselves, as they now do," Pretty Shield commented years later. "They listened to their fathers, married the men selected for them, and this, I believe, is the best way."

As in many tribes, Crow men were often polygamous, that is, they had more than one wife at a time—it was a sign of prosperity. In fact, men often married sisters. If a man proved to be a good husband to his first wife, her parents were glad for their other daughters to also marry him. So it was with Goes Ahead, who was already the husband of Pretty Shield's older sister, Standing Medicine Rock. Pretty Shield was proud and excited to be engaged to Goes Ahead. She liked his kindness and bravery and admired his hunting skill. She also found Goes Ahead *eechik*—attractive.

The marriage took place three years later, when Pretty Shield was sixteen. The wedding was, she recalled, "a happy affair," and Pretty Shield settled contentedly into married life. When she moved in with her new husband, she brought her widowed aunt to live with them too. All was well at first, but the following year, something terrible occurred. A smallpox epidemic hit Pretty Shield's camp. About one hundred Crow people died. Pretty Shield herself caught the disease, but she recovered.

Later, Pretty Shield's younger sister, Two Scalps, became Goes Ahead's third wife. Pretty Shield loved her husband, and she and her sisters got along well, though Pretty Shield believed she was Goes Ahead's favorite. When, after saving another Crow in battle, he gained the right to paint his wife's face for the celebration, he chose Pretty Shield for the honor. He also let her ride his warhorse and carry his shield. As it happened, she was the only one of his wives to have borne children, which may account for his favoritism.

Together, Pretty Shield and Goes Ahead had five children, three girls and two boys, but one girl and one boy died as babies. Crow people mourned intensely when loved ones died, and after her children's deaths, Pretty Shield lost the desire to live. For two months, she wandered between her lodge and the hills beyond her camp, eating little and sleeping on hard ground. All the while she hoped for a medicine-dream, or vision, that would help her go on.

Finally, walking through the hills one day, Pretty Shield thought she saw up ahead a woman who had died four years earlier. She realized the woman was a spirit. The woman spirit stopped beside an anthill and called Pretty Shield over. With her heart nearly bursting with fear, Pretty Shield listened as the spirit instructed her to tell the ants what she wished for. The spirit then vanished. Pretty Shield followed her instructions, asking the ants for good luck and a good life. A vision of a war-eagle in a beautiful lodge came to her, and from then on, Pretty Shield was able to communicate with ants. These "busy, powerful little people," as she called them, became her spirit helpers, the source of her "medicine," or power. Listening to the ants and following their advice, she claimed, helped her become a "wise-one," capable of healing sickness and helping mothers give birth. With her interest in life renewed, Pretty Shield hurried back to her family.

In Crow culture, healers were special. It was believed that their powerful spirit helpers guided their work. Healers knew how to talk with patients and listen, observing their body language and facial expressions. Sometimes Pretty Shield healed through touch, gently pushing pain out of a patient's body. She also gathered plants with healing properties and made medicines from it. Healers knew how to gather each plant, what time of year to harvest it, and which parts to use. Take the white-flowered yarrow, for example, which the Crow called chipmunk tail. Its leaves, which could be picked in any season, had many uses. It helped stop bleeding, heal wounds, and cleanse the body internally. Another plant, lomatium, was rarer. The Crow used this plant, which they called bear-root, for pain, cold and flu, and especially childbirth. The root could be dug up only in the autumn, secretly and with a special ceremony. It was then roasted and peeled. Pieces would be sliced off as needed. Pretty Shield always carried a big bear-root with her in case of emergency.

For a time, it looked like Pretty Shield had everything a Crow woman could want: a good husband, children, extended family, meaningful work, and plenty to eat. But developments in the wider world were beginning to unbalance her life and the lives of her people. Since the time she was born, things had been changing rapidly for Montana's tribes. Although the Crow had signed a treaty with the U.S. government in 1851 giving the tribe 38.5 million acres of territory, in 1868 the size of the reservation was radically reduced, to 8 million acres. Later, when miners hit gold on reservation land, the government shrank the boundaries again to make more of the land public. By 1872, the year Pretty Shield got married, the government was actively trying to force the Crow and other tribes to give up their nomadic ways and settle on small farms on their reservations. Yet Pretty Shield and other Crow could not discard their ancient ways of life so easily.

During most of the 1800s, Crow men sometimes served as scouts for the American army, since the army's enemies—the Lakota, Cheyenne, and Arapaho—were also the Crow's enemies. In the summer of 1876, a number of Crow warriors, including Goes Ahead, scouted for General George A. Custer at the Battle of the Little Bighorn, where Custer was killed and the U.S. Army was defeated. The following year, the army hit back hard, forcing the Crow's enemies to surrender or flee. After that, with no competitors in their hunting grounds, the Crow felt safer.

At the same time, however, a different kind of competition was arriving in Crow country. White miners and settlers were streaming into the area and taking over Crow land. Worst of all were the white buffalo hunters, who killed bison just for their hides. The U.S. government encouraged the slaughter, knowing that if their main food source was destroyed, the Indians would become dependent on government food supplies and stay on their reservations. By the time Pretty Shield was about thirty, around 1886, so few bison were left that the Crow had to give up their traditional hunting way of life. Later, Pretty Shield remembered this painful time:

> The whole country . . . smelled of rotting meat. Even the flowers could not put down the bad smell. Our hearts were like stones. And yet nobody believed, even then, that the white man could kill all the buffalo. Since the beginning of things there had always been so many! Even the Lakota,

bad as their hearts were for us, would not do such a thing as this; nor the Cheyenne, nor the Arapahoe, nor the Pecunnie [Blackfeet]; and yet the white man did this, even when he did not want the meat.

The Crows' transition to the reservation was miserable, as Pretty Shield described:

> We believed for a long time that the buffalo would again come to us; but they did not. We grew hungry and sick and afraid. . . .
>
> Then white men began to fence the plains so we could not travel. . . . We began to stay in one place, and to grow lazy and sicker all the time. [N]ow, with everything else going wrong . . . our leaders began to drink the white man's whisky, letting it do their thinking. Because we were used to listening to our chiefs . . . we listened to them now; [but] our wise-ones became fools, and drank the white man's whisky.

By 1894, Pretty Shield and Goes Ahead were living on the reservation, in the town of Crow Agency. There, they were surrounded by the same people they had always lived with, except now families lived in houses on regular streets, bought their food in stores, sent their children to school, and attended Christian churches. Adjustment to this new life was difficult. The food supplies that the government promised the tribe were commonly of poor quality, if the shipments arrived at all. Because people could no longer hunt very much, and because their farms were frequently unsuccessful, the tribe had no way to supplement government rations, so food was often scarce. Hunger, poverty, and disease killed Crow people by the hundreds. Between 1865 and 1910, the number of tribal members dropped by half, from an estimated 3,500 to 1,740.

Church was one new thing that many Crow embraced. For decades, Christian missionaries had been visiting native tribes throughout the West. The Crow were no exception. By the late 1800s, many of them had converted. Some combined the new beliefs with traditional ones, while others gave up Crow spiritual practices entirely.

In 1896 Goes Ahead, Pretty Shield, and their second daughter, Little Woman (also called Helen), became the first three members of Crow Agency's Congregationalist church. Goes Ahead embraced Christianity completely, seeing Christ as a true and impressive warrior, and the Christian God as an extremely powerful chief. To prove his devotion, he threw his precious medicine bundle, a collection of sacred items, into the river. Pretty Shield promised her husband that she, too, would give up traditional Crow beliefs, and she tried to keep her promise, especially while Goes Ahead lived. But she could never let her old ways go completely.

In 1919, Goes Ahead became ill. Knowing he was going to die, he chose a favorite spot at the edge of town by the Little Bighorn River. His family erected a tipi, where he and Pretty Shield stayed until his death. Afterward, Pretty Shield received a few marriage proposals, but she had no interest in remarrying, remaining a widow for the rest of her life. By that time, she had many grandchildren, and she took comfort in spending time with them.

Pretty Shield's daughter Little Woman had seven children with her husband, George Hogan. When George was around age seven, he had been taken away to an Indian school in Pennsylvania and hadn't returned to the reservation for thirteen years. He grew used to eastern things there, and when he returned and fell in love with Little Woman, he built her a beautiful house in Benteen, about ten miles south of Crow Agency, complete with hardwood floors, Persian rugs, fine furniture, and even a record player.

Sadly, in 1924, when George and Little Woman's youngest child was only a year old, Little Woman contracted tuberculosis and died. Mourning her daughter's death, Pretty Shield asked George if she could raise his and Little Woman's children. He agreed. He later remarried, but he always remained part of his first family's lives.

To raise the children, George gave Pretty Shield the house he had built for Little Woman in Benteen. Crow custom dictated that, after her death, all of Little Woman's fine things must be given away, so the house Pretty Shield and the kids moved into was practically empty. They made do, though, and it would be their home for the next seven years.

Only a short time after Little Woman's death, Pretty Shield's older daughter, Pine Fire, also died, and Pretty Shield adopted her two kids too. Now, at age sixty-eight, she was raising nine children by herself, the youngest one an infant. Life had become very challenging for Pretty Shield. As Goes Ahead's widow, she received a small government check each month for her late husband's service as an army scout, but it was not enough to cover the large family's expenses. Sometimes the grandchildren barely had enough to eat. But Pretty Shield knew how to survive, and she kept her brood together. In the Crow way, neighbors and friends helped, sharing what they had. Hunters, including Pretty Shield's son-in-law, George, dropped by with meat.

Even though she lived in a house now, Pretty Shield spent much of her time outside, and she continued to rely on traditional skills. She harvested edible and medicinal wild plants and gathered her own firewood. She washed clothes in the river, butchered and pounded game meat on its banks and scraped and tanned animal hides. For a long time, until she got used to it, Pretty Shield hated the smell and taste of beef, much preferring bison and other game. Unlike her grandchildren, who were growing up in a different world, she never learned more than a few words of English. But some modern things pleased old Pretty Shield. She started using soap to scrub stains from clothes instead of sand and liked manufactured cups, combs, and needles. One of her favorite meals was hardly a traditional Crow dish: canned tomatoes and macaroni.

The youngest of Pretty Shield's grandchildren was Alma Hogan. As an adult, Alma would write a book about growing up with Pretty Shield. Of course Pretty Shield loved all her grandchildren, but Alma became her kaalisbaapite ("kah-LEESH-bah-bee-dah"), or "grandmother's grandchild." A kaalisbaapite is a sort of apprentice to the grandmother. He or she is expected to pay close attention to the grandmother and learn everything she teaches. In exchange for this special education, the kaalisbaapite stays with the grandmother and helps her as she gets older. Unlike most children, whose parents watch over them and provide everything they need, a grandmother's grandchild has many responsibilities and little time to play.

In changing times, Pretty Shield's traditional knowledge may have seemed outdated, but it was all she had to offer. Neither grandmother nor grandchild could imagine it, but in the future, the knowledge Pretty Shield gave her granddaughter would enrich Alma's life greatly, as well as the lives of others. In teaching Alma, Pretty Shield was trying to help her, but she was also trying to preserve Crow culture. Through Alma, she hoped, essential traditions and the reasons behind them might reach future generations.

And so Alma learned Pretty Shield's way of doing everything from bathing to butchering, from collecting firewood to playing traditional games. Alma took a special interest in gathering and cooking wild foods and in making medicines from plants. Pretty Shield taught her kaalisbaapite all about such medicines and about Crow healing techniques. Most important, and at the base of it all, Pretty Shield was teaching Alma what makes a good life and a good person, according to Crow values.

In addition, Pretty Shield was a storehouse of tribal legends, history, and songs for her granddaughter. "Grandma had a song for everything," Alma recalled. Singing was part of daily Crow life, associated with both practical tasks and spirituality—traditionally, the two were not separate. Pretty Shield was deeply spiritual, rising before dawn every day to go outside and converse with God. Often she prayed so hard and for so long that when she returned, she was soaked with sweat.

Fiercely protective of her grandchildren, and with few material resources at her disposal, Pretty Shield called on her faith to keep her loved ones safe. Once, in Benteen, the radio warned of a huge storm coming. Soon, the wind was roaring like a freight train. Pretty Shield hurried her grandchildren to a root cellar, but she herself did not go down. When Alma, worried, sneaked up to find her, she saw Pretty Shield standing outside, one hand raised, her braids blowing straight out behind her. She was praying fervently, asking God to spare her grandchildren's house. Suddenly, the wind shifted direction. Awed, Alma believed that Pretty Shield had turned the storm.

Alma's older siblings and cousins went to school in the town of Crow Agency, some ten miles from Benteen. Twice a day, Pretty Shield drove a wagon with her grandkids through the river and several miles down a road to the nearest bus stop. Little Alma, however, stayed home until she was nearly eight. During that time, numerous government officials knocked on Pretty Shield's door to tell her Alma had to go to school. Every time, Pretty Shield told them Alma was sick. At last, however, Pretty Shield felt her kaalisbaapite's traditional education was complete and that she needed modern knowledge too. She agreed to send Alma to school.

Around the same time, Pretty Shield made another decision. She was seventy-five now, and the rides to and from the bus stop were exhausting. She moved the children into Crow Agency to be closer to school. The family lived in a one-room shack. Furnishings were minimal; they slept in buffalo robes on the floor. By this time, some of Alma's older siblings had married and were living on their own, but Pretty Shield still cared for the younger children.

In March 1931, after the move to Crow Agency, a strange request made its way to Pretty Shield's ears. A white man, a writer, was looking for a female Crow elder willing to tell her life story. The man, Frank Bird Linderman, had lived among several Montana tribes and was a proven friend to Indian people. The Crow called him "Sign Talker" because although he spoke only English, he was skilled at the sign language that tribes used to talk with one another.

Recognizing how drastically Indian life was changing, Linderman devoted himself to capturing tribal histories and traditions before they were forgotten. He had already interviewed the Crow leader Plenty Coups and published his story as a book. By sharing the story of one Crow man, Linderman hoped to educate the American public about the plight of reservation Indians. The book was well received, but Linderman realized that, for a full picture of how Crow life used to be, he should also talk to a woman. Few Indian women felt comfortable, however, having long, personal conversations with non-Indian men. When Pretty Shield agreed to talk to Linderman, therefore, it was a bold step.

Pretty Shield told Sign Talker that she would tell him anything he wanted to know and hold nothing back. Why? Because she knew it was important—it would be terrible if the way of life she'd known as a girl was forgotten. Over several weeks, Pretty Shield met with Linderman and recounted her life to him. In addition to using sign language, the two communicated through a Crow interpreter, Pretty Shield's friend Goes Together. Most days, the man and two women met in an old, empty schoolhouse, but sometimes they talked under the trees in the local park instead, or at Pretty Shield's house, over hot coffee. Alma remembered Linderman as a wonderful man, and his gifts, often silver dollars, were much appreciated.

Linderman tried to get Pretty Shield to talk about her life after the buffalo disappeared, but she wouldn't. Talking about that time made her too sad. Crow life had changed so much, and not for the better, she felt. "I'm living a life I don't understand. I feel like I'm losing my children to this new world of life that I don't know."

Linderman had great respect for Pretty Shield, as did everyone who knew her. The superintendent of the reservation told Linderman, "[Pretty Shield] is a good woman. I do not know how some of these people could have lived without her. She is charity itself. She has mothered the motherless." Linderman's book, originally called *Red Mother* but later retitled *Pretty-Shield: Medicine Woman of the Crows*, was published in 1932. It not only helped preserve Crow culture, it also introduced the world to a hard-working, funny, caring, honest, and admirable human being named Pretty Shield.

Crow women had always helped one another and their communities, but in Crow Agency, that tradition became formalized in the Crow Women's Club, which Pretty Shield joined after the family moved back. The club was part of a national organization of women's clubs across the country that focused mainly on improving health and education in their communities. Sometimes Pretty Shield even traveled with other club members to meetings in Helena, Billings, and elsewhere.

Eventually, at the urging of her granddaughters, Pretty Shield acquired a few modern conveniences. She bought a washing machine, though she refused to touch it. She did, however, agree to stop washing her clothes in the river and let the girls use the machine. Pretty Shield even bought a car, but again, it was mostly for her granddaughters. The one time she tried to drive it, she smashed through a woodpile and ended up in the coal shed.

Meanwhile, Alma had started school. After a short period of adjustment, getting used to sitting still and speaking only English, Alma did well in her classes. She made good grades and enjoyed sports and drama. Outside school, she sang in a quartet, took tap-dancing lessons, and joined the Girl Scouts. But Alma sometimes got into mischief as well. As she later recalled, in the sixth grade, she was sent to the principal's office for some small offense. She was shocked when the principal whipped her hands with a rubber hose. No adult had ever hit her before. Traditionally, the Crow did not believe in punishing children physically. Alma ran home and showed her swollen hands to Pretty Shield. Furious, Pretty Shield grabbed a hatchet and marched back to the school, Alma in tow. Without knocking, she stormed into the principal's office and, brandishing the hatchet, told him, "You bad!" After that, the principal thought twice about using a hose on students.

After sixth grade, Alma was sent to an Indian boarding school in Pierre, South Dakota. Because she was so close to her grandmother, it was very painful for Alma to be away from her, and she knew it was painful for Pretty Shield, too. Making it worse, Alma hated the school. Discipline was strict, and she sometimes found worms in her food but was forced to eat it anyway. In spite of her misery, she couldn't go home. Her sister Mayme believed the education Alma was receiving was worth the suffering, and she convinced Pretty Shield that staying at school was best for Alma. Two years later, in 1940, Alma went on to attend the Indian high school in Flandreau, South Dakota. In 1942, however, she left school to help her sister Pearl, who was by then a working mother in Tacoma, Washington.

By 1944, Alma was back home. That year, Pretty Shield, now eighty-eight years old, became ill, and on April 30, surrounded by her grandchildren, she peacefully passed away. Life had changed so much, and though Pretty Shield never gave up, and devotedly raised her grandchildren to adulthood, Alma believed that all the changes broke her grandmother's heart. Pretty Shield was buried in the same grave as her husband, Goes Ahead, in the Custer National Cemetery at the Little Bighorn Battlefield National Monument.

Pretty Shield's granddaughter and kaalisbaapite, *Alma Hogan Snell, who became an expert on traditional Crow foods and an author. Here she is in her kitchen in 2000, posing for a book about pies.* —Courtesy Kristin Loudis, KrisinLoudisPhotography.com

After her grandmother's death, Alma experienced difficult times, but the memory of Pretty Shield's love and lessons kept the young woman going. Eventually she married her true love, Bill Snell, an Assiniboine man she had met in high school, and raised a family. Through it all, Alma, Pretty Shield's kaalisbaapite, remained true to her grandmother's teachings. Alma embraced modern life, but she also talked with birds and ants, used wild plants for healing, and recounted ancestral Crow stories as Pretty Shield had done. What's more, after retiring from a career of work and travel, Alma began sharing her knowledge by teaching classes, giving presentations, and writing books and articles. The book she wrote about growing up with Pretty Shield, *Grandmother's Grandchild: My Crow Indian Life*, was published in 2000. Shortly before she died in 2008, Montana State University awarded Alma Hogan Snell an honorary doctorate degree for her work in Crow cultural preservation.

Pretty Shield and her grandchildren experienced painful transitions during their lives. In the case of Pretty Shield, the changes were as huge and radical as if, in a different kind of story, space aliens had invaded and taken over. In contrast, Pretty Shield's grandchildren, growing up in the 1920s through 1940s, were more like pioneers, feeling their way along in a new world where the rules were seldom clear. Despite everything, strengthened by their love for one another, the family held together and the children made their way.

Pretty Shield's legacy has endured. Her commitment to Indian people continues through the Pretty Shield Foundation, founded by her great-grandson Bill Snell, Jr., in 1997 to help Native American communities across the continent. In addition, Pretty Shield's honest, poignant story as recorded by Frank Bird Linderman, as well as her granddaughter Alma's informative and equally honest writings, are gifts of information and inspiration, not just for Crow people but for people of all backgrounds, everywhere.

JEANNETTE RANKIN

BUILDING TOWARD PEACE

Jeannette Rankin was a fixer. Born and raised on a ranch in western Montana in the 1880s and '90s, she learned early how to get things done. The daughter of a builder-engineer, she seemed to inherit her father's quick grasp of mechanical problems and solutions; perhaps at a different time of history, when women had more opportunity, Jeannette would have followed in her father's footsteps and become a builder. Instead, she applied her knack for spotting a problem and fixing it to society itself. For her entire life, she worked hard to make the world better, especially for women and children, approaching problems with the enthusiasm and stubborn determination it seemed she was born with.

Jeannette's problem-solving ability showed early on. One day, when she was only eight or nine, her father's new haying machine seized up. As he and his ranch hands scratched their heads over the problem, Jeannette, who had been watching the whole time, spoke up. She showed the men where the machine was blocked. As the workers set about removing the obstruction, Jeannette's father scolded them for knowing less than a little girl. Thanks to her, the machine was soon humming again.

Jeannette's quick eye and mind were matched by a compassionate heart. On the ranch, she often jumped in when she witnessed suffering. When she was about twelve, noticing that one of her father's horses

Jeannette Rankin as a young woman; no date. —Courtesy Montana Historical Society Research Center, Montana Historical Society, Helena, Montana

had torn its shoulder on barbed wire, Jeannette had the ranch hands wrestle the horse to the ground while she grabbed some supplies. She washed the wound and quickly, efficiently sewed it up. Another time, Jeannette's dog caught his paw in a trap. She realized she had no choice but to amputate his foot, which she did. While her pet healed, she sewed a leather boot for the stump, and he wore it for the rest of his life.

As an adult, Jeannette's efforts to fix the whole world began in earnest when she became involved with the campaign for "woman suffrage"— women's right to vote. For five long years, she crisscrossed the country, working tirelessly to convince people in one state after another that society would improve if women could vote. Next, Jeannette ran for the U.S. House of Representatives and won, becoming America's very first congresswoman. She is also famous for her opposition to war—in particular, voting "no" in Congress not once, but twice, against major wars. By the end of her life, Jeannette was respected around the globe as a leader in the movement for world peace.

———————•••———————

Jeannette Pickering Rankin was born on her family's ranch on Grant Creek, just outside Missoula, Montana Territory. The date was June 11, 1880, nine years before Montana became a state. She was the eldest of John and Olive Rankin's seven children, six girls and one boy.

John Rankin, born in Canada, came to Montana as a young man in the 1860s. Although he had received only about three years of schooling, John was an expert builder. Arriving in the budding village of Missoula around 1870, he went into business. In addition to churches, homes, and other buildings, John built some of Missoula's first bridges. He even served a term as a Missoula County commissioner. In 1878, John invested in a 1,480-acre ranch up Grant Creek, a few miles from town. There he raised sheep and, later, cattle; he also operated a lucrative sawmill on his property and ran several businesses in town.

Also in 1878, at a local dance, John met Missoula's new schoolteacher, Olive Pickering, who, longing for adventure, had moved west from New Hampshire. Taken by this plucky young woman, John courted her, soon winning her over with his good looks, work ethic, and financial success. The following August, John and Olive married and settled in at the ranch.

After Jeannette, John and Olive's first child, came Philena, born in 1882, then Harriet (Hattie), Wellington (the only boy), Mary, and Grace. The youngest, Edna, was born in 1893. Sadly, when Jeannette was only eleven, before Grace and Edna were born, nine-year-old Philena died of a ruptured appendix.

The three oldest Rankin siblings began their education at the one-room school in Grant Creek. Then, in 1885, John built an elegant ten-room house in Missoula. From then on, the family spent winters in town, where the kids attended the local schools, and summers at the ranch. The Rankin house was the first one in Missoula with central heating and hot and cold running water. There was even a bathtub. At the very top

Rankin family; no date. Left to right: front row, John, Mary, Edna, Grace, Wellington, Olive; back row, Jeannette, Harriet; on the table is a photograph of Philena. —Courtesy Montana Historical Society Research Center, Montana Historical Society, Helena, Montana

of the three-story home, John added a fancy cupola from which to look out over town.

As a former teacher, Olive emphasized education. She kept a pull-down map of the United States in the dining room, and the Rankin household, both in town and at the ranch, overflowed with books. Even so, Jeannette did not really like school. She was somewhat timid in class, and her mind went blank "when confronted with a piece of paper," as she later described. She managed to make average grades, but she preferred the open air, hardy physical work, and freedom of the ranch to a stuffy classroom.

If Jeannette was quiet in school, within her family she was a leader. As the oldest daughter, she helped her mother a lot around the house, cooking, cleaning, and taking care of the younger children. By the time Jeannette was thirteen, in fact, Olive, who had grown weak and overweight from physical and also possibly mental illness, withdrew from running the household and, instead, let her firstborn do it. Jeannette cooked nearly all the meals, sewed nearly all the family's clothes, baked the bread, and even read to her younger siblings before bed each night. It was a lot of work and responsibility for a teenager, and Jeannette did not enjoy it. Only her sense of duty kept her going.

Jeannette also worked hard for her father, whom she adored. From the time she was little, John took a special interest in his eldest daughter. He trusted her reliability, initiative, and good judgment, discussing business and other matters with her like an adult. In turn, she was eager to help and please him. Once, John was trying to sell one of his downtown properties, but the buyer balked because the building had no sidewalk in front. In those days, sidewalks were made of wooden planks. John resigned himself to losing the sale, but teenage Jeannette grabbed some tools and lumber from the sawmill, and in no time, constructed a sidewalk. The building was sold.

Jeannette and her siblings were vital to their father's business ventures. When they were only between the ages of ten and fourteen, Jeannette, Harriet, and Wellington ran their father's sixty-five-room downtown hotel practically by themselves. Whenever she was needed,

Jeannette also filled in at John's lumber camp, cooking for the workers. She even knew how to run the sawmill. John encouraged his children to be responsible and self-starting. He expected a great deal of them, yet he did not criticize how they went about getting things done. His attitude may help account for the healthy self-confidence with which the Rankin kids approached their lives.

Belonging to Missoula's earliest community of settlers also contributed to that confidence. Growing up within a small population where everyone knew and tolerated one another, quirks and all, endowed the Rankin kids with an inner security that they seldom seemed to question. And the Rankins did have their quirks. Jeannette herself described her family as "gregarious loners," meaning they were outgoing and talkative, yet underneath, they preferred keeping to themselves.

Olive and John tended to be permissive with their children, and the house was often chaotic. Arguments between the kids, often over current events, could grow so heated that they threw things at each other, even glasses of water. As adults, they would go on disagreeing, yet the Rankin siblings always stood by one another. The extreme passion they exhibited as kids showed up later in the drive with which they accomplished their goals.

Jeannette graduated from high school in 1898, then enrolled at the University of Montana, which had been founded in Missoula only three years before. In addition to her studies, she played basketball there, even breaking her nose in one game. Majoring in biology, Jeannette received her B.S. degree in 1902. Later, all five of her siblings followed her to the university. Wellington transferred from the University of Montana to Harvard University, near Boston, Masssachusetts, where he earned his BA and, later, a law degree.

As Wellington and Jeannette got older, they grew closer, despite the four-year gap between them. In adulthood, Jeannette would rely on her younger brother for support and advice on how to manage her life and career. Jeannette would become the most famous Rankin, but most of her siblings also made names for themselves. Wellington grew up to be a wealthy and renowned trial lawyer. In 1920, he served as Montana's state attorney general, and by the time of his death he was one of America's largest landowners. Edna, the first woman to earn a law degree at Montana State University, worked in the birth-control movement both nationally and internationally. Harriet became a dean at the university, and Mary taught English there.

After graduating from college, Jeannette wasn't sure what to do with her life. She received, and turned down, several marriage proposals. She was not interested in having children, feeling like she had already raised one family—her sisters and brother. Teaching school like her mother seemed to be a natural choice for someone so experienced with children, so she took a job teaching at a local school in Missoula. After only one school year, however, she decided she didn't like it.

In the fall, Jeannette moved about 150 miles southeast to teach in Whitehall, Montana, but that was worse. She quit after the first semester and returned to the family ranch in December of 1903. Teaching children, it seemed, was not Jeannette's gift. She wanted to do something different, something bigger that would make a difference in the world.

In the meantime, back in Missoula, Jeannette's ability with a needle and thread came in handy when one of the city's finest dressmakers and hatmakers hired her to sew. Sewing wasn't the career Jeannette had in mind, but until she figured out what to do next, it was good, steady work. For the rest of her life, Jeannette could fall back on sewing when she needed to earn money.

In May 1904, shortly before Jeannette's twenty-fourth birthday, her father came down with Rocky Mountain spotted fever, a disease carried by ticks, and he died. The family was devastated, especially Jeannette. Wellington came home from Harvard to handle the business and financial interests his father had left behind. Olive and the girls each received a moderate amount of money, giving them a measure of security for the rest of their lives. Still, Jeannette wanted to work. She just didn't know what kind of job would suit her.

Wellington returned to Harvard in the fall of 1904. That winter, he became sick, and Jeannette hurried to Boston to care for him. He recovered quickly, but Jeannette decided to remain on the East Coast a little longer—and ended up staying six months. In Boston, and also in

New York City, Jeannette saw deep urban poverty for the first time. In the inner-city slums, thousands of families, many of them recent immigrants from Europe who did not speak English, lived crammed together in poorly heated tenement buildings without adequate sanitation. Seeing such miserable conditions ignited Jeannette's inborn compassion—and her desire to fix the problem of poverty.

Upon returning home to Missoula, Jeannette helped out at home and took a class, by mail, in furniture design. At the same time, she couldn't stop thinking about the poverty she'd seen in Boston and New York. She began reading more about the topic of poverty and what some Americans were doing to help. One of them, Jane Addams, had started a "settlement house" in Chicago, called Hull House, for the working poor—mainly, newly arrived immigrants. Settlement houses were created to help such families find housing, education, jobs, and health care. The staff at the settlement houses, she learned, were trained in a new field called social work.

Perhaps because she had worked so intensively throughout her childhood, it was hard for Jeannette not to have meaningful or "definite" work, as she put it, in her life. By 1907, she had become restless and blue. She felt she needed a change, so in the late fall, when she was twenty-seven, Jeannette traveled to San Francisco to visit an uncle. In that city was a well-known settlement house, like Hull House in Chicago, called Telegraph Hill. Intrigued, Jeannette paid the place a visit.

At Telegraph Hill, Jeannette observed the social workers' efforts to help suffering families. Seeing her interest, the staff asked her if she wanted to help, and she said yes. As a volunteer, Jeannette looked after children, learning about their lives and those of their families. Desperate for jobs, poor immigrants and other disadvantaged people endured low pay, long hours, and terrible working conditions, especially in factories, where men, women, and even children labored. In those days, laws in many states allowed kids as young as six to work, and workers often toiled six or even seven days a week and up to sixteen hours a day. In the future, Jeannette would find herself advancing new labor laws to protect people from being so exploited and overworked.

After four months at Telegraph Hill, Jeannette became convinced that as a social worker, she could help fix the terrible problems she saw in her country. She felt she had found her life's goal at last. In 1908 she left San Francisco for New York City, where she enrolled in the social-work program at the New York School of Philanthropy.

Jeannette wasn't the only one hoping to end the suffering of the poor. The early 1900s saw the evolution of the "Progressive Era" in America, and women were taking the lead. Progressives wanted to reform American government and pass laws that would curb government corruption; eliminate child labor; ensure the safety of workers, the purity of food, the health of newborns; and many other improvements.

In New York, Jeannette met a number of brilliant, passionate female activists dedicated to changing their world. In addition to helping the poor, these women believed in women's suffrage, or right to vote. At that time, only four American states, all in the West, allowed female citizens to vote in any election. Progressive men and women thought that because most women were concerned about the welfare of their families and communities, female voters would support laws that would bring about change. It was therefore vital, Progressives felt, for women to be able to participate fully in elections. It was also a matter of simple fairness. The link between women voting and societal change was a seed planted in Jeannette's mind.

Upon graduating in 1909, Jeannette returned west. After spending the summer in Montana, she took a job as a social worker in what was supposed to be a new, better kind of orphanage, or children's home, in Spokane, Washington. After working in Spokane for a short time, Jeannette transferred to another facility in Seattle run by the same organization, the Washington Children's Home Society. In addition to orphans, these homes took in kids whose families couldn't afford to raise them. The goal was to find them adoptive parents, but to Jeannette's horror, nearly half of the children who were adopted were later returned. Poverty had damaged many of the kids' physical and mental health so much that any new placement was almost guaranteed to fail. Even worse, thirteen of the children living at the home that year died.

Frustrated, Jeannette concluded that social work was not enough to change society's ills. Ever the fixer, she wanted to prevent problems in the first place, and that could only happen through new legislation. America's laws needed to change, and Jeannette decided to devote herself to making that happen. First, she decided to get training. In the fall of 1909, she enrolled at the University of Washington in Seattle to study political science, economics, and public speaking.

While a student at the university, the seed that had been planted in Jeannette's mind in New York sprouted. Remembering the link between social-reform legislation and women voting—the idea that women in particular were likely to support such legislation—Jeannette began working for women's suffrage in Washington State. Ultimately, American suffragists wanted a national constitutional amendment that would expand voting rights to all women. In the meantime, their strategy was to campaign state by state, convincing male legislators and voters in individual states to give their female citizens the vote. Now, in the spring of 1910, the Evergreen State was the suffragists' next target.

As a first step, Jeannette volunteered to put up posters for the campus suffrage organization, the College Equal Suffrage League. She was so enthusiastic and did so well that the group's leaders offered her a paid position working on the state campaign. Jeannette threw herself into the job. From experienced coworkers, she learned how to organize "grass-roots" campaigns and persuade voters. She would always remember the advice of one savvy leader: "Rely on facts rather than argument. . . . Convert the indifferent—there are thousands of them; let the incorrigible alone—there are only a few."

After so many false starts, Jeannette had finally found work that felt truly meaningful to her. Traveling through county after county in Washington, Jeannette discovered what worked and what didn't. With practice, she overcame her natural shyness, so much so that public speaking became one of her greatest skills. She spoke mostly in small settings, such as public schools, churches, taverns, and people's homes, but she also gave talks at big venues such as community centers, universities, union halls, and even the state capitol. Jeannette's favorite place to speak, however, was street corners. There she could reach all kinds of people, not just those interested enough to attend a speech.

The suffragists' hard work paid off. In November of 1910, the men of Washington State voted to enfranchise (grant voting rights to) women. The campaign had won! With her newfound skills, Jeannette was hired to work on the campaign in New York State and, after that, in California. Sometimes she was sent to rural areas to speak with voters. Other times, she lobbied state legislators.

Generally, suffragists presented many logical arguments to convince Americans that women should vote. Surprisingly, it wasn't just men who opposed suffrage; many women did too, believing that they already had enough influence through their husbands. What about women who were single or widowed, Jeannette and other suffragists countered, and had no husband? Was it fair that working women, who paid taxes, had no say in how that money was spent? Some Americans felt that women simply don't belong in politics. In response, Jeannette would give the example of a traditional woman, a mother at home nursing a child with typhoid. Good sanitation would have prevented her child's illness in the first place. Shouldn't mothers be able to vote for candidates who support better sanitation?

Jeannette held political opinions about things besides women's suffrage, too. Earlier, in Seattle, one of her suffragist friends, Minnie J. Reynolds, had shared her views not only about voting, but also about war. Minnie believed that war of any kind was wrong, and that problems between nations could always be solved in other ways. The enormous suffering and loss caused by war only made the problems worse. Jeannette was convinced that Minnie was right. She and Minnie viewed war as a woman's issue because it took away the fruits of their labor— their sons, their communities—and destroyed them. No matter what the circumstances, Jeannette came to believe, war was never worth the costs. This belief is called pacifism.

Between work trips, Jeannette headed home to Montana to rest. On the campaign trail, she was always beautifully dressed, and in Montana, she took time to sew new clothes while talking politics and planning strategy with Wellington. They often discussed the suffrage struggle in Montana. Even while Jeannette was working to expand the vote across the nation, as of 1911 her own home state had yet to pass women's suffrage. Although many Montana women had been campaigning for years to get the vote, they had not been able to convince the state legislature to pass the law.

In February 1911, upon hearing that a new suffrage bill had been introduced in the Montana general assembly, Jeannette headed to Helena. There, she became the first woman to speak before the state legislature. Wearing her abundant brown hair pinned up under a wide-brimmed hat, Jeannette made her case and urged the legislators to support the bill. The lawmakers listened respectfully to her well-reasoned arguments, but in the end, although the House voted yes, the Senate voted no. Montana women would have to wait for their turn at the polls. With Jeannette Rankin in their corner, however, they would not have to wait much longer.

Jeannette returned to the campaign in California, where the suffragists saw victory in November. After that, she tried again to get suffrage passed in New York State. By 1912, she had crisscrossed the continent twelve times by train and automobile. In subsequent years, she would help on campaigns in thirteen more states as well as in Montana and Washington, D.C. The results were mixed, but in most of the states she campaigned in, it would be 1917 or later before suffrage passed. In the meantime, Jeannette kept working and learning.

In March 1913, the National American Woman Suffrage Association (NAWSA), a group in which Jeannette served as an officer, organized a huge parade in Washington, D.C. It was held the day before the inauguration of President Woodrow Wilson, who opposed the movement. Among the more than five thousand female marchers were Jeannette and her sister Edna. But people opposed to suffrage, mostly men, disrupted the parade, shouting insults, pushing women, pulling down banners, throwing things, and even spitting on the marchers. The event turned into a riot, but the local police did nothing. Finally, the National Guard arrived and restored order.

The incident made headlines. Because the men were so aggressive and ugly, the public sympathized with the suffragists. Even those who disagreed with the marchers' cause were outraged. The incident made people more aware of the suffrage issue and of the viciousness of the opposition. Support for the suffragists grew.

Before the year was out, Jeannette quit the NAWSA to focus on suffrage in Montana. Arriving home, she connected with the state's existing suffragists. Setting their sights on the 1914 legislature, Jeannette and her Montana colleagues redoubled their efforts, hanging posters, writing letters, distributing pamphlets, giving speeches, and talking to voters in person. Jeannette herself logged over six thousand miles driving around the state, visiting as many places and people as she could and building a network of political volunteers. Soon the name Jeannette Rankin was known throughout Montana.

In November 1914, Montana women's suffrage passed—albeit narrowly, by only 52 percent. No matter: the Treasure State had become the tenth state in the union to grant women the right to vote in any election. Needless to say, Jeannette was elated. She also felt empowered. Her effort and dedication had achieved results. Now the question was, what's next?

Needing a rest and a change of scenery to think things over, Jeannette took a trip to New Zealand in 1915. It was not just a vacation. The women of New Zealand had been voting since 1893, and Jeannette wanted to learn more about civic life there. For months, she traveled around that nation, talking to people and observing the culture. New Zealand had laws protecting workers, children, and the elderly. Public health clinics and public parks seemed to be everywhere. Jeannette was impressed with how well the government treated its citizens. America could take a lesson from this nation, she must have thought. It was this trip, perhaps, that inspired her to take her next step in politics.

Back home, Montana's growing population had given the state a new, second seat in the U.S. House of Representatives. Upon her return from overseas, Jeannette began working toward a bold idea. What if she ran for that seat? She was now thirty-five and politically experienced. The suffrage campaign had built a strong political network, and eager female voters stood ready to exercise their power at the polls. Many of them had heard of or had even met Jeannette on the suffrage trail, and most viewed her with respect and gratitude. But no woman had been elected to the U.S. Congress before. Perhaps seeing a woman serving in Congress, Jeannette thought, was just what the country needed to prove that the so-called weaker sex was more than capable of handling political office.

In Missoula, Jeannette gathered friends and family and announced her intention to run for the U.S. House of Representatives. She was met with skepticism. Some people thought she should aim lower and run for the state legislature first, to see whether a woman could win an election at all. One friend felt that Jeannette should not run for any office—she would only make herself a laughingstock. Certain suffragists in the East also thought that Jeannette would lose and feared that her failure would make things harder for other women trying to enter politics. They believed that a better-known woman from an eastern state would have a greater chance of winning and therefore should be the first to run for Congress. But Jeannette was politically shrewd. She knew her own abilities and had sized up her state. She agreed that she might not be the best candidate, but she felt sure she could be elected.

If others were doubtful, Jeannette's family was not. Her siblings stood fully behind her. Wellington, by then extremely successful, offered to be her campaign manager and to help finance her campaign. Although Jeannette did not consider herself a member of either political party, the Rankins had traditionally been Republicans, so she chose to run as a Republican. In those days, the party lines were not as clear-cut as they are now; both parties had progressive, moderate, and conservative members.

After an energetic primary campaign, in August 1916 Jeannette was nominated as one of the Republican Party's two candidates for the U.S. House. Now she had to win the general election in November. In addition to her fellow Republican opponent, she ran against two Democrats and two Socialists. Since there were two open seats, the two candidates who received the most votes—regardless of party—would go to Congress. In other words, even if Jeannette placed second, she would win a seat.

Once again, Jeannette traveled the state exhaustively, this time for herself, telling voters what they could expect from her in Washington, D.C. In addition to supporting a constitutional amendment to give all American women the vote, she would introduce and support laws to improve the lives of the poor, especially children. To better serve Montana's farmers and ranchers, she educated herself about wool tariffs, grain inspection, and farm loans. She also shared her opposition to war, a stance she linked to the suffrage movement, since war, she believed, was a woman's issue.

By this time, 1916, World War I (then called the Great War) had been raging in Europe for two years. There was some talk of the U.S. getting involved, which most Americans opposed. It's not that they were pacifists—most people believed in fighting back if directly attacked. They simply weren't sure about sending American boys into a conflict that was not America's concern. Fortunately, at this point, U.S. involvement in the war seemed unlikely, so when Jeannette spoke of her belief in total pacifism, it probably seemed like an interesting or quaint idea to most people, not a seriously radical one.

The press largely ignored Jeannette on the election trail, but she drew large crowds whom she inspired with her engaging and effective speaking. Her sisters all pitched in to help, and Wellington wielded his influence with prominent Montanans to boost her campaign. Friends and fellow suffragists rallied around Jeannette, including former reporter Belle Fligelman in Helena, who managed Jeannette's publicity and wrote speeches for her (see chapter 6, Frieda and Belle Fligelman). Later, when Jeannette became a congresswoman, Belle and Jeannette's sister Harriet would work for her in Washington.

On Election Day, November 6, 1916, Jeannette cast her first-ever vote for herself. That evening, she went to bed thinking she had lost. Not all of the votes had come in yet, particularly from the rural areas, but the newspapers reported that she was way behind in the count. It took three days for all of the ballots to be counted. When the final numbers were tallied, the candidate, the state of Montana, and the entire nation were astonished: Jeannette Rankin had been elected the first female member of Congress.

In the same election, Woodrow Wilson won his second term as president. During his reelection campaign, Wilson had promised to keep America out of the Great War. In January 1917, however, the German government violated a pact it had signed with Wilson and began attacking American civilian ships with submarines. The U.S. also learned of a secret German plan to persuade Mexico to turn against its northern neighbor. Outraged, Americans began to support entering the war.

After the first German attacks on ships in February, Wilson severed diplomatic relations with Germany. Yet he still hesitated to bring America into the war. The Germans attacked several more times in March, torpedoing U.S. ships. Wilson was reaching his breaking point. However, the president does not have the power to declare war; only Congress does. If Wilson decided war was necessary, he would have to call an emergency session of Congress, and there would be a vote.

In February 1917, as all this was happening, Jeannette headed east to prepare for her service as America's first congresswoman. Congress was not scheduled to meet for its first regular session until December, but Jeannette meant to spend those months preparing for her new role. In New York, she bought new clothes, not just for work but for the many social events she would be attending. She also gave interviews and speeches, including a talk on democracy at Carnegie Hall in March. After that, Jeannette left for a speaking tour in the South. Her trip was cut short, however. On April 2, President Wilson called for an emergency joint session of Congress eight months early. It was no mystery why. Both the Senate and the House would be voting on a declaration of war.

In the meantime, public opinion had shifted dramatically in favor of retaliation. Nearly everyone Jeannette knew, including Wellington, advised her to vote for war. They believed that if she voted contrary to popular opinion, her political career would be over. Her fellow suffragists also feared that a "no" vote from Jeannette would make women look weak, hurting their chances to pass nationwide women's suffrage. Jeannette listened to their arguments, but as a pacifist, she was torn. She refused to say how she would vote—in part because she herself didn't know.

April 2 arrived—Jeannette's first day in Congress. Flowers from well-wishers filled her office. When she entered the House chamber, her colleagues gave her a standing ovation. She was sworn in with other new members and took her seat. Then the president entered to make his case for declaring war on Germany. The debate was on.

Members of Congress argued and deliberated for days. Hour after hour, Jeannette listened to her fellow representatives present their opinions, the overwhelming majority arguing in favor of war. She deliberately opened her mind to see if any of their arguments made more sense to her than pacifism.

On April 6 at 3 a.m., the roll was finally called for votes. Jeannette was visibly anxious as she stood to cast her first vote in Congress, but her voice was clear. "I want to stand by my country, but I cannot vote for war." Although Jeannette was in the minority, she was not alone. Forty-nine other members of the House also voted no. Of course, America did go to war, emerging victorious in November of 1918.

In voting against the war, Jeannette had stood by her principles, but it did cost her. Many congressmen refused to work with her on legislation, making her less effective in her job. Still, she did the best she could, working on bills for social reform—for example, equal pay for men and women—and many other issues. During her term, she helped pass the national women's suffrage bill in the House, only to see it fail in the Senate. Nevertheless, she was glad to have had the opportunity to vote for it.

Despite her difficulties, Jeannette's service in office did subtly affect public opinion. People saw that a woman in Congress did not seem so unnatural. Some Americans named their daughters after Jeannette. In the end, though, Wellington was right: her unpopular vote against the war had doomed her political career, at least for a long while. Running for reelection in 1918, Jeannette lost.

When her term ended in March 1919, Jeannette regretfully left Washington and went back to Montana. She had loved being a congresswoman. One thing made her feel better: the national women's suffrage amendment seemed poised to succeed. In May 1919, the 19th amendment to the U.S. Constitution, granting suffrage to women, passed the House, and two weeks later, the Senate. The states officially approved it in August of 1920. Now all American women, except Native American women, could vote in elections (American Indians were not permanently granted voting rights in every state until 1957). For most women, however, the passage of the amendment was a triumph.

Meanwhile, in 1919, Jeannette was chosen as one of six American delegates to the Women's International Conference for Permanent Peace, held in Zurich, Switzerland, in May. In Europe, Jeannette witnessed firsthand the devastation the Great War had caused—ruined buildings, mass graves, thin and sickly children. Seeing war's aftermath confirmed her belief in peace as the core ideal she wanted to strive for. When she returned to the U.S., she spent the next two decades lobbying legislators in Washington and traveling the country speaking about peace.

Most of Jeannette's peace work was focused in the east, particularly in Washington, D.C., yet she spent her breaks in Montana, staying as a guest with her mother or Wellington. In 1924, after years of long car and train trips between the eastern U.S. and Montana, Jeannette decided to move closer to her work. By train, the trip from Montana to Washington, D.C., took four days. She was drawn to the American South, which she had gotten to know during her suffrage days. She enjoyed the region's sunny weather and down-to-earth folks, some of whom even seemed to have pacifist leanings. The South was affordable, too—a plus for Jeannette, who had never earned or saved much money. Fortunately, that did not trouble her; she believed in living simply and inexpensively. After looking around, she bought a sixty-four-acre farm in rural Georgia, near the university town of Athens and less than a day's train ride from Washington, D.C. It would be a permanent home base from which to organize for peace—and for the first time, a place of her own.

On the property, near the hamlet of Bogart, Georgia, Jeannette had carpenters build her a simple house. Unlike the stately home she had grown up in, her little cottage had very few conveniences—no electricity or indoor plumbing. Jeannette's old fascination with building and engineering resurfaced as she devised her own heating system, using pipes and an old car radiator connected to the fireplace. Outside, she planted acres of trees, bushes, and vines.

Although the farm was her own, Jeannette did not live alone. Shortly after she bought the place, her sister Edna, recently divorced, brought her two children, Dorothy and John, to live there while she remained in Montana. Because Jeannette still traveled frequently, her elderly mother, Olive, also moved in to help with the kids. The family bought a cow for milk and butter, and harvested peaches and pecans from Jeannette's orchards. In addition to her family members, Jeannette had many visitors on the farm, and soon she added a few extra bedrooms to her little abode.

Jeannette adored her nephew and niece, and she was brokenhearted when John died in an accident at age seven. She and her niece Dorothy remained close for the rest of Jeannette's life.

After settling in on the farm, Jeannette got back to work promoting world peace. At home she wrote letters, articles, and speeches. On the road, in coordination with various antiwar groups, she gave talks, attended meetings, and lobbied legislators. Jeannette also worked for peace locally. In Bogart, she started recreational clubs where local girls and boys learned swimming, crafts, and games. Jeannette also told them stories and tried to instill in them "the habit of peace." She worked to "convert" her adult neighbors to peace as well. In Athens in 1928, she and other area pacifists formed the Georgia Peace Society.

In the summer of 1932, Jeannette, working with some national antiwar groups, helped organize a peace "march." For this event, she personally led a motorcade from Washington, D.C., to the national Republican and Democratic conventions in Chicago. The sign on her car said "NO MORE WAR." Little did Jeannette know, however, that world events were building toward another war.

After Adolf Hitler gained power in Germany in 1933, he became very aggressive toward nearby countries. Japan, too, was showing aggression, invading China in 1937. Two years later, Imperial Japan, Nazi Germany, and Fascist Italy signed a pact of alliance against a number of European nations—all of which were American allies—as well as China and some other countries. Soon afterward, Hitler invaded Poland, and war was officially declared in Europe. France, Great Britain, and the other Allied nations appealed to the United States for help.

As with World War I, many Americans were initially against involvement in an overseas conflict. As the hostilities grew worse, however, the American public became torn over whether or not to support the Allies in their fight to stop the Nazis. Although nothing was announced, President Franklin Roosevelt seemed to be preparing for war. In response to these tensions, Jeannette got busy. In 1937 she organized a children's peace parade in Georgia, and over the next few years, she went on dozens of tours, speaking against war. She also lobbied Congress to support peace measures and spoke on the radio. But would that be enough?

In 1940, in a final effort to keep the United States out of the war, Jeannette decided to run for Congress again. Although she lived much of the year in Georgia, she summered in Montana and still considered it home. Running for office there, where she and her family were known, made more sense than running in Georgia. As before, Wellington lent his financial and moral support.

Now nearly sixty, with fluffy white hair, Jeannette ran a brilliant campaign in Montana, appealing particularly to women voters. Once again, she traveled to town after town, talking to people. Persuasively, she encouraged citizens to write antiwar letters to elected officials. She went on the radio to plead her case against war. In her speeches, she maintained that the way to keep America secure was to strengthen its citizens by providing education and health care, enacting labor laws, and building up infrastructure.

Jeannette won the Republican primary in June 1940, and in November, she won the general election by more than nine thousand votes. Congressional sessions now started at the beginning rather than at the end of the year, so in January 1941, Jeannette found herself back in Washington, D.C. This time, Jeannette was not the only woman in Congress. There were nine others, eight in the House and one in the Senate.

During her first year in the new Congress, Jeannette offered several antiwar proposals, but all were defeated. War seemed inevitable. On

December 7, 1941, in a surprise assault, Japanese planes bombed U.S. Navy ships at Pearl Harbor, Hawaii. Whatever antiwar sentiment lingered in America instantly evaporated. The country had been attacked! President Roosevelt called an emergency session of Congress, urging a declaration of war on Japan.

Jeannette was traveling when she heard the news. Heavyhearted, she returned to Washington. Friends and colleagues began calling and coming by, urging her to support the war. Wellington, in particular, advised her not to vote against it. Certainly Japan's aggression justified fighting back! To escape the flood of pro-war voices, Jeannette got in her car and drove around the city while she thought it all over, arriving at the Capitol in time for the session. Later she recalled it had been like "driving to my execution."

When Jeannette took her seat, the issue was brought to a vote essentially without debate—unlike the prolonged discussions of twenty-four years earlier. Jeannette objected to the lack of debate on such a serious matter and tried repeatedly to protest, but the Speaker of the House coldly ignored her, finally ruling her out of order.

Jeannette could have chosen to abstain from voting. But instead, boldly, she voted no. "As a woman I can't go to war, and I refuse to send anyone else," she said. Immediately, boos and hisses erupted around her. In the end, 388 representatives voted for war and 41 abstained; in the Senate, the vote was 82 for and 0 against. Jeannette Rankin cast the sole congressional vote against World War II.

As she left the House chamber after the vote, Jeannette was met with an angry, jeering crowd. She was forced to duck into a phone booth, where she called for an escort to her office. Soon, telegrams denouncing Jeannette for her vote were pouring in from Montana and around the country. Wellington agreed with her critics, saying she had let her country down and telling her that Montanans were overwhelmingly against her. Some of her friends never forgave her for her antiwar vote.

While it seemed like everyone was against her, a few citizens thanked Jeannette for her stand. Others said that, though they disagreed with her vote, they admired her courage. It was the right to disagree, they said, that made America great. Even so, Jeannette knew that after her term ended in 1943, she would not win another. She returned to Montana to spend time with her family, especially her mother, Olive, who was now nearly ninety and in poor health. Besides, Jeannette had no home to return to in Georgia. Her little house in Bogart had burned down while she was serving her term.

In 1945, without the money to rebuild at Bogart, Jeannette sold the property and moved to a smaller farm in nearby Watkinsville, Georgia. She named the place Shady Grove. Now in her sixties, Jeannette became friendly with a neighboring black family, the Robinsons. At first, she experimented with creating a house from rammed earth, but ended up settling into an abandoned sharecropper cabin on the property, making improvements with help from the Robinsons. For one thing, she added a sunny annex with a dirt floor covered with tarpaper and rugs. Rustic like her previous house, at least it had electricity. As in the house in Bogart, Jeannette took creative, even eccentric approaches to providing heating and plumbing for the house, such as setting a toaster on the floor for heat and using an airplane chemical toilet.

After the war, in 1946, Jeannette took off for a six-month tour of India. She had long admired the nonviolent philosophy of Mahatma Gandhi, and she wanted to observe East Indian society. The following year, after her mother's death, Jeannette returned to Georgia, but traveling the world and experiencing other cultures became her new passion. Over the next twenty-five years, she would return to India six more times and visit Asia, Africa, Europe, and South America. When Jeannette embarked on her last world tour in 1962, she was in her eighties. She would visit India one last time at age ninety.

In between overseas trips, Jeannette kept pushing hard on the issues she cared about, foremost among them being peace. She also worked on the political campaigns of candidates she supported. In 1961, Montana State College in Bozeman (now Montana State University) awarded Jeannette an honorary doctorate degree for her political work.

While the 1950s through the early '70s were a busy and exciting period for Jeannette, she also suffered personal pain and grief as three of her siblings died—first Grace in 1954, then Wellington in 1966, and finally Mary in 1971. Jeannette experienced physical pain as well.

Few people, even close friends, knew that she had an unpredictable, agonizing condition that had tortured her for decades, a disorder known as tic douloureux ("TICK doo-luh-RUH"), which caused excruciating stabs of pain in her face. The only possibility for a permanent remedy was surgery to sever a facial nerve, but Jeannette feared the operation would affect her ability to speak. So for most of her life, she simply endured the pain.

In earlier years, Shady Grove had been full of people—Jeannette's family members and many others. Now, in her eighties, Jeannette was usually alone, though the Robinsons and other neighbors watched out for her and she, them. Many elderly women, she realized, were in the same boat, without immediate family to care for them. What if they cared for one another? she wondered.

With some of the money she inherited from Wellington, Jeannette, ever the innovative builder, decided to put it to use on her latest idea. On her property she built a large, round building where ten women could live together. At the center was a big open living area and kitchen, with bedrooms around the perimeter. Residents would take turns cooking, Jeannette envisioned, and would care for one another when ill. In the end, though, Jeannette never found any women to live in the house, and the building remained empty except for occasional guests.

By the mid-1960s, the United States had become embroiled in another foreign conflict—the Vietnam War. Jeannette had been speaking out against the idea of sending U.S. troops to Vietnam since the late 1950s, but under President John F. Kennedy, the first Americans were deployed to South Vietnam in 1961 to fight the communists of North Vietnam. Over the next decade, U.S. participation escalated dramatically under Presidents Lyndon Johnson and Richard Nixon. Unlike World War II, however, the Vietnam War was not popular, so Jeannette's peace work received a good deal of public support.

Not everyone appreciated Jeannette's antiwar activities, though. The U.S. government did not like citizens protesting the war it was invested in. Jeannette was among many Americans at this time who were watched and monitored by the FBI (Federal Bureau of Investigation).

In 1967, the House of Representatives observed the fiftieth anniversary of Jeannette's first term in Congress. Jeannette welcomed the publicity as a chance to voice her antiwar beliefs. Leaders in both the peace movement and the women's movement of the '60s took notice of her reappearance into the limelight. They were planning a dramatic protest, and Jeannette Rankin, with her illustrious history and longtime antiwar efforts, was the perfect choice to lead it.

In January 1968, eighty-seven-year-old Jeannette Rankin stood in the streets of Washington, D.C., at the head of a line of thousands of women, most dressed in black, ready to march to protest the war. The marchers had been inspired by a challenge Jeannette had thrown out the previous May: "It is unconscionable that ten thousand boys have died in Vietnam, and I predict that if ten thousand American women had mind enough they could end the war, if they were committed to the task, even if it meant going to jail." The long parade of protesters, calling themselves

On a cold day in January 1968 in Washington, D.C., Jeannette Rankin (front row, with glasses), nearly ninety years old, marches in the protest parade named in her honor.
—Courtesy Bettman/Getty Images

the Jeannette Rankin Brigade, marched in silence, under gray skies, to the Capitol, where Jeannette and a few other women, including the wife of Dr. Martin Luther King, presented their antiwar petition to Congress.

After this event, Jeannette kept going, writing letters, giving interviews, lobbying Congress, and traveling the country making speeches against the war. The years were beginning to catch up with her, and she was suffering from failing eyesight and intensifying pain from the tic douloureux. Finally, when she was eighty-nine, Jeannette had the operation on her facial nerve. Afterward, as she had feared, her speech did become slurred, and half of her face was paralyzed and drooped, but she carried on. In March 1970, just before her ninetieth birthday, she fell and broke her hip. That did not stop her from attending her June birthday celebration in Washington, D.C.

Even with her failing health, Jeannette kept making speeches, giving press interviews and appearing on television to talk about peace. In 1972, when Montanans gathered in Helena to write a new state constitution, Jeannette spoke at the convention as a distinguished guest. The same year, in recognition of her lifelong efforts on behalf of women, Jeannette became the first recipient of the National Organization for Women's Susan B. Anthony Award.

Since the late 1960s, in addition to her home in Georgia, Jeannette had kept an apartment in Carmel, California, where her sister Edna lived. As Jeannette's health deteriorated, she stayed in California more frequently, especially after a small stroke weakened her further. It was there in Carmel, on May 18, 1973, just weeks before her ninety-third birthday, that Jeannette Rankin died quietly in her sleep. Her ashes were scattered over the Pacific Ocean—appropriate, since "pacific" means peaceful.

In her will, Jeannette left a modest amount of money to help older women go back to school. This grew into the Jeannette Rankin Foundation, which over the years has helped hundreds of women over age thirty-five transform their lives through education. The foundation operates out of Athens, Georgia, but it accepts applications from any state. The foundation is only a small part of Jeannette Rankin's legacy, however.

Since her death, Jeannette has been honored in many ways throughout the nation and around the globe. In 1980, to commemorate her one-hundredth birthday, an eight-foot-tall bronze statue of Jeannette was dedicated in the Montana Capitol rotunda in Helena. Five years later, after a replica statue was made for the state capitol, Montanans sent the original to Washington, D.C., where it is one of two statues representing their state in the National Statuary Hall.

In her hometown of Missoula, one of the oldest buildings at the University of Montana was renamed Jeannette Rankin Hall in 1983. The following year, Missoulians founded the Jeannette Rankin Peace Center downtown, and a small park just across the Clark Fork River from the site of her family's house also bears her name.

In 1993, Jeannette was inducted into the National Women's Hall of Fame in Seneca Falls, New York. In addition, books, articles, films, and websites about her abound. Several of the books have been translated into or were originally written in other languages—evidence of Jeannette's international impact. Forever restless, this girl from Missoula envisioned a better world and spent her life pursuing that vision. Her courage and conviction will continue to inspire women and men for generations to come.

LENA MATTAUSCH, BRIDGET SHEA, AND THE **WOMEN'S PROTECTIVE UNION**

SISTERS IN SOLIDARITY

In September 1890, an announcement appeared in the *Helena Independent*:

> The women's protective union of Butte City, Mont., will give their first grand ball on the 23d of September, 1890, at Miner's Union Hall. A cordial invitation is extended to all respectable people. Already there have been 700 tickets sold and the ball promises to be the greatest event of the season.

The Women's Protective Union (WPU), a labor union for working women, had been established in Butte only three months earlier. It was not created to give parties, of course (the ball was probably a way to gather support), but to "protect" its members—that is, to fight for their rights, for fairness, and for a better quality of life at work and beyond. As the *Butte Daily Miner* reported the day after the WPU's first meeting on June 5, "The ladies of Butte . . . are not going to be behind their brothers in demanding their rights. Last evening a representative assemblage

Women's Protective Union staff and members during a holiday food drive, date unknown. Lena Mattausch is pictured at far left, with Virginia Paynich (fourth from left), Helen Guest (left of Virginia), and Blanche Copenhaver (far right); the other members are unidentified.
—Courtesy Butte–Silver Bow Public Archives, Butte, Montana

of the working women of the city met . . . and organized a protective association."

Little is known of the thirty-three women who met in Butte that night. We know the name of the founding president, Mrs. Delia Moore, but the other ladies mentioned in the article were identified by their last names only: a Miss Jencks was vice president, and Mrs. E. M. Hughes and Mrs. Lamont were appointed, along with Mrs. Moore, to write the organization's constitution and bylaws. The other women who attended the meeting, including "dressmakers, milliners, waitresses, sales ladies," and others, are not listed by name. A complete roster of the founding members of the WPU and further details about how the union came about have never been found. Since the WPU shared space with other unions in the Miners Union Hall, it's likely that early records of the WPU were lost in 1914, when, during a time of rivalry between various miners' unions, one group bombed the union hall to smithereens.

If the WPU had been a person—a woman, of course—she would have been over eighty years old when she finally "died" in 1973. To this day, like a beloved matriarch, the WPU is remembered proudly, not just in Butte but everywhere the history of labor struggles is honored.

The WPU was in its prime when Lena Mattausch ("muh-TOSH") and Bridget Shea ("SHAY"), working together, were two of its main leaders—from the 1910s through the 1940s. Lena and Bridget's lives were not much different from those of the hundreds of other working women in Butte. As admired and respected as they were, they never seemed to consider themselves more important than the hard-working women whose hard-earned union dues paid their salaries. They probably would not have wanted to be singled out among the other women who led the union before or after them. Still, within the story of the WPU, Lena and Bridget stand out. Their ideals and actions carved them a special place in labor history.

———•••———

Many early American labor unions did not admit women, but it was not long before working women—usually single, often immigrants—began organizing their own. The first all-female union in the United States, the United Tailoresses of New York, formed in 1825 and held its first strike, for "a just price for our labor," in 1831. Even before that, working women banded together, if unofficially, to demand change. In 1734, for example, maidservants in New York City united to boycott male employers who beat them.

Even within unions that included them, however, women workers were few in number and weak in power. One of the first major unions in America, the Knights of Labor, founded in 1869, allowed female members after 1878, but the women's influence was limited. This inequality gave rise to women-only unions. The WPU in Butte, Montana, became one of the most powerful.

What is a union, anyway? Labor unions are groups of workers who, by joining together, increase their clout with their employers. Even in a small company, one worker alone may not have the power to make a difference when problems arise; in fact, speaking up may put his or her job at risk. But when workers band together, their bosses are not able to cheat, abuse, or take advantage of them so easily. As a group, they can protest mistreatment and ask for higher pay, shorter hours, or better working conditions. Solidarity, making decisions as a group and sticking together no matter what, is the heart and soul of unions. To encourage solidarity and to acknowledge the equality of all members, unionists, especially in the past, often addressed one another as "Sister" or "Brother," as in "Sister Mattausch" or "Brother Jones."

Union members elect leaders to meet with employers on their behalf. Leaders negotiate terms for the workers' contracts, which set pay scales, working hours, benefits, workplace conditions, and other provisions. Sometimes, if negotiations over a contract fail, the union will decide to strike—that is, to stop work and walk out. Strikes are meant to remind employers of workers' crucial importance to their company. If successful, they force employers to address the workers' needs and rights.

Most unions were (and many still are) organized by "craft" or "trade"—that is, by occupation. Miners had their own union, carpenters had theirs, and so on. The WPU was different. It was open to any working woman, no matter what her occupation, unless she already belonged to another union (for example, in 1902, telephone operators in Butte, who were mostly female, formed their own union). So, over the WPU's lifetime, its members would include, among other workers, waitresses, cooks, dishwashers, theater usherettes, factory workers, janitresses, laundresses, midwives, dressmakers, hatmakers, domestic servants, teachers, car hops, sales clerks, typists, cashiers, bookkeepers, a female chimney sweep, and even a fortune teller.

When the WPU was founded in 1890, not everyone took it seriously. The *Anaconda Standard* reported, "The idea of a union of servant girls, chambermaids, and dressmakers was so unique and comical that the new union has been the subject of endless jokes." But the members of the WPU weren't joking. As the city of Butte would soon see, they were dead serious. Blessed with a series of leaders who combined toughness, intelligence, and caring warmth, the WPU, like no other organization or individual before or perhaps even after it, helped women workers in Butte get ahead. It is hard to overstate the difference the union made in both its members' lives and those of their families.

In addition to fighting for better wages and working conditions, the WPU provided assistance to its members outside the workplace, helping them find housing, health care, child care, and legal services. Influenced by the Progressive ideas sweeping the country in the late nineteenth and early twentieth centuries, the union established the Women's Industrial Institute, where women could not only rent clean, affordable rooms but also take classes in English, job skills, personal hygiene, child care, citizenship, and other areas. In addition, the union opened a library, and later, it served as a sort of employment agency, matching employers and workers.

Particularly in the early days, WPU members took their status as union "sisters" seriously, and their union reflected their unique experience as women. For instance, the WPU kept a supply of clean white infants' dresses for members whose babies died, so they could be buried with dignity. Infant death was common in Butte, especially among the poor. Members who were seriously ill received flowers.

When the WPU was founded, Butte was already known for its labor unions. With 1,800 members in 1880, the Butte Miners Union was the largest, but there were many other smaller unions as well. In fact, by 1900, Butte had thirty-four different unions, earning it the nickname the "Gibraltar of Unionism."

The city of Butte began as a rough-and-tumble gold-mining camp in the 1860s, but after miles of copper veins were discovered, the population boomed, and the city became known as "the richest hill on earth." By 1884, five thousand men toiled in copper mines below the city. Only six years later, that number had tripled. In 1900 Butte's mining industry was paying out $1.5 million per month to workers, one of the largest payrolls in the world. The mines operated around the clock. To oblige the miners, many restaurants and taverns stayed open twenty-four hours a day.

Serving this army of miners, most of them single and without families, was another army—an army of working women, including boarding-house landladies, chambermaids, laundresses, seamstresses, shop girls, and restaurant workers. Restaurants in particular provided jobs for many women and girls. Besides waitresses, restaurants needed cooks, kitchen helpers, dishwashers, and other food-service workers. Among the most fondly remembered of these workers were the "bucket girls," who, in cafes and boarding houses, packed the miners' metal lunch buckets with hearty repasts that might include sandwiches of cold meat between great slabs of bread, hard-boiled eggs, pasties (meat turnovers), cake, and a container of milk or hot tea. Other women worked as "yard girls," who helped prepare food for the never-ending round of meals. So-called because they often worked outside, even in winter, yard girls plucked whole braces of chickens, unpacked pounds of fish from barrels, peeled hundreds of potatoes, and shucked dozens of oysters with sharp knives.

In the early twentieth century, working women were often looked upon with disdain, or at least with pity. Especially up until World War II, if a woman was married, particularly if she had children, American society expected her to stay home and keep house. Even among poor families, husbands were supposed to be the sole breadwinners. If a man could not support his family on his own and his wife had to work to make ends meet, it was a bad reflection on the family. Nevertheless, some wives did have jobs.

Attitudes toward working single women, including poor widows, were hardly more generous. The burden on widows with children was especially heavy, and because of the mines, Butte had a lot of widows. Mining was truly treacherous work. Legend has it that in Butte, you could not walk the streets at any given time without hearing, somewhere, a woman wailing in grief. One historical study showed that in Butte, between fifty and a hundred married Irish immigrant miners died in mining accidents each year. In 1910 alone, the mines created 434 Irish widows and 1,117 fatherless children. After a male head-of-household's death, not only did his widow need to go to work, but often, older daughters left school to help the support the family.

Making things even harder, most jobs available to women offered low wages and little appreciation. While traditional women's occupations such as cleaning, serving food, providing child and elder care, and making clothing were essential to the smooth functioning of society, they were neither valued very much nor respected. Especially vulnerable to disrespect were immigrant women from non-English-speaking countries who could barely speak English. Opportunities for such women were mostly limited to low-paying manual labor. Yet even the English speakers seldom knew how to read and write, meaning that the most they could aspire to was a service job such as a waitress or elevator operator. Society saw poor working women as, at best, unimportant and, at worst, disposable. This attitude meant that women workers were particularly subject to employer exploitation. If their boss told them to do extra work or work longer hours for the same pay, there was little they could do about it. Even physical abuse often had to be tolerated. Anyone who complained would likely lose her job. The WPU set out to change all that.

The union had made some progress by the time Lena Mattausch and Bridget Shea joined up, Lena around 1909 and Bridget in 1917. For example, in 1903, the union won a battle to limit workdays to ten hours (as opposed to eleven, twelve, even fourteen or more), and this rule was soon adopted in Chicago, Seattle, Denver, and San Francisco.

Both Lena, born in Montana, and Bridget, an immigrant from Ireland, spoke English and had some formal education, which no doubt helped them become leaders in the WPU. Both served as business agents, an official in charge of the union's day-to-day affairs; later, Lena became the union's financial secretary and Bridget became the union president. The help and inspiration they had received as WPU members motivated them, as officers, to ensure that all "WPU girls" were treated just as well. Lena and Bridget's efforts through the decades would help bring the union to its peak of power and influence.

Lena Mattausch was born Lena Antonioli in Butte around 1888. Her father, Peter, was an Italian immigrant who established a dairy farm near Ramsay, just west of Butte. In 1881 he married another Italian immigrant, Theresa Botini. Over the next sixteen years, the couple had nine children, all but one of them girls. Lena was the fourth child. At the farm, the older girls bunked in a cabin on the property, while the younger children stayed in the house with their parents. The Antonioli kids were able to get some education, probably at the small school in Browns Gulch, a mile or so from their home.

As dairy farmers, the Antoniolis worked hard. For extra money, Theresa sold milk, eggs, and wild watercress in Butte, traveling there by horse and wagon. Sadly, when Lena was about eleven, her mom died in childbirth. Two years later, the baby died too.

After Theresa's death, Lena's three older sisters petitioned Butte's courts to have their father, Peter, removed as their guardian. The court records for this case were sealed, so it's impossible to know why the girls initiated this break with their father, but we do know that the court granted their petition and appointed a neighbor as their guardian. Not long afterward, the sisters moved into Butte and found jobs.

Lena, along with her younger siblings, remained with Peter, but seeing her sisters go to court and win may have been a powerful education for her. Not only did the sisters stand up to their father, the highest authority in most people's lives, they also successfully navigated the justice system of the day.

In 1903, at age fifteen, Lena married a thirty-three-year-old Italian American named Giuseppe (Joe) Cereghino. Sadly, Joe turned out to be abusive, and the couple soon divorced. At some later point, Lena may have married and divorced again, though no documentation for this marriage has been found. In any case, Lena had no children.

Eventually, probably shortly after her divorce from Joe, Lena joined her sisters in Butte and started working somewhere, perhaps in a restaurant or a laundry. By 1909, if not earlier, she had joined the Women's Protective Union. A few years later, Lena would meet Bridget Shea and begin what would become a formidable team in the WPU.

Bridget Murphy, later Bridget Shea, was born in Ireland around 1883, making her about five years older than Lena. The youngest of eight children born to John and Mary Murphy, Bridget grew up in a mining area on the southwestern coast of Ireland, near Cork. Although it was unusual for a girl at that time and place to be educated, Bridget went to school and learned to read and write in both Gaelic and English.

Bridget grew up during a time of Irish struggle against English rule. The Irish people were overwhelmingly Catholic, while their British rulers were Protestant. The hostility between the two went deeper than religion. Centuries before, England had colonized Ireland, and the British monarchy slowly began to dominate the Irish people, stripping them of economic and political power. In the mid-1800s, on top of the political disputes came a severe famine in Ireland, which led to thousands of impoverished Irish immigrating to, among other places, America. This migration continued well into the twentieth century.

Growing up in this time and place, Bridget developed an acute awareness of injustice. Not everyone reacts to such circumstances with a desire to change them, but Bridget did. Later, in America, she would support from afar the Irish people's efforts to throw off the British and rule themselves. More generally, she would always be motivated to help people experiencing hardship.

Around the turn of the twentieth century, Bridget's brothers and sisters joined the great migration out of Ireland. The destination they chose, since they came from a mining area, was Butte, Montana, America's mining epicenter. They also probably knew that Butte was practically a little Ireland; at that time, an estimated 25 percent of Butte's population was Irish. In 1902, according to records, Bridget, about nineteen years old, also left the old country and joined her siblings in Butte.

When she was an old woman, Bridget would tell her grandchildren about the day she first arrived in Butte. Looking out the window as her train started down toward the city, Bridget saw air so thick with smoke and pollution that the sky was dark, even though it was daytime. Doubts about her new home filled her mind, but she knew she would be with her family. It didn't take long for her to adapt.

A few years after her arrival, in 1905, Bridget married a miner who had also emigrated from Ireland, James J. Shea. James was as passionately patriotic about Ireland as Bridget was, which may have made for a strong bond between them. A year or so after Bridget wed James, she had a child, a boy, but sadly, he died when he was only eighteen months old. Infant deaths happened frequently in Butte due to its pollution and poverty. Bridget went on to have four more children, though, all of whom survived. James Francis was born in 1908, Neil in 1910, Emmett in 1913, and Eileen in 1915. The Shea family lived in a comfortable home on West Quartz Street, near their church.

In 1917, when Bridget was in her thirties, her husband's love for Ireland led to tragedy. The Sheas were like a lot of other Irish immigrants who supported Irish independence from across the sea. Even after they became U.S. citizens, many sent their hard-earned wages "home" to help the cause. Some Irishmen even formed informal militias in which they trained for battle, in case an armed struggle against the British ever erupted in Ireland, so they would return and fight. James Shea belonged to such a militia in Butte. As a husband, James needed his wife's permission to join such a militia. Bridget had given him her permission without hesitation—a sign of how much the Irish cause meant to her.

In the end, however, the Sheas' Irish patriotism led, according to an article published in June 1917, to a painful upheaval in the family's life. On June 26, 1917, the *Butte Daily Post* described how, two months earlier, on April 19, James Shea killed a man in a Butte bar. According to the article,

James was wearing his blue militia uniform when an Englishman insulted him, and worse, insulted Ireland. Some witnesses, the article recounted, said James acted in self-defense. Nevertheless, he was convicted of manslaughter (murder that is not premeditated) and sentenced to two to four years in jail. He entered Montana State Prison on July 11, 1917.

Bridget's world was turned upside down. As so often happened to women in Butte, Bridget had lost her breadwinner. Scrambling to support

Bridget Shea with her husband, James, and children (left to right) James, Eileen, Emmett, and Neil, 1917 —Courtesy Butte–Silver Bow Public Archives, Butte, Montana

her four kids, she found a job as a waitress. Luckily, unlike some women in Butte, Bridget had lots of family in town who helped her with child care. It was at this time that Bridget joined the Women's Protective Union.

Sadly, Bridget would have to support herself for more than two to four years. In October 1918, James died of influenza during the worldwide flu epidemic of that period. After his death, Bridget wore only black for the rest of her days. In later years, Bridget seldom if ever talked about this terrible time in her family's life.

While the year 1918 was awful for Bridget, Lena had better luck. That summer, when she was around thirty, she married mine electrician Frank Mattausch, a man she would stay with until his death decades later. The couple never had children, though after Lena's sister Ida died, they took in her daughter.

In the meantime, the WPU had grown into a force to be reckoned with. By 1903 the union was well organized and represented hundreds of women and girls in Butte. The WPU's work also extended beyond Butte to the national level, as members advocated for federal reforms such as health insurance and retirement funds.

The WPU welcomed its first African American members in 1907. While the union prided itself on not drawing the "color line," there was an exception: Asians, particularly the Chinese. Butte had a large population of Chinese immigrants, but discrimination against them in Montana and the United States in general was severe in those days. Not until 1944, when the WPU wanted to organize Butte's Chinese noodle parlors, were Asian women allowed to join.

Also in 1907, the WPU came under the umbrella of a much larger union, the Hotel Employees and Restaurant Employees Union, yet WPU members insisted on keeping the union's original name, its women-only membership, and its policy of accepting workers of any occupation. In fact, the struggle to remain independent and gender specific would be a theme throughout the WPU's history, as many larger unions tried to pursuade the women to merge with them. Even though the WPU always succeeded in keeping itself separate, its affiliation with and support of the larger unions gave it more power. Because the WPU was so strong, its members knew that whatever problems they faced on the job, they were not alone. They always had the support of their network of "sisters" as well as that of the larger labor community.

What kinds of problems did WPU workers encounter in their jobs? Reports from union meetings provide examples. In 1916, at the local tamale factory, employers made one shift of women work longer hours than they were allowed to. The WPU brought this violation before the courts, which fined the employers fifty dollars each. In other cases, the union even had employers arrested for rule violations. Another method the union used to pressure employers was to boycott businesses that treated workers unfairly, meaning union supporters refused to buy from, or use the services of, that business until its owners did the right thing.

The union's method of last resort was to strike. Strikes were a big risk. No work meant no pay, so workers and their families had to suffer, and there was no guarantee that the union would win. In addition, strikes put strain on unions. Under pressure, decisions about tactics became crucial, and disagreement and bad feelings were hard to avoid. Yet if members of a union felt a strike was worth it, they knew other unions would support it and even join in.

In return for the benefits of belonging to the union, WPU members had to follow strict rules. Every month, after paying their dues, each member received a union pin. Anyone who forgot her pin was fined. WPU member Mildred Laitinen remembered that putting her pin on before work was as automatic as combing her hair. Members were also required to attend one or two union meetings per month. The same meeting was held twice in one day to accommodate both daytime and night-shift workers.

On the job, the union forbade WPU members from doing any work outside their occupation, so even if, for example, a waitress was not busy and the dishwasher was overwhelmed with dishes, the waitress could not step in to help wash them. Breaking any union rule usually led to a fine. While this may seem harsh, WPU members understood that only through tough discipline could the union achieve the best results for its members. Nearly everyone paid her dues and fines, followed the rules, and attended the meetings without complaint.

In fact, the women so loved, respected, and appreciated the WPU that union meetings were actually something to look forward to. Before each one, members received a special password, which was required to get in. Although the meetings weren't exactly entertaining, they kept members informed about happenings across the city and about labor issues that affected them. No matter how "lowly" her job, each woman was respected and given a voice. Big decisions were made through a vote of all members. After the meetings, WPU members often went out together, sometimes to a local ice cream shop, to continue discussing issues and to socialize.

Two of the most beloved WPU leaders were Sister Lena Mattausch and Sister Bridget Shea. When it came to getting things done for the union, Lena and Bridget were an unbeatable team. Long after James's death, Bridget continued to dress in dark clothes for her union work, deciding it was more professional and even somewhat intimidating. Lena, the taller of the pair, did the same. Indeed, these two women, who had the power to shut down businesses with a boycott or even a strike, managed, for years, to fill the hearts of Butte employers with terror.

No problem was too small for Bridget and Lena to "straighten out," as WPU secretaries taking notes at meetings often put it. For example, one employee showed up for her usual two-hour shift but wasn't needed, and she was sent home with just 25 cents of her wage. The WPU fought for, and won, her pay for the whole two hours. In another instance, a girl working in the hospital kitchen got black pepper in her eye and had to go home. The hospital docked her pay, but the WPU got it reinstated.

Usually, Lena and Bridget worked out problems with employers peaceably, through discussion, but they did not hesitate to get tough when necessary. Bridget, in particular, was known to chase rule-breaking employers with a broom until they promised to do better. As Mildred Laitinen remembered, speaking of Bridget, "The bosses used to kind of quiver when she came around."

Lena and Bridget worked together for more than three decades, from 1917 to 1949. Both were official union officers, but they mostly served as "walking delegates," and walk they did, side by side, up and down the steep streets of Butte. Dropping in unannounced at the cafes, theaters, hotels, candy stores, and factories where WPU members worked, they looked for rule violations, whether committed by the employers or by their own "girls." They also monitored the working conditions, ensuring that the women were safe and comfortable. Uncooperative employers might be reported to the trades council.

By 1920, the WPU had some four hundred members. That year, the union held its first big strike. The union had presented a proposal for wage increases to the employers association in Butte, but the plan was rejected. Joining with the Cooks' and Waiters' Union, WPU cooks, waitresses, dishwashers, yard girls, and other food-service workers walked out of their jobs, shutting down nearly every restaurant and cafe in Butte. WPU members who did other types of work as well as members of other unions also struck in solidarity, until about one thousand people were on strike, with more threatening to join.

After almost a month of striking, the unionists won a pay increase. Perhaps even more important, WPU strikers succeeded in establishing their union in every eatery in town. In other words, every restaurant owner agreed to let their workers belong to the WPU.

After 1920, the mines in Butte began to decline and the city's overall population shrank, yet the WPU continued to grow. By the end of World War II, it had nearly a thousand members, and the women were getting better jobs. No longer limited to lower-paying occupations such as waitress and housekeeper, many women in Butte now worked as bookkeepers, stenographers, nurses, and teachers.

In the meantime, the WPU and other unions in Butte had won their members benefits that were nearly unheard of in most parts of the country. Work shifts were limited to eight hours, six days a week; anyone who worked longer than that was guaranteed overtime pay. Workers were also entitled to sick leave and paid vacation days. Over the years, the WPU and other unions had gained all this without resorting to a strike. In 1949, however, after weeks of negotiations failed to secure a desired pay raise and extended benefits for WPU members, talk of a strike began to circulate.

Toward the end of May, the bosses made their final offer, which some members, including Bridget Shea, the president of the union, were at first inclined to accept. In the end, however, on May 27, after much contemplation, WPU members made the hard decision to strike. Lena Mattausch was chosen chairwoman of the strike committee. On June 9 WPU workers walked out of their jobs.

Usherettes at Butte's American Theatre, circa 1940. These hard-working women were probably members of the WPU. —Courtesy Butte–Silver Bow Public Archives, Butte, Montana

Joining the strike, to show support and solidarity, were members of other Butte unions, including teamsters (drivers), restaurant workers, and carpenters. At the WPU office, strikers signed up to picket in two-hour shifts. A picket is a group of strikers standing in a line or walking in a circle, usually holding signs and often chanting, in front of the business establishments being protested. Because customers are reluctant to show sympathy with employers or get caught up in trouble, they seldom cross picket lines, and businesses lose money. The WPU women organized an around-the-clock picket at the entrance of the elegant Finlen Hotel, discouraging guests from staying there.

Usually, picketers carry signs raised high for all to see. Instead, WPU picketers pinned yellow banners on their clothes that said "On Strike!" so their hands would be free. Why? Because many of the women were mothers who had to bring their small children with them to the picket line. As one member explained, "You can't carry a child and a picket sign at the same time."

On the second day, Lena encouraged the strikers: "We are not afraid. We have the right to demand a living wage. . . . We mean business and we are going to win this strike."

As the strike stretched on, letters of support poured in from unions around the country; many sent money to help the strikers with their expenses while they were not working. Local grocers and bakers donated food. Ordinary citizens began wondering why the employers didn't give the women what they asked for.

The strike was working, but not without a cost. The solidarity that had always been so strong among members began to suffer. Disagreements surfaced. Were union leaders asking for enough or holding out for too much? Also, the differences between members' occupations began to matter. Why, for example, should elevator girls, factory workers, and janitresses suffer when the fight really impacted just waitresses? Resentments built, rumors circulated, and fingers were pointed.

Finally, after seven weeks, the WPU won its demands for higher wages and better conditions. But damage had been done to the union. The WPU would survive, but the strike created rifts that would not heal.

One of these rifts, sadly, was between Lena Mattausch and Bridget Shea. After working together for thirty years, Lena and Bridget's close work relationship, and presumably their friendship, ended. It's uncertain what broke them apart, whether it was disagreement over tactics, money, leadership decisions, or something else completely. They both continued to work for the WPU, but things were never the same. Luckily, though, the WPU itself, under a succession of excellent new leaders, continued to look out for its members and to help the community for twenty-four more years.

Times were changing, however. Since the end of World War II, many unions had begun to lose power as companies grew larger and larger. "Chain" stores, restaurants, and hotels, whose corporate offices were thousands of miles away, began replacing local businesses. With size came power. Negotiating with huge companies about local workers' issues was a challenge, though for many years the WPU managed that challenge, winning further benefits for its members, including a five-day workweek. But by the early 1980s, Butte's mines, which had once defined the city, had all closed, and with them, other businesses. Scores of people left Butte in search of work, and for decades the city suffered severe economic decline. By then, many of the unions in Butte, including the WPU, were gone.

The end of the WPU came, ironically, with the introduction of laws intended to help women. With the women's movement of the 1970s, gender inequality came to be seen as a problem to be addressed. Laws were passed to force all-male organizations to allow women members. At the same time, however, the laws also forced all-female organizations to admit men, the WPU among them. When the U.S. Department of Justice demanded that the Women's Protective Union change its policy (and its name), WPU president Blanche Copenhaver's first response was "Over my dead body." But the union had no choice. In 1973, the WPU merged with the Cooks' and Waiters' Union to become a new, co-ed union, the Culinary and Miscellaneous Workers Union, Local 457, which was later absorbed into the Hotel Employees and Restaurant Employees Union, today known as UNITE HERE.

As for Lena and Bridget, they lived out their lives mostly in happiness, Lena with her husband and siblings and Bridget with her children. Bridget was particularly proud when one of her sons became a Catholic priest. Her dinner table at her Irish-style cottage, with its lace curtains and bright geraniums at the windows, was usually full of family, which eventually included many beloved grandchildren. When she died on March 22, 1955, around age seventy, the WPU was still going strong. Bridget's house in Butte is now a historic site, part of the Butte-Anaconda National Historic Landmark District.

Unlike Bridget, Lena outlived the WPU by several years. Most of her sisters and her brother lived nearby, celebrating holidays together and helping with each other's kids. Lena lost her husband, Frank, in 1956, but she lived over twenty more years, passing away on April 5, 1979. She was about ninety.

Bridget, Lena, and all the women of the Women's Protective Union left a legacy of working women helping one another, proving that they could improve their lives and their futures by banding together. Perhaps most significant of all, the WPU gave women working in some of the lowest paid and least respected jobs a strong sense of pride, dignity, and power. In many Butte families, multiple generations of women belonged to the WPU, nourished by the support and solidarity that came with membership.

Since its demise, the WPU has been studied and written about by historians of labor unions and the women's movement in the United States. The fact that it is still remembered generations later with awe and respect attests to its enduring impact on thousands of hard-working women in Butte, Montana.

Frieda Fligelman in Europe; no date —Courtesy
Montana Historical Society Research Center, Montana Historical
Society, Helena, Montana

*Belle Fligelman at the University of Wisconsin, in
the outfit she wore to address the Wisconsin state
legislature in support of women's suffrage, 1913*
—Courtesy Montana Historical Society Research Center, Montana
Historical Society, Helena, Montana

6

FRIEDA FLIGELMAN AND BELLE FLIGELMAN WINESTINE

POLITICS AND POETRY

On a Saturday afternoon in January 1977, the Second Story Cinema, a new performance space in Helena, Montana, was filled to overflowing. Onstage, a petite elderly woman in colorful clothes was reading poetry aloud. The poems were her own. Spellbound, members of the audience craned forward, listening. Each time the reader finished a poem, the crowd responded with a heartfelt sigh or a laugh of delight—and always, applause.

> Waiting to concoct a poem
> I am a prancing horse,
> Pawing impatiently
> And shying in a semi-circle
> To tease the rider on.
> My head shakes and tosses,
> As if it knew it wore a silver harness.
> And it is proud and will be off,
> Whirring against the wind
> Made by its speed,
> Hoping the rider is a hero
> Worthy of his heed.

The poet was Frieda Fligelman. Most audience members recognized Frieda, if they did not actually know her. She was often seen walking briskly through the streets of downtown Helena, standing on the sidewalk in deep conversation with someone, or attending a community event.

Two people in the audience knew Frieda very well. One was a woman around Frieda's age and height, with sparkling, lively eyes and a sprig of greenery in her white hair. She was Belle Fligelman Winestine, Frieda's beloved younger sister. Beside Belle was her husband of fifty-nine years, Norman Winestine.

This poetry reading was long remembered by those who attended. Perhaps Frieda's poems were memorable because they were so honest. In them, she bravely shared her soul, expressing, with astonishing passion, life's pain and joy, love and loss, hope and disappointment. Many years later, Frieda's poems would be gathered into a book. Today, she basked in the audience's admiration.

Belle, her sister's biggest admirer, was a local legend in her own right. A journalist, writer, and political activist, she spoke out for women's suffrage (voting) in the 1910s and for social justice throughout her life. Frieda shared Belle's Progressive ideals and also fought for reform. Later, however, she pursued another path. In addition to writing poetry, she spent many years—a good number of them overseas—as an independent scholar of language and culture.

As children, the Fligelman sisters embraced the ideals of their father and of their Jewish faith, and in their pursuit of those ideals, they lived their lives to the fullest. They also earned a special place in Montana history.

———•••———

Growing up in Helena, Montana, in the late 1800s, little Frieda and Belle Fligelman were pretty lucky. They lived in an elegant home with servants. Their father, Herman, owned the nicest clothing store in town, called the New York Store, where ladies and gents bought high-quality outfits and fabric. As walking advertisements for the store, Frieda and

Belle always wore beautiful clothes. Their parents looked forward to the future, when their two daughters would marry, raise families, and lead lives of culture and ease.

Herman Fligelman wasn't always rich. Born Jewish in Romania, Herman faced serious persecution in his native land. Sometime around 1882, at about age twenty-two, he arrived in America with just ten dollars in his pocket. In New York City, he washed dishes and unloaded ships until he had enough money to move west—to Minneapolis. There, he worked laying streetcar tracks, saving up for a supply of fabric and other "dry goods," intending to sell them to miners in Montana. Moving to Helena, Herman sold his merchandise from a pushcart on the street. Later, his first wife, Minnie, would sew his fabric samples into bright, patriotic quilts.

As Herman established his little dry-goods business, he learned to speak English through interacting with his customers. Knowing that to move forward, he would need to read and write in English as well, he spent some of his hard-earned money on a tutor. In 1885 Herman partnered with three other businessmen and opened a shop in Helena called the New York Dry Goods Store. Not long after that, he had enough money to bring his six siblings over from Romania. He also sent for a childhood friend, Minna (Minnie) Weinsweig, who had agreed to become his wife.

Herman and Minnie were married in 1888. In January of 1890, Minnie gave birth to Frieda in Helena, and Belle came along the following spring. Tragically, very soon after Belle's birth, Minnie died. Herman's sister and brother-in-law moved into Helena from nearby Marysville to help care for the girls, and three years later, Herman remarried. The girls grew up believing that their stepmother, Getty Vogelbaum (sometimes recorded as Vogelman), was their birth mother. Only many years later did they learn the truth.

Getty, an immigrant from Germany, was demanding. She insisted on a spotless house and was strict with Frieda and Belle. Even when they played outside, she made them wear white gloves. To avoid getting the gloves dirty when they fell down, the girls learned to fall on their elbows. To discipline her daughters, Getty often swatted them with a yardstick. If

Frieda Fligelman at age nine, 1899. Photo by Taylor, Helena, Montana. —Courtesy Montana Historical Society Research Center, Montana Historical Society, Helena, Montana

Belle Fligelman at age eight, 1899. Photo by Taylor, Helena, Montana. —Courtesy Montana Historical Society Research Center, Montana Historical Society, Helena, Montana

their behavior pleased her, however, she might treat them to candy or ice cream downtown. As hard as Getty tried to make Frieda and Belle live up to her high standards, she could not dampen their independent spirits. As Belle later put it, "We were brought up to be ladies. It didn't take."

Early Helena was an exciting place to grow up. After the city was selected as the Montana state capital, it celebrated with a big parade that Frieda, age four, watched from her father's shoulders. Belle remembered the parade, too, recalling that it happened at night and was followed by fireworks. In the winter, with other kids, the sisters raced on sleds, sliding down the streets below Mount Helena, often crossing the trolley tracks on Benton Avenue. Miraculously, they never collided with a trolley. All year round, the girls enjoyed swimming at the Natatorium (indoor pool) at the elegant Broadwater Hotel. In those days, women and girls wore bathing suits that included full skirts, bloomers, and stockings, for modesty.

Everyone in Helena knew the Fligelmans. The New York Store was a main source of cloth and clothing, and Herman was known for his kindness, allowing customers, during hard times, to buy on credit until they had more money. For these reasons, the Fligelmans, like strands in the cloth they sold, were firmly woven into the larger community of Helena. Yet at the same time, as Jews in a mostly Christian town, the Fligelmans stood apart. Frieda and Belle believed that this contradiction—being part of the community but also separate—gave them an unusual perspective that they came to value.

Of course, the Fligelmans weren't the only Jewish family in Helena. In fact, when Herman arrived in the city around 1882, an organization called the United Hebrew Benevolent Society, founded by early Jewish settlers, had existed for over twenty years. By the late 1870s, Jewish citizens were active in Helena's board of trade and the city council. In 1890, the year Frieda was born, the community began building a synagogue in Helena, Temple Emanu-El, finished the following year. The Fligelmans attended services there, and on Saturday mornings, Frieda and Belle went to Sabbath school at Temple Emanu-El, where they learned Hebrew and studied the Jewish holy books.

While Helena, like much of early Montana, was largely tolerant of different racial and religious groups, the Fligelman girls did experience some prejudice because of their faith. For example, Belle remembered being taunted in the sixth grade by some boys who chased her with snowballs and called her names. Many Christians were ignorant about Judaism and based their beliefs about Jews on myths and stereotypes. Others simply feared and distrusted anyone different.

The girls' father, Herman, approached the problem of prejudice patiently. Once, after Frieda had been picked on for being Jewish, he said, "Perhaps it's a good thing that the Jews never became a powerful nation—otherwise, [we] might have oppressed other peoples, too." Herman embodied the Jewish ideal of a good person. Later, Frieda remembered, "I thought it was . . . wonderful . . . to be Jewish. For Catholic and Protestant children, God was in heaven; for our family, God was the idea of goodness." A quote inscribed on a wall at Temple Emanu-El read, "Know ye truth and goodness." Frieda loved those words.

The Fligelmans weren't extremely religious, however. For example, their home was not kosher, meaning they did not follow the strict Jewish laws about what and how to eat. The family did, however, observe the Sabbath (Saturday), which forbade work or vigorous play until sundown. Sometimes, after Sabbath school, Frieda and Belle would secretly sew doll clothes while Getty napped.

At Sabbath school and at home, the sisters learned stories and lessons from the Torah, or Hebrew Bible, and another Jewish holy book, the Talmud. But their most enduring moral lessons came from their father. He would often tell his girls, "Let's be reasonable. Civilized people don't do that sort of thing. Civilized people do things that are pleasant to live with and are respectful of other people."

Herman loved learning and read several newspapers each day. At the dinner table the family often discussed current events, and Herman kept a large dictionary nearby so Frieda and Belle could look up words they didn't understand. The house overflowed with books. After supper, the family read aloud together, usually classics like *Alice in Wonderland* and Shakespeare plays. Getty taught the girls to recite German poetry.

Frieda showed an early interest in languages. Helena, known as the "Queen City of the Rockies," attracted immigrants from a wide variety of cultures. Frieda remembered that, as a child, she enjoying listening to Helena's Chinese residents speak. In addition to German, which Getty often spoke at home, and Hebrew, Frieda later learned French, Spanish, and many other languages. In the future, language would be central to Frieda's career.

Belle, for her part, took to writing. When she was nine, she sent a story she had written to a popular magazine, *Ladies Home Journal*, for publication. The letter she got back began, "Dear Madam." Belle was so thrilled to be called "Madam," she hardly noticed that her story had been rejected.

In high school, Frieda was an especially good student and would graduate a year early. Belle, however, just "scraped along" in high school, as she later recalled. Yet she had her own talents, especially writing, and she worked on the school newspaper.

In her junior year of high school, Frieda, contemplating her future, told her parents that she wanted to go to college. Herman and Getty were aghast. Upper-class girls like Frieda and Belle were expected to go to "finishing school" to learn how to behave in high society and attract a wealthy husband. Finishing schools focused on etiquette, grooming, and skills that refined ladies were expected to possess, such as piano playing, ballroom dancing, French, and good penmanship. As future wives and mothers, it was believed, girls had no reason to go to a university. The answer, Herman and Getty told Frieda, was no.

Frieda refused to accept that answer. She told her parents that if they wouldn't send her to college, she would earn the tuition money herself. With that, fifteen-year-old Frieda went searching for a job. Everyone she asked told her she was too young. Frustrated, she came home and threw herself, weeping, on her bed. Finally realizing how much it meant to her, Herman and Getty relented and agreed to send her to college. In this way, Frieda blazed the trail for her sister. If Frieda went to college, Belle knew she would get the same opportunity.

After graduating from high school in 1907, Frieda attended the University of Minnesota. She took additional classes through the summer, so she was ready for her senior year of college by the fall of 1909. At that point, she decided to transfer to the University of Wisconsin in Madison, which, she'd heard, had wonderful economics and political science instructors. At the same time, Belle was ready to start her freshman year of college. She chose Wisconsin, too, to be with Frieda. In Madison, the sisters shared a room in a boardinghouse.

Outside class, Frieda and Belle participated in social and political activities on campus. Frieda was a member of the Equal Suffrage Club, the Ethical Culture Club, and many other groups. Belle was involved in student government, sports, and, with her love of writing, the student newspaper and the yearbook. Both girls belonged to a women-only speech and debate club.

The University of Wisconsin was a center of Progressivism, a political idea that was sweeping the country at that time. Progressives, both Democrats and Republicans, wanted to improve society by passing laws for women's suffrage, aid to the poor, safe food, better working conditions, and more. Both sisters were drawn to Progressive ideals and the women's suffrage movement, and they would soon become involved in political activism.

After graduating from college in 1910, Frieda, now age twenty, continued her education at Columbia University in New York, planning to earn an advanced degree, or PhD. Influenced by her father's and her religion's high regard for education, she had always felt, from a young age, an almost sacred passion for ideas. This passion drew her naturally to academia—the world of education, research, and scholarship that takes place at colleges and universities. With her lively yet disciplined mind, Frieda wished to devote her life to expanding human knowledge by teaching at a university.

At Columbia, Frieda wanted to take a class on the U.S. Constitution, but she learned that the professor didn't accept women students. Undaunted, she wrote a letter to the university's admissions board explaining why she wanted to enroll:

Dear Sirs,

It seems indeed unnecessary for an American citizen to give reasons why she should wish to study the constitutional law of her country. But in view of the fact that it has been suggested that I do so, I will state that since so many laws which are considered desirable by civic-minded people have been declared unconstitutional by the Supreme Court, I have a great desire to know why.

Very truly yours,
Frieda Fligelman

Frieda was admitted into the class.

While in New York, Frieda remained politically active, marching in a national women's suffrage parade. After a year in that city, Frieda took a break from school and returned to Helena. That year, 1911, she began working for the city's newly founded YWCA (Young Women's Christian Association). The YWCA was a national organization founded in the mid-1800s to provide safe lodging for young single women coming into cities to attend school or to work. YWCA staff helped women find employment and assisted them in other ways. By the early twentieth century, the organization had chapters across America.

A respected doctor in Helena, Maria Dean, had founded that city's YWCA. Although it was a Protestant organization, Dr. Dean got the local branch started by inviting each house of worship in town, no matter what denomination, to send two young women from its congregation to help. From Temple Emanu-El came Miss Frieda Fligelman, eager to lend a hand. So effective was Frieda that the group wanted to hire her as its first secretary. However, a problem arose. The national YWCA organization did not allow non-Protestant members to hold office or even to vote.

Dr. Dean and the other YWCA members appreciated Frieda's work—and the support of the Jewish community—too much to exclude Jewish women in this way. The Helena YWCA decided to forgo the support and resources that national affiliation would bring, instead choosing to be independent so they could hire anyone they wished. Although the national YWCA would change its policy decades later, in the meantime the Helena Y remained the only unaffiliated chapter in America.

Frieda became the Helena YWCA's first secretary in 1911. Part of her job was to interview new arrivals, see what they needed, and help them find it. For two summers, Frieda also worked for Montana women's suffrage by setting up a booth at the state fair, and she spoke at at least one suffrage meeting in Montana. In 1912 she wrote an essay, "Early Laws of Montana for Women," that appeared in the *Anaconda Standard*. It was her first published work.

Meanwhile Belle, continuing at the University of Wisconsin, was writing, too. She edited the "women's page" of the student newspaper and the women's activities section of the yearbook, and she wrote for the university magazine. In her senior year, she was elected president of the Women's Student Government Association. One day, while serving in that role, Belle got a call from a woman from Wisconsin's leading suffrage group, who asked her to speak before the state legislature in support of a women's suffrage bill. Belle supported suffrage, but she hadn't thought much about the specific reasons why women should vote. With just a few hours to prepare, she quickly read up on suffrage, spoke to other women about it, and gathered her thoughts into a speech. That evening, she bravely presented her speech to the legislators, afterward receiving loud applause. With that, Belle, like her sister, became a passionate advocate for women's suffrage. Over the next several years, she would devote much of her time and energy to that cause.

After earning her bachelor's degree in 1913, Belle worked briefly at a newspaper in Milwaukee, Wisconsin. From there, she worked in New York City as a freelance writer, then traveled abroad, probably for the first time. Back in Helena in 1914, she soon became the first female reporter at the *Helena Independent*, writing articles on the suffrage movement and women's rights. On the side, she composed charming and funny pro-suffrage poems, which appeared in various newspapers. Humor, Belle believed, was often an effective way to get points across.

The year Belle came back to Helena, 1914, a suffrage bill was introduced in the state legislature. Montana suffragists were organizing a big push to get the word out and sway voters to support it. In June, Belle was assigned to cover a speech by Jeannette Rankin, Montana's leading suffrage activist, in Lewistown. Belle had never reported on an event outside Helena, so she was nervous, but she went.

Rankin impressed Belle greatly. "When Miss Rankin came forward to speak," she later recalled, "the air became electric." At another suffrage rally the next day, Rankin spoke again, this time joined by others, including Belle herself. In this way, Belle and Jeannette Rankin became acquainted.

Spending much of that summer of 1914 working for suffrage, twenty-three-year-old Belle adopted Jeannette Rankin's controversial technique of speaking on street corners. In those days, it was scandalous for a lady to make public speeches out on the street, and the first time Belle did it, she was terrified. Mustering her courage, she staked out a spot near the Helena post office around noon, expecting a lunch crowd. To her surprise and discomfort, no one came by. After waiting uneasily for an audience, she finally just started "talking to the world." It wasn't long before passersby began to gather. As she went on, her nervousness subsided. She kept it up for several days, getting better each time.

When Getty got wind of her daughter's activities, she was horrified. Though she was not opposed to women's suffrage, Getty considered Belle's methods disgraceful. She warned Belle that if she made another speech on the street, she should not bother to come home. The next day, however, Belle was back on the street corner. That evening, she checked into a hotel and charged the room to her father. After that, Getty reluctantly gave in.

Expanding her campaign beyond Helena, Belle drove a horse and buggy to outlying areas, including some rough mining towns. Once, she traveled all the way to the town of Augusta, where she positioned herself right outside a saloon. At that time, respectable women avoided drinking establishments. Once again, Belle began speaking to the air until, one by one, the male patrons stumbled out of the bar to listen. She must have made quite an impression: during Augusta's next election, someone wrote on the ballot "Belle Fligelman" for sheriff.

Belle's dedication, along with that of the other Montana suffragists, paid off. In the November 1914 election, the state's women's suffrage law was passed.

By that time, Frieda was in California. The previous year, she had received a fellowship (similar to a scholarship) to study economics at the University of California in Berkeley. She had enjoyed her time in Helena and her job with the YWCA, but she was ready to return to graduate school.

At Berkeley in 1913, in addition to economics, Frieda studied statistics, law, anthropology, and sociology. Anthropology is the study of ancient and modern cultures. Sociology, the field that Frieda would eventually choose, is also a study of culture but is more focused. Sociologists examine how people behave in groups, including how they organize their societies, create governments, conflict with each other, and so on, in order to understand how to deal with social problems.

Upon finishing her fellowship in 1914, Frieda put her learning to use in jobs at the U.S. Commission on Industrial Relations and the U.S. Bureau of Labor Statistics, then returned to Columbia for her final year of study for her PhD, or doctorate degree, in sociology. To become a professor, Frieda would need a doctorate. In 1916, at age twenty-six, Frieda passed the tests required for the degree, but in order to receive it, she still needed to complete a research paper called a dissertation. However, Frieda wasn't sure what to write her dissertation about.

The work of a French philosopher named Lucien Levy-Bruhl intrigued her. Levy-Bruhl maintained that "primitive" peoples were not capable of reason or analysis. Although he did not say that they were inferior, he did insist that they were different, mentally, from people of European heritage. Frieda strongly disagreed with Levy-Bruhl's conclusion—that less developed societies had simpler thought processes. For her dissertation, she started working to disprove it. But the work grew overwhelming. She decided to take some time to think more about it. Students often take years to write and turn in their dissertations.

Meanwhile, Frieda took a series of short-term jobs for state and federal government agencies around the U.S. She compiled research on social issues like housing, health care, family income, and prison reform. The jobs involved collecting information, organizing it, and crunching the numbers. Frieda was a whiz with statistics.

Back in Helena, Belle, now the editor of a new paper, the *Montana Progressive*, received a phone call one day in 1916. It was Jeannette Rankin. She was in Helena, she told Belle, and wanted to ask her about a big decision she had just made. She was going to run for Congress. What did Belle think? "I think it's wonderful," Belle replied. "I'll be right there." She walked directly to Rankin's campaign office and started working to get her elected (see also chapter 4, Jeannette Rankin).

As a journalist, Belle could especially help Jeannette with campaign publicity, encouraging the Montana newspapers to write about the candidate and her issues. Few of the state's newspapers gave Jeannette Rankin much coverage, but Belle did her job well enough that Jeannette credited her with helping her win the election. Afterward, Jeannette, America's first congresswoman, asked Belle to come with her to Washington, D.C., as her secretary and personal writer. Jeannette's term was due to start in December 1917, but in April, the president called a special early session. Ready or not, Belle hurried to Washington with Jeannette.

Jeannette was a mesmerizing speaker but greatly disliked writing. During her first year in office, nearly all of Congresswoman Rankin's speeches, written statements, and articles were actually composed by Belle. In addition, Belle answered letters to the congresswoman. So much mail poured into Rankin's office—two large sacks a day, from every state and around the world—that Jeannette employed four secretaries. Most congressmen had just one.

Belle's job was intense. The women in the office worked from 9 a.m. until dinnertime, with lunch at their desks. After dinner, Belle returned and worked some more. Her boss, Jeannette, seldom quit before 10 p.m. Sometimes, at the end of a long, hard day, Jeannette would suddenly need an important speech written right away. Belle might stay up late writing it, only to have Jeannette deliver an entirely different version, off the cuff, the next morning.

The nation was still marveling at the fact that there was a woman in Congress. Sometimes visitors stopped by the office just to look at Jeannette, to see what a congresswoman looked like. One day, a group from another government agency stopped by the office for such a visit. Among them was a bright-eyed fellow named Norman Winestine. Belle liked Norman immediately. A graduate of Yale College, he was, like Belle, a writer. "I was lost the first time I saw him," Belle remembered later. "He was just the right kind of person for me."

In April 1918, Belle sent a telegram to her parents in Helena. It read, "Dear Father and Mother, Norman and I have decided to be married. Sorry you can't be with us. Belle." Herman and Getty telegraphed back, "Who is Norman?" As it turned out, they would not meet him for a while.

Belle quit her job with Jeannette Rankin and, after the wedding, headed off to Europe with Norman. She wasn't sorry to leave politics behind—for now. She had gone to the Capitol believing that Jeannette could make great, sweeping changes in America. The reality left her disillusioned.

Belle and Norman moved to Paris, intending to work there as writers, but making ends meet turned out to be difficult. In 1919 the couple came back to the United States, staying in New York City, where their first child, Minna, was born. The family returned to Europe, but the following year, Belle and Norman gave up on Paris and went back to New York. Here, they had their second daughter, Judith. Later that year, the Winestines decided to move back home to Helena, where Norman joined Herman in running the New York Store, or Fligelman's, as it was now called. It had become Helena's most elegant department store.

The same year Belle returned to Montana, Frieda went overseas. After a year of teaching economics at Mills College in Oakland, California, thirty-year-old Frieda was ready to travel and expand her education in Europe and the Middle East. Thanks to some money her father had set aside for her, she was able to explore and study freely, though sometimes she worked. In 1921, the government of Palestine (now Israel) hired Frieda to study immigration to that country, so for several months she lived in the city of Tel Aviv. Throughout the 1920s, she traveled in Europe and northern Africa, working, studying, and observing.

In Paris, Frieda took courses at the National School of Oriental Languages. Language had always appealed to her, but even more than the languages themselves, Frieda realized, she was fascinated by their role in people's lives—the interplay of language with politics, economics, history, law, culture, and psychology.

In Frieda's view, history and even everyday life overflowed with examples of language affecting society. One such example is propaganda. Often used in wartime and during political campaigns, propaganda is language meant to persuade people to adopt a certain point of view, usually through emotional appeals and dramatic images. Another example is the language of immigrants in a new country. Whether or not newcomers can speak their adopted country's language, as well as how well they speak it and with how strong an accent, affects their opportunities for employment, education, and social acceptance. Language can even be a tool of domination. Sometimes conquered or oppressed people are forbidden to speak their native tongue in their own country, which stifles their culture as a whole. As Frieda knew, this had happened to native tribes in Montana. These were some of the ideas that Frieda explored at the National School of Oriental Languages.

At the school, Frieda enrolled in a class in Fulani ("fuh-LONN-ee"), a language spoken by the nomadic Fulani people of West and Central Africa. In Frieda's day, many citizens of developed countries considered people like the Fulani inferior because they lived more simply than those in the technology-oriented societies of Europe and America. Frieda remembered the work of Lucien Levy-Bruhl, which she'd studied at Columbia. Levy-Bruhl believed that since "primitive" peoples did not use modern technology and often had no written form of their language, they had an entirely different way of thinking. For example, they did not understand basic scientific concepts such as cause and effect. They related to the world through feeling, not intellect and logic.

Frieda Fligelman didn't buy Levy-Bruhl's notions, and she decided to put them to the test. If the Fulani people indeed could not think logically, it would, she presumed, be reflected in their language. It was true that the Fulani language did not include words for, say, "electricity" or "telegraph," but Frieda doubted that that meant they didn't think logically, morally, or philosophically. To try to prove it, she figured out an apples-to-apples method for comparing Fulani with western European languages—specifically, French.

Using a Fulani-French dictionary, Frieda spent a year sorting Fulani and French words into categories and comparing them side by side. Aside from technological words, the two languages covered all the same bases. When it came to logic, intellectual reasoning, and what Frieda called "moral richness," they were no different. Based on her findings, she wrote two academic papers, which she hoped she could use as her dissertation for her long-awaited PhD.

Frieda's work was absorbing, but she was becoming increasingly lonely overseas. While Belle had found Norman and had children, Frieda had never married. She had fallen in love several times, but it was always with a man who was unavailable or not interested.

In Paris, to deal with her feelings, Frieda began to write poems. Some expressed her longing for love.

BRIDGE
Give me long, lithe kisses
To build a bridge
Over the charm of my waiting.
Give me strong embraces
For the stakes
To hold my bridge
Between the earth and sky.

Many of Frieda's poems reveal a deep sadness. The life she had always imagined for herself, which included a soulmate and children, was not coming to pass. Yet other poems sparkle with joy and optimism. Writing poetry brought Frieda such pleasure that, even in the midst of pain, she could find hope.

UNREQUITED
I am so lonely and so desolate
Yet happiness buds out from me
Like tender shoots
along the trunk

of a withered tree
whose entrails have been
gnawed away by storms,
But whose initial sap
seems inexhaustible.

Frieda turned to poetry not because she felt sorry for herself, but to explore, bravely, some of the gloomier emotional states that all human beings experience sometimes. "In general," Frieda once wrote, "life is terrible but very interesting—and the purpose of the mind or spirit is to cope." Through her poetry, Frieda was able to cope with her intense emotions and connect with other people.

CURES
For bitterness, for rancor,
Only one cure:
Widen the circle,
Stand further off,
Or higher up.
For unrequited love,
The miracle of love itself.
For utter loneliness
Effort born of dreams.

Frieda would always struggle with loneliness, but she had Belle for support. Even though their life paths took them in different directions and they rarely saw each other, Belle, through her letters, had become an anchor of stability for her passionate, strong-willed sister.

Unlike her unlucky sister, Belle was quite happy. Back in Helena, she was busy raising her family, but she still wrote on the side—stories, poems, nonfiction, children's literature, and plays. She especially loved poetry, which she said should "lift you off the ground"—that same feeling you have on a swing of "just sailing into the air."

Belle had her third child, Henry, in 1924. When she was pregnant, she had designed her own maternity dresses. Pleased with the result, she sent six of the designs to a women's magazine that published sewing patterns for readers. As usual, Belle was ahead of her time. The rejection letter she received back stated that the magazine "does not mention babies before they are born"—in other words, pregnancy was not considered an appropriate topic for the public, even in a women's magazine.

Always keeping busy, Belle enjoyed inventing things, including suspenders with amusing phrases on them and cereal shaped like numbers. She also dabbled in painting. Above all, despite her disillusionment with the government in Washington, she never ceased working on political and social causes.

Still on her own, Frieda remained abroad for twelve years. While there, she translated a French book into English, though it would never sell well. Later, she tried to get her poems published, but only a few ever appeared in print during her life. However, in 1931, both of her papers on Fulani were accepted by academic publications. She summarized her conclusions as follows:

> (A) the native African Negro language, judged by Fulani, has ample moral richness as an instrument of twentieth century ordinary daily life; (B) in its figurative expressions and its many nuances of meaning . . . it has an artistic and psychological richness . . . such that Western languages could usefully borrow from it.

Upon their publication, Frieda's meticulous and innovative papers won praise as the first studies of their kind.

In 1932, back in Helena, Frieda and Belle's father, Herman, died. Later that year, partly in his honor, Belle decided to run for Montana state senator. Her slogan, playing off her petite stature, was original— "Smaller and Better Senators"—but she did not win.

Meanwhile, Frieda returned to America. In New York, she submitted her research papers to Columbia as her dissertation in sociology. Unfortunately, the professor she had worked with before had died while Frieda was away. The new professor rejected Frieda's work. He said it belonged in another academic department, linguistics (the study of language), not sociology, and he saw no overlap between the two subjects. Yet a few decades later, Frieda's work would be recognized not only as legitimate sociology but as a breakthrough into a new field of study called "sociolinguistics"—sociology combined with linguistics. In the future, sociolinguistics would be taught at universities around the world. But in 1932, Frieda Fligelman was a scholar ahead of her time—which is often a frustrating place to be.

Frieda had discrimination to deal with, too. She was a fiercely opinionated Jewish female intellectual at a time when American universities favored male, traditional, Christian faculty. The upshot was that with no PhD, Frieda could not fulfill her dream of becoming a full college professor. She might be able to attend conferences and occasionally participate in scholarly debates, but without university credentials, most academics would look down on her. She would never have the resources of a big university to help her continue her work. She was entirely on her own.

From New York, Frieda returned to Berkeley, California, where she kept busy studying and researching on her own. A topic she had first hit upon while at Columbia bloomed into an area of research that fascinated her for the rest of her life: the study of people's beliefs, especially the assumptions that underlie human beliefs. People can believe that their actions are good or necessary, Frieda saw, yet if their belief is based on erroneous assumptions, they can cause terrible harm. Frieda saw her theory come to life inside Nazi Germany. If only the assumptions underlying beliefs could be isolated and analyzed like tiny organisms in a lab—some of which cause sickness—it might be possible, Frieda believed, to prevent some strife and harm. In addition, she remained politically active. During World War II, she raised money to bring elderly European Jews, persecuted by Hitler, to America. She also traveled frequently, visiting her family in Helena as often as she could.

In Montana, Belle, too, worked on societal issues, sometimes by employing her writing talent. For example, in the 1930s, she fought for Montana women's right to serve on juries—a right that, surprisingly, didn't arrive with suffrage. Among other things, she wrote a short play in which two women sorted out the pros and cons of the jury issue. The play was distributed to women's groups across Montana to be performed at meetings. The Treasure State finally granted women the right to serve on juries in 1939, but it wasn't until the late 1960s that women in every state would gain that right.

In 1948, Frieda, age fifty-eight, moved back to Helena. Belle needed her sister's help caring for their aging stepmother, Getty. Frieda settled into an apartment a few blocks from Belle and Norman. Her home overflowed with books and papers. At one point, a friend remembered, even the kitchen sink contained books. The mess exasperated Frieda, who told visitors, "I didn't degenerate into this. I am a hero for putting up with it." On the other hand, books were a comfort to her. "I am never lonely," she insisted. "I have with me the greatest minds of the last ten thousand years." When the apartment next to hers became available, Frieda rented it, too. She dubbed her combined adjacent apartments the Institute of Social Logic, reasoning that, since no impressive-sounding educational institution wanted her, she would create one of her own. There Frieda continued to study, do research, and write. Among her many projects was a sociolinguistic textbook with course outlines and a translation of a seventeenth-century Spanish play about Christopher Columbus, published in 1950.

In Helena, Frieda's acute loneliness subsided. With Belle and Norman, she attended practically every cultural event, lecture, and political meeting in town. Frieda was always the first person to ask questions. On the street, she was famous for starting up conversations with strangers, especially foreign visitors, and inviting them over for dinner. She and Belle shared their writing at readings and spoke at events. Both sisters were members of the Montana Institute of the Arts, the League of Women Voters, and many other groups. It no doubt pleased Belle to see her sister content at last.

The people of Helena treasured Frieda, with her signature purple beret, and Belle, who always tucked a sprig of green leaves in her hair. Belle said the sprig was symbolic. "I always thought it would be wonderful to be a tree . . . it's the branching out, getting the most out of and giving the most to life, that's important." The sisters' optimism,

Norman and Belle Winestine at a Montana Club celebration, May 1983, Helena, Montana. (Note greenery in Belle's hair.) Photo by Gene Fischer. —Courtesy Gene Fischer

humor, intelligence, generosity, and community involvement inspired everyone they knew, and even people they didn't know.

The Helena newspaper office was located behind Frieda's apartments, and she was well-liked among the journalists. Reporters getting off the late shift would see her lights burning and know she was in there, working away. These fellow writers were inspired by Frieda's dedication to the life of the mind.

Sometimes people would ask Frieda if, after traveling the world, living in Helena was boring for her. She responded that boredom only afflicts the unimaginative. For sociologists, she wrote, "Life is [always] interesting wherever there are at least three people."

Although Frieda was never fully accepted in international academic circles, she maintained a vigorous correspondence with scholars across the globe. She refused to be closed out of the world she treasured, academia. Finally, when she was nearly eighty, her sociolinguistic work achieved some scholarly recognition. In 1968, the American Association for the Advancement of Science (AAAS), an old and prestigious organization, elected her a fellow, or special member. In 1973, she was invited to write a paper about her early work in sociolinguistics and read it at the World Congress of Sociology the following year. When the collected conference papers were published as a book, it was dedicated to Frieda Fligelman, "who, more than four decades ago was received by closed minds . . . and who, nevertheless, never lost her vision but lived to see it vindicated." Frieda was also recognized in her hometown, receiving, in 1972, the Electrum Award for her contribution to the arts in Helena.

Of course, by this time, the 1970s, Helena was a very different city from the one Frieda and Belle had known as kids. For one thing, although the population had grown, the Jewish community had dwindled. Back in the 1930s, Temple Emanu-El's proud twin onion-shaped domes were removed and the building was sold. Many other changes had also occurred. The Broadwater Natatorium, where the sisters used to swim, was closed after earthquake damage in 1935. Most poignantly, their father's store, Fligelman's, was sold in 1958, becoming McDonald's Department Store. Yet Frieda and Belle weren't ones to live in the past. "If I am well," Frieda said, "I want to live another ninety years. . . . I am in a state of thrill all the time."

Both sisters remained sharp and active until the end of their lives. In letters, Frieda and Belle sometimes referred to "beautiful old age" as something they both aspired to. The phrase may come from a 1929 poem by D. H. Lawrence, which describes old age as a time of peace and fulfillment. It's safe to say that both Frieda and Belle achieved beautiful old age, radiating the beauty of a life lived fully, honestly, and artistically.

Frieda died in 1978, collapsing from a heart attack after answering the door to accept a delivery of groceries. She was eighty-eight. Belle died of a stroke seven years later, in 1985, at age ninety-four. Norman passed away the following year. With the lights of both Frieda's apartments and the Winestine family home now dark, Helena mourned. Frieda, Belle, and Norman were all buried with other family members in Helena's Jewish cemetery, the Home of Peace, near Capital High School.

The Fligelman sisters will always be remembered. In 1999, fourteen years after her death, Belle Fligelman Winestine was named by the *Missoulian* newspaper as one of the one hundred most influential Montanans of the twentieth century for her work for women's rights. In addition to her academic work, Frieda's main legacy is her poetry. In 2008, many of her poems from the 1920s through the 1970s were finally collected into a book called *Notes for a Novel: The Selected Poems of Frieda Fligelman* and published to much acclaim.

From the start, Frieda and Belle pursued learning, worked hard for causes they believed in, and lived lives of their own choosing. Inspired by the ideals of their faith, they refused to let the prejudices of the day deter them from their goals. Their contributions to Helena, to the state of Montana, and to the world secured the Fligelman sisters a permanent place in political, literary, and intellectual history.

Isabelle Johnson, date and photographer unknown
—Courtesy Museum of the Beartooths, Columbus, Montana

ISABELLE JOHNSON

In January 1972, one of America's most prestigious museums, the Amon Carter Museum in Fort Worth, Texas, hosted a solo exhibit of a certain contemporary Montana painter's work. Seventy-five of the artist's paintings covered the walls, and among the crowd who came to see them were art lovers from around the West as well as art critics from New York. Also at the exhibit were two elderly sisters from Montana, who flowed through the galleries, greeting people and chatting about the paintings.

The scenes of trees, mountains, flowers, sheep, cattle, and ranch buildings weren't depicted exactly, the way they would be in a photograph. Instead, many of the images were just suggestions of these things, created by a few lines, shapes, and colors. Yet the paintings were alive with movement, capturing the feeling of their subjects more accurately, the artist might argue, than a camera could.

Every scene, every building, and even the sheep were familiar to the two older women. That's because one of them was the artist herself, Isabelle Johnson, and the other was her sister Grace. The paintings had been done at the Johnson family's ranch near Absarokee, Montana. This show at the Amon Carter was the most high-profile exhibit Isabelle had ever had. Yet she had never painted to gain fame or money. She painted because making art fascinated her.

———•••———

Isabelle Jonette Johnson was born in 1901 near the hamlet of Absarokee, Montana, about sixty miles southwest of Billings, and grew up on the family ranch. Her parents, Albert and Irene Johnson, were married in January 1898 and had their first child, their son Ingwald, less than a year later. Three girls followed, all three years apart: first Isabelle, then Grace in 1904, and Pearl, the youngest, in 1907. To her siblings, Isabelle was "Sis."

The Johnsons were a very close family. In fact, all four of the children would live and work together on the ranch all their lives. Except for Ingwald's disastrous marriage and quick divorce when he was just a teen, the Johnson siblings never married. They all stayed on the homestead until their deaths.

Isabelle's story started when Albert and Irene, both Norwegian immigrants, met while working at a large cattle ranch in Castle, Montana, near White Sulphur Springs, in the 1890s. Albert drove wagons and worked with horses on the ranch, and Irene was a cook and housekeeper. The day after they were married—interestingly, by a female pastor—they left for Absarokee, just north of the majestic Absaroka and Beartooth Mountains, where Albert had bought a homestead from a discouraged rancher, on land that was previously part of the Crow Reservation. The newlyweds brought four horses with them; two, a pair of white mares trailing behind the wagon, were a wedding gift from their former employer.

The buildings on the Johnson homestead were right on the banks of the Stillwater River. The main house was big, clean, and white, and next to it, Irene planted a flower garden. Nearby, a bridge crossed the river along the main road between Absarokee and Big Timber. At first, Albert farmed cooperatively with his neighbors in the Stillwater Valley. The residents pooled their money, and with $4,000 they bought and shipped a Percheron draft horse all the way from France. They then bred Thomas, as they named him, with local mares, producing a line of sturdy workhorses that the farmers either used themselves or sold. In addition to farming, Albert and Irene raised cattle on their homestead, and they made a modest but comfortable living.

The Johnsons and other Stillwater residents, who came from all kinds of backgrounds, helped one another raise houses and barns, harvest crops, cut ice from the river, and celebrate milestones and holidays. In 1899, Albert Johnson joined with other townspeople to build the first church in downtown Absarokee, even though it was Congregationalist and the Johnsons were Lutheran. The area's Lutheran congregation, founded in 1895, met in a plain building on a ranch four miles south of town until, in 1917, Albert and other members built a more permanent church in downtown Absarokee. The citizens of Absarokee also created a public school system from scratch, beginning with the Sandstone elementary school in 1910; the high school was built seven years later.

Isabelle started first grade young, around 1905. The Sandstone School had not yet been built, but not far from the Johnson ranch at the time was a one-room log schoolhouse in the Grove Creek area. When the teacher there left, the Johnsons switched Isabelle and Ingwald to another small school, Beaver Creek. The brother and sister rode an old horse about three miles to get there.

Even out in the country at a time of early settlement, Isabelle found art. As a small child at the Grove Creek school, she remembered seeing an older boy dig chunks of gumbo (clay mud) out of the road and shape them into sculptures of birds and animals. Watching a piece of earth transform, through skill, into something recognizable and beautiful enthralled little Isabelle.

As an adult, Isabelle would credit her artistic inclinations to the fact that her parents came from rural Europe. Rural people everywhere tended to make, rather than buy, whatever item they needed, whether it was a tool, a piece of furniture, or a house. Yet Isabelle's parents came from an old-world tradition that went beyond the practical, adding a little color or decoration to make a thing beautiful as well as useful. She saw her parents as coming from a line of "natural craftsmen." As a girl, sharing that creative spirit, she covered the walls of the family home with drawings.

In 1911, when Isabelle was ten, the Johnsons stopped raising cattle and bought their first band of sheep. Sheep ranching would be their focus for the next three decades (many years later, though, labor shortages during World War II would force the family back to raising cattle).

Like most ranch kids, Isabelle and her siblings were expected to help out around the place. Their parents taught them that there is no such thing as women's work and men's work. Both genders, they believed, needed to know how to do "inside work" (traditionally, women's) and "outside work" (traditionally, men's). Albert and Irene had other ideas about work, too. Their upbeat motto was "Your play should be your work and your work should be your play." Because of this philosophy, the Johnsons generally enjoyed themselves, their work, and their neighbors. When it came time to move the sheep into the mountains for summer grazing, for example, the family invited friends along, turning the trek into a campout. The notion that work should be joyful may well have influenced Isabelle's eventual decision to become an artist.

Isabelle started high school in Absarokee as a member of its first class in 1917, but both she and Ingwald went away to Billings to finish school, living as boarders with a local family. During this time, Isabelle took some art classes, but she did not yet dream of becoming an artist. You were either born an artist, she believed, or you weren't, and she didn't feel she was one.

In 1920, when she was nineteen, Isabelle suffered a life-threatening accident. As she described it, she was out in the fields when the lever of a farm machine struck her, cutting open her skull. Thanks to the local doctor, her own youthful resilience, and her family's skillful nursing, Isabelle recovered. Some historians suggest that Isabelle's accident drew the Johnsons even closer.

Albert and Irene believed wholeheartedly in education. All four Johnson kids not only graduated from college but went on to earn higher degrees as well. When one or two of them were away at school, whichever siblings remained at the ranch took up the slack at home. Isabelle herself attended the State University of Montana in Missoula (now called the University of Montana), where she took some art classes but majored in history. After graduating in 1922, she taught school in the small town of Fromberg, east of Absarokee, for two years.

Isabelle loved learning and was always hungry for more education. In 1924 she crossed the country to attend graduate school at Columbia University in New York City. Upon earning her master's degree in history, she returned to Montana to teach that subject at Billings High School. In Billings she shared a house with her sister Grace, who taught home economics at the same school. On weekends they drove home in their big colorful jeep to help out on the ranch.

Teaching for a few years then returning to school became a pattern in Isabelle's life. She would teach until she had saved enough money to take more classes. In 1932, she studied political science in Los Angeles for a year at the University of Southern California. While there, she also signed up for an art class at the respected Otis Art Institute (now called Otis College of Art and Design).

Isabelle's teacher at Otis was part of a blooming artistic movement of the time called Modernism. Many American artists were experimenting with new, Modernist techniques and freedom of expression. Instead of trying to capture in paint exactly what a scene or subject looked like, these artists wanted to convey the essence of what they saw through shape, color, and line, allowing the viewer to experience more than a simple picture. These ideas, and the challenge of achieving them, hit home with Isabelle. Her interest in art blossomed into a passion. Finally it dawned on her: with study and hard work, perhaps she could be an artist after all.

In her later years, looking over her life, Isabelle recalled several major lessons, or moments of sudden understanding, that she experienced in her growth as an artist. One occurred while she was at Otis Art Institute. She was thrilled when one of her landscape paintings was chosen for an exhibition of student work. Arriving at the exhibition, Isabelle searched for her painting. As she went through the gallery, she passed works by well-known masters, such as James Whistler. By the time she spied her own painting on the wall, her perspective had changed. Compared to the great paintings, she thought hers "looked just like raw beefsteak." In other words, she realized that she still had a long way to go as an artist. The experience taught her never to be "conceited about a painting." Art was not about personal achievement, she believed. It was a process of learning and becoming, which never ended.

Early in her student years, Isabelle was drawn to the great French painter Paul Cezanne. His work impressed her more than that of any other artist. Originally, Cezanne had been an Impressionist painter like Jean Renoir and Claude Monet, but his later work led to a new movement in Modern art known as post-Impressionism, which in turn led to other Modernist genres, such as Cubism. Something about Cezanne's style spoke to Isabelle, and she chose him as her master—the artist who would serve as her ideal and her inspiration.

Isabelle took art classes again in the summer of 1938, this time at the Colorado Springs Fine Arts Center. There she studied under Henry Varnum Poor, who would become one of her most important teachers. A guest instructor in Colorado, Poor was also a professor at Columbia University in New York, where, seven years later, Isabelle would study with him again.

In 1939 Isabelle went to New York and enrolled at the Art Students League. This was the setting for another of her major lessons. The teacher of her drawing class, making his rounds of the students, highly praised her work. She was of course pleased, but after the instructor moved on, Isabelle overheard two students behind her say, "No wonder he thinks she's good, she's not trying to learn to draw, she's trying to do like he does." The comment, she remembered, "went through me like a knife." She realized it was true—she had been trying to conform to her teacher's expectations. In that moment, Isabelle understood that art is not about pleasing another person, it's about finding your own artistic vision, which no teacher can teach. It can only come from inside you.

In between these educational breaks, Isabelle went back to the family ranch, where she continued to help her parents and siblings manage the property. During the Great Depression of the 1930s, as neighboring land went up for sale, Albert had been wise enough to buy it, and the ranch had grown to six thousand acres.

Isabelle returned to New York in 1945, this time to Columbia University, and reunited with her teacher Henry Varnum Poor. The following year, Poor invited her to be one of the first twenty-five students in an experimental school that he and other artists were starting in Maine. Called the Skowhegan School of Painting and Sculpture, it remains a well-respected school for visual artists to this day. Isabelle jumped at the chance to go.

One day at the Skowhegan School, Isabelle was painting outside when one of the teachers suggested she try "modernizing" her work by turning every line she saw in the landscape into a more aggressive, "slicing" kind of mark. In other words, he told her to exaggerate what she saw before her. Intrigued, Isabelle played with the technique. "I was having a real good time after he left, [slicing] this way and that way." Then her teacher, Professor Poor, happened to come by. What was she doing? he asked. She replied that she was doing what the other teacher told her to do. Poor clearly disagreed with him. He sat down with Isabelle and ended up spending the whole afternoon with her, discussing the differences between real art and "false" art.

In real art, Poor maintained, there is no exaggeration. You might dramatize, simplify, or emphasize, but the great painters, including Isabelle's favorite, Cezanne, followed nature's lines. "It was as though someone had pulled up a blind," Isabelle recounted. Isabelle cherished such insights, and she was always pursuing new ones. "We have to prepare ourselves for those moments when the shades are drawn up," she said. From her conversation with her teacher, Isabelle was thrilled to discover she was already seeing the world the way Poor described, she just hadn't realized it.

Seeing what was really there before her became Isabelle's main interest and endeavor as an artist. But what exactly does that mean? Vision can be tricky. What we think we see is not always what is really there. Our eyes tell us that a muddy river is brown, for instance, yet if we really look, we can see much more—in a certain light that water might reveal shades of pink and yellow and dark green. Similarly, we might assume that both of a person's eyes are identical, but when we really look, we see that one is slightly larger than the other and is shaped differently. Isabelle devoted herself to the challenge of really seeing things and communicating what she saw through painting.

Out on the Johnson ranch, date unknown. Isabelle, at right, with her youngest sister, Pearl.
—Courtesy Museum of the Beartooths, Columbus, Montana

When she finished at the Skowhegan School, Isabelle thought about staying in the East, where it was easier for artists to find work. But her mentor Henry Poor convinced her that her talent was needed in the West, which was an "art desert," as he put it. He meant that art in the West was not changing with the times, and included little variety. Modern art had hardly appeared in the region yet, let alone taken root. "You go home and make the desert bloom," Poor told Isabelle.

In Montana, Isabelle knew, traditional art ruled. To most Montanans, art was "representative," meant to capture scenes realistically. Typical of this style was the work of beloved "cowboy" artist Charlie Russell and similar western artists, who portrayed lively and poignant scenes of early life on the range. While that kind of work was important and valuable, it did not include the Modernist ideas that were sweeping the art world, ideas that Isabelle felt were just as important. Modern artists like Isabelle saw it as their job to ask, What can art reveal about the world today? And how can I, as an artist, help answer that question? However, in art

126

classes in Montana, these concepts were barely being discussed. Few if any galleries in the state exhibited Modern paintings.

In 1949, after working on her own paintings for two more years, Isabelle got a chance to reach out to local art students when Eastern Montana College (now Montana State University Billings) hired her to teach art history, painting, drawing, and printmaking. Because education had changed Isabelle's life and helped make her an artist, she embraced the chance to guide budding artists in the same way. Later, in 1954, she was appointed head of the art department, a position she held until her retirement in 1961.

Just as her own best teachers had done, Isabelle engaged her students in serious discussions about art and the challenges of being an artist. "Look and see for yourself," she urged them. "You can make an awful lot of mistakes before you really begin to see. In fact some of us never do."

The students loved "Izzie," as they called her among themselves (though they always addressed her as Miss Johnson). She both nurtured and challenged them, inviting small groups back to her house for hot chocolate and lively debates about art. She worried that one of her students, Ted Waddell, who worked every night until 3 a.m., wasn't getting enough sleep, so she bought a cot and set it up in the tool room for him to nap. Waddell, like many of Isabelle's other students, would become a vital member of the next generation of Montana Modern artists.

While teaching, Isabelle also continued to paint—and to learn. "I think an artist never arrives. I think you're always trying to become one." She still drew inspiration from the work of her master, Paul Cezanne. Of all Cezanne's paintings, Isabelle most liked his landscapes, in which he often depicted the mountains and the natural world near his home in France. Likewise, Isabelle found that the scenes from her own home on the Johnson Ranch—its landscapes, its people, its animals both wild and domestic—provided all the views she needed to make art. Her friend Bill Stockton remarked that looking at Cezanne didn't teach Isabelle "how to paint, how to design, or how to draw. [It] taught her only how to look with the eyes of a poet at the very things she loved. She learned on her own how to transfer that love into the images we see now."

*Isabelle Johnson,
location unknown,
circa 1940s*
—Courtesy Yellowstone
Art Museum, Billings,
Montana

Painting fit well with ranch work, Isabelle found, which was lucky since she was, after all, still a rancher. After helping to move animals to an upper pasture, for example, or to expand the ranch's irrigation system, she still had free time to sit alone and sketch or paint.

In 1954, Isabelle took a sabbatical (a year off from teaching). College professors take sabbaticals in order to concentrate on their own personal projects. In Isabelle's case, she used the break to travel to Europe for the first time. Crossing the Atlantic Ocean on a ship, she visited ten countries, though she spent most of her time in Italy, France, and Spain. She explored museums great and small, as well as historic churches, formal gardens, archaeological sites, and natural areas. With the biggest museums, like the Louvre in Paris, Isabelle would go back day after day, slowly absorbing the art in one or two exhibit areas at a time. Viewing the real-life originals of paintings she had seen only as pictures in books was a life-changing experience for her. A photographic copy doesn't show a painting's extraordinary details, its true colors, the artist's brushstrokes. Standing before the great works, Isabelle could see how the artists, including her own master, Cezanne, had laid down the paint and layered it to create certain effects.

Isabelle was in her fifties when she visited Europe. The things she saw on the trip changed the way she viewed the world, which in turn transformed the way she painted. As one artist friend, Bill Stockton, said about her, "She insisted on growth. Most of us lack sufficient humility to learn in our later years. [It was] perhaps the secret of her greatness."

When Isabelle returned home, she appreciated the Johnson Ranch and the Stillwater Valley even more. "The mountains here are not only majestic," she said, "they're colorful. The further I went, even to Europe, and came home, the more wonderful these mountains were."

Isabelle's mother, Irene, passed away in 1957, and her father, Albert, followed two years later. This left Isabelle and her siblings to look after the ranch. In addition to doing ranch work, Isabelle kept teaching until 1961, when she retired. At last, at age sixty, she could devote most of her time to painting. By then, she had her own studio, an old miner's cabin that her father and brother had hauled out to the ranch for her several years before and converted. The whole family had been glad when Isabelle got her own space because until then her artwork, in all different stages, had been strewn all over the house. Now, only her finished paintings of people, animals, landscapes, ranch buildings, and flowers were displayed, and displayed with pride.

Isabelle's siblings were indeed proud of their sister, and they admired and supported her work. Of all her fans, her brother and sisters could uniquely appreciate how her paintings captured the essence of the harsh but beautiful world they had all grown up in and loved. After Isabelle stopped teaching, her siblings' support became more important than ever. Having enjoyed decades of mutual encouragement and meaningful discussions among teachers, colleagues, and students in Billings, Isabelle now worked in near isolation. Few people around Absarokee understood her work, since traditional art still prevailed in Montana. "For some, going home is an easy way out," wrote Isabelle's friend and former student, Donna Forbes. "For Isabelle, it was a bold thing. It took courage."

Even if they didn't always understand her artwork, Isabelle frequently gave pieces away to neighbors and townspeople. With time, they came to appreciate her artistic approach. One neighbor, looking at a woodcut Isabelle had made of a horse he once had, said, "Her art is different from a lot [of artists].... It's interesting how she really pulled out the character of that horse."

Isabelle wasn't alone in her efforts to build an oasis in the "art desert." Another of Montana's earliest Modern artists lived only 130 miles away, in Grass Range, where he ranched with his family. Like Isabelle, Bill Stockton had grown up on a ranch, studied art, and painted mostly agricultural and natural subjects. Whenever they got the chance to visit and talk, the two friends helped, encouraged, and inspired each other. "From Isabelle, I learned that what was around me was all important," Bill said.

Both Isabelle and Bill publicly exhibited their work occasionally, mainly in their home state. In 1964 Montana's first art museum featuring contemporary western art, the Yellowstone Art Center (now Yellowstone Art Museum) opened in Billings, and two years later it mounted a show of Isabelle's work, her biggest exhibition to date. Still, Isabelle never pressed very hard to promote herself or her work, nor did she vigorously try to sell it. If she sold one or two paintings per year, she was pleased.

Due in part to her lack of interest in fame and fortune, Isabelle's art was never as recognized as it deserved to be. Some observers believe that another reason she and her work are not better known is that she was a woman in an art world dominated by men. Nevertheless, Isabelle was highly respected by many in that world and is considered a significant artist in her genre. She played a major role in establishing and stimulating Modern art in Montana, not only through her own work but also through teaching and nurturing new generations of dedicated artists.

While Isabelle's work was mostly overlooked and underappreciated in the larger art world, it did receive some important, if belated, national recognition. In 1970, when Isabelle was sixty-nine, a stranger knocked on her door and introduced himself as Mitch Wilder, director of the renowned Amon Carter Museum in Fort Worth, Texas. Wilder said that the director of the Yellowstone Art Center had told him about Isabelle and had urged him to go look at her work. Flattered, Isabelle invited Wilder in. After examining her paintings for hours, he offered to exhibit her work in a one-woman art show at his esteemed museum. He selected seventy-five paintings to be in the exhibition. Isabelle was thrilled.

When the show opened two years later, Isabelle and her sister Grace traveled to Fort Worth, where they were treated like royalty and enjoyed themselves immensely. After all those years of working in near obscurity, Isabelle had to admit that the warm spotlight felt good.

Aside from occasional exciting episodes such as the Texas show, the last decades of Isabelle's life mostly flowed with the rhythms of the ranch and the natural world as she and her siblings tended the animals and the land. The Johnson "kids" all worked together and took care of one another, as they always had. A letter Isabelle wrote in 1971 proves that at age seventy, she still did hands-on ranch work. "We have been riding for the cattle—first time in my life that after three days in the saddle I have a blister in an unmentionable place."

In her retirement, Isabelle became more involved with her small community of Absarokee. She went to church on Sundays, debated the merits of the town's school system with neighbors, had coffee with friends, and, still fascinated by history, spent time as a volunteer on local history projects. Of course, she also continued making art on the ranch.

Isabelle had always enjoyed painting and drawing outdoors when possible. "She liked to get the fresh air into the composition," one of her students remembered. Her favorite time for painting outside was, surprisingly, winter. During that bare, muted season, the landscape could not hide its underlying structure and basic colors behind bright vegetation. As she worked, her watercolors often froze in the cold air, but she found she liked the effect—the colors freezing on the paper created an interesting texture.

A good example of Isabelle's cold-weather painting is a watercolor called "Seventeen Below and the Ducks Are Frozen In." One frigid morning in 1973, Ingwald burst into the house and called to his sisters. Some ducks were stuck in the river, he said—their feet were frozen in the ice. The siblings were concerned, but no one could help the birds. If people approached them, they might try to fly away, and in the struggle, tear off their ice-locked feet.

This Isabelle Johnson painting, Old Willows, Winter *(1948), is a good example of her winter paintings.* —Courtesy Yellowstone Art Museum, Billings, Montana

Although she couldn't rescue the ducks, Isabelle thought, she could capture this rare moment by painting them. Immobilized, the ducks would be perfect models. Bundling herself in her warmest clothes and grabbing her paintbrushes, watercolor paints, and paper, she headed out to the river. The view from the roof of the lambing shed, she quickly decided, was the ideal vantage point for her painting.

Tossing up a few bales of hay for a windbreak, seventy-one-year-old Isabelle climbed onto the roof and settled in to paint. Her head bobbed as she looked up at the scene, then down at the paper, working rapidly before her water and paint froze solid. The lines she painted were strong and free, freezing onto the paper the second she laid them down. It was not long before she had to stop. For now, the colors were just suggestions anyway. She would work more on the painting later, in her little studio by the house. She had an excellent memory for landscapes.

As Isabelle gathered up her materials, she felt a flood of warmth on her face. She looked up. The sun had come out, making the icy river and surrounding snow sparkle. As the sun hit the water, the ice started melting. Isabelle watched as her models finally freed themselves and disappeared.

The year after she made the duck painting, Isabelle and her sisters lost their brother, Ingwald. After his death, running the entire ranch was too much for the aging sisters, so they leased out most of their land for neighbors to use.

A few years later, when she was in her late seventies, Isabelle took a bad fall from a horse. The accident slowed her down, but she recovered. Bowing (a little) to age, Isabelle stopped painting outside in the cold, especially after she discovered that sitting by the windows in the house or her studio, she could see and paint just fine. This meant looking at the same scenes from the same perspective, but she knew no two paintings would ever be the same. As livestock moved about and the weather changed, every scene looked different and presented her with a brand-new challenge.

In 1983, Isabelle was honored in Montana with the Governor's Arts Award. At last, the people of her home state recognized her contribution to western art through her paintings and teaching. The following year, sadly, her youngest sister, Pearl, died, followed by Grace four years later. Without her lifelong companions, Isabelle was lonely on the ranch, but her devotion to art kept her going, even through cancer and, later, a stroke. Finally, however, in her late eighties, she had to stop painting, at least at the level she always had. At this point she returned to her first love, history, writing numerous short papers about the Stillwater region and its past, including both historical facts and her own recollections. In these writings, Isabelle shared memory after memory of the special valley she had grown up in and depicted in her art. Though unpublished, they serve as important historical source material.

Near the end of her life, as she grew frailer, Isabelle hired a woman to live with her and help take care of her and the property. Her long-time neighbors across the river also looked out for her, visiting often. One morning, not long after her ninety-first birthday, Isabelle asked her caregiver to walk her out to the garden to look at some flowers, called western stars, they had recently planted. There, in the garden her mother had planted long ago and she and her sisters had tended, Isabelle Johnson died a peaceful death. She is buried in Absarokee's Rosebud Cemetery with her family.

Because none of the Johnson siblings had children, they all left their money and property to charity. Upon Isabelle's death, some of her money went to build a local history museum, the Museum of the Beartooths, in nearby Columbus, Montana, which to this day houses Isabelle's writings and the bulk of the Johnson family's papers, photographs, and artifacts. Isabelle left all of her artwork—more than one thousand separate paintings, drawings, and other works—to the Yellowstone Art Museum in Billings.

The Johnson family ranch, too, was donated. Isabelle left the property to Montana State University in Bozeman. The income it produced was used, in accordance with Isabelle's wishes, to help support the university's veterinary-science program. Later, the university sold the ranch to an artist couple, Peter and Cathy Halstead, who developed it, along with adjacent land, as a combination working ranch and arts venue, with sculptures scattered across its rolling hills. Today, the Tippet Rise Art Center, which opened to the public in 2016, hosts concerts, student workshops, and other events.

Isabelle Johnson believed that all art is spiritual, in the sense that, when creating, "you have to rise above yourself and connect yourself with humanity as a whole." Through her own work, Isabelle pursued that connection with the larger human community. With unending dedication and hard work, she carved her artistic path, doing her best to live by the same advice she gave her students: "Forget everyone else and get down to business and work, work, work." The result was a legacy of artworks for countless generations to enjoy, and for herself, a long, full, rich, and beautiful life.

8

ALICE GREENOUGH ORR AND MARGE GREENOUGH HENSON

It was 1937. In the basement of Madison Square Garden, New York City's premier indoor arena, bronc-riding sisters Alice and Marge Greenough sat together on bales of hay. Soon, the parade kicking off one of America's biggest rodeos would begin. Alice, the elder sister, had been in New York's rodeo several times before, but this was Marge's first competition at Madison Square Garden. To pass the time and calm their nerves, the duo played a hand of cards. Alice and Marge, both in their thirties, looked glamorous in their colorful silk western outfits. Around them, other rodeo cowboys and cowgirls chattered and laughed as they readied their horses, brushing, saddling, and bridling them. The livestock—hundreds of horses, bulls, and other animals stabled in the basement during the rodeo—seemed to share the people's excitement.

When the word came to mount up, the Greenough sisters laid down their cards, hurried to their horses, and swung into their saddles. At the signal, all the performers spurred their steeds forward onto a winding ramp that led up to the arena. Above their heads, eighteen thousand spectators roared with excitement. As the riders burst into the

Alice (left) and Marge Greenough getting ready (with help from a friend) at Madison Square Garden (date unknown) —Courtesy Carbon County Historical Society and Museum, Red Lodge, Montana

cavernous arena, the roar became deafening, the bright lights blinding. The performers circled the ring in formation, looking up and waving.

For a professional rodeo athlete, performing at Madison Square Garden, one of the most prestigious rodeo venues in the country, was a career milestone. But truth be told, Marge and Alice loved any competition, large or small. Rodeo gave them the chance to do what they loved best: to test their riding skills against other athletes and perhaps walk away with prize money and a title. One day, in fact, Alice would win the women's bronc-riding championship here at Madison Square Garden. But not quite yet.

Years later, when they were old, both sisters counted the trip up that winding ramp as their favorite memory. That is saying a lot, since, for over three decades, Alice and Marge led successful, exciting careers as two of America's best-known rodeo cowgirls. As performers and competitors, their lives were demanding, but the sisters lived them with relish and had a lot of fun along the way.

———•••———

Horses were in the Greenough sisters' blood. Growing up, Alice and Marge, along with their siblings, practically lived in the saddle. Their father, Benjamin Franklin "Packsaddle Ben" Greenough, had, in one way or another, depended on horses for his living ever since moving to southeastern Montana, where he would eventually buy a ranch and raise his eight kids. Early in life, Ben, a wiry man with sharp blue eyes, became a gifted packer and horse trader. He was said to have won the first official bronc-riding championship in Montana, in the 1890s. Ben's larger-than-life personality influenced Alice, Marge, and his other children greatly over the course of their lives.

The details of Ben's youth and his migration to Montana vary widely among different sources, so the facts are hard to pin down. We know he was born in 1869 and grew up in the northeastern United States, but it seems his family moved around quite a bit when he was a child. At a young age, Ben lost his mother, and then, after his dad moved him and his four younger brothers to New York City, his father died too. Until around age fifteen, Ben lived in a New York orphanage. Then he left, hopping trains and working his way out west. In 1886, at age seventeen, he arrived in Billings, Montana.

In Billings, Ben found work as a porter at the Headquarters Hotel. Part of his job was tending the fireplaces in all the rooms. The person Ben bought firewood from was none other than Martha Jane "Calamity Jane" Canary, who lived outside of town at that time, overseeing a crew of woodcutters. Ben always paid Jane for the wood in two payments. This was because Jane, fearing she would get drunk and gamble her men's wages away, had her trusted young friend hold half of the money until the next morning. Calamity Jane was just one of the western icons Ben reputedly brushed shoulders with during his first decade in Montana— others were mountain man "Liver-Eating" Johnson; famous Crow army scout Curly; and Crow chief Plenty Coups.

The following spring, Ben began cowboying for ranchers on the Crow Reservation, about sixty miles south of Billings. There, he learned horse trading, that is, buying, selling, and swapping horses. Over the next few decades, horse trading would become a major source of income for Ben Greenough and his family. His herds would number some three hundred horses or more at a time.

Around 1893, Ben relocated to Red Lodge, Montana, and filed a homestead claim in an area called Fox, north of Red Lodge, along Rock Creek. Here he began breeding horses, particularly a sturdy mix of Morgan and Clydesdale breeds. He took them on the road to sell them, sometimes going as far as the Midwest. On one such trip in 1894, Ben stayed in a boarding house in rural Illinois and befriended the owner's daughter, Myrtle Webb. For the next five years, the two exchanged letters.

In Red Lodge, in addition to other activities, Ben learned the art of horse packing. This skill involved evenly distributing loads of supplies on the backs of horses or mules and tying them securely, as well as managing the strings of pack animals carrying the loads. Packers sometimes worked as guides, too, organizing and leading trips into the wilderness for out-of-towners interested in hunting or fishing. Becoming a master of all these skills, Ben lived up to his nickname, "Packsaddle Ben." With his brother Bill, who had also come to Montana, Ben forged one of the first pack trails across the formidable Beartooth Plateau between Red Lodge and the mining town of Cooke City, a distance of more than sixty miles, and he traveled it often.

In October 1899, Myrtle took the train west to Billings, where she and Ben were married. The newlyweds settled at the Fox ranch, living in a log house Ben had built. Myrtle was tiny (she weighed under a hundred pounds) but tough. Between 1901 and 1910, she had eight children. From oldest to youngest, they were Vena, Alice, Frank, Ida, Thurkel (Turk), Mae, Margaret (usually called Marge or Margie), and Bill. Alice was born on March 17, 1902, and Marge on November 14, 1908.

The first five Greenough kids were born while the family lived at the Fox homestead. There, summer through fall, Ben was often away on

Myrtle and Ben Greenough at the Fox homestead, north of Red Lodge, circa 1905. The children sit on a horse that Ben had persuaded to lie down. Left to right are Alice, Vena, Ida, Frank, and baby Turk. —Courtesy Carbon County Historical Society and Museum, Red Lodge, Montana

pack trips, carrying supplies to Cooke City or guiding paying customers on trips. This left Myrtle alone with the children for weeks at a time. In addition to preparing food and other household chores, Myrtle hauled the family's water, chopped the wood, tended the animals, and cared for her ever-increasing brood. Years later, Alice looked back on her mother with awe, marveling at all she had managed. "I never in my life heard one word of complaint from my mother," Alice remembered.

In 1906, because of the hardships and isolation of life at Fox, Myrtle and Ben decided to move the family to the city of Billings, where the three youngest Greenoughs would be born. There, on a ten-acre lot on the outskirts of town, near the famous Moss Mansion, Ben dug the basement for a house. He never finished the house, so, for fifteen years, the family lived in the basement. Blankets divided up the open space. Ben and Myrtle slept in one "room" and the girls in another. The boys bunked in the kitchen.

From the time the children were very little, their parents sat them on horses, and by age three or four, they were riding. As they grew older, their father taught them how to drive teams, to pack horses, and especially, to "break" new broncs, that is, teach untrained horses to tolerate a rider. In the horse trade, breaking broncs was a never-ending job. The extra step was worth it, though, since gentle, manageable horses brought better prices than wild, untrained ones. Ben's method of teaching his children this skill was tough. After divvying up a herd of unbroken horses among the kids, Ben would tell them, "Ride 'em or walk!"

The most common technique for breaking a horse was simply to mount it and endure its bucking until it became exhausted and gave up. The sharp rocks that littered the corral gave the Greenough kids extra incentive to stay on the backs of their mounts. "Nobody," Marge later said, "could get bucked off on those rocks and live." Without realizing it, the children were training for a future of rodeo competition.

As soon as they were old enough, the kids joined their father on pack trips. In the early summer, Ben would head out from Billings with a herd of horses, riding up into the Beartooth Mountains, where he set up a base camp, usually at serene Beartooth Lake. Once the camp was set up,

Ben bid his children goodbye and continued farther into the mountains with his pack string, leaving the youngsters alone with the rest of the horses for weeks at a time. To teach them self-sufficiency and especially willpower, a characteristic he playfully dubbed "Old Willy," Ben left them with the barest necessities—fishing hooks and line, a few canned goods, and an ax. While there, the children were expected not only to survive but to work, breaking the horses.

Some people questioned Ben Greenough's unusual child-rearing methods, leaving the kids like that in the wild, but Ben would respond, "I never lost a kid or a horse in my life." His children always maintained that they enjoyed the rigors of their mountain camp, and they had a lot of fun. Alice recalled that, when they weren't working with the horses, they challenged one another to races and fishing contests. Once, they made a raft and enticed a favorite horse aboard for a ride on the lake.

While Ben and the older kids were in the mountains, Myrtle stayed home with the younger ones. The family grew rutabagas and strawberries and sold them, along with fresh eggs, for extra money. During Ben's long absences, the family's Billings neighbors, the O'Donnells, kept a protective eye on Myrtle, helping out if she ran low on food or money. Sometimes they hired the Greenough youngsters for odd jobs around their dairy farm, giving the family a small boost.

In the fall, the Greenough family reunited in Billings. The kids went to school in town, riding there on horseback. Each child had only one set of school clothes, so after school, they changed into their "play" clothes while their mom washed the school outfits, then hung them by the stove to dry. By the time the kids woke up the next morning, Myrtle had their clothes pressed, their breakfast and lunches made, and the bread ready for baking. Myrtle also taught her girls domestic skills. Sewing in particular would come in handy for Marge and Alice in the future, when they would make all their own rodeo outfits.

In 1915 Ben, always on the lookout for work opportunities, briefly traveled with a small, regional Wild West show called "The Passing of the West." These frontier-themed traveling shows were very popular from the late 1800s to the early decades of the 1900s. They were similar to rodeos, except the focus was more on entertainment and storytelling than on competition. In his part of the show, "Packsaddle Ben" demonstrated his skills with a pack string to appreciative audiences.

During Ben's time with "The Passing of the West," Alice, thirteen, and Marge, seven, spent time with their father at the show. One of the other performers was the great Fannie Sperry Steele. Originally from Helena, Montana, Fannie had, three years earlier, competed against the best of her peers to become the world champion "lady" bronc rider at the first Calgary Stampede, a lavish rodeo in Alberta, Canada. Fannie was one of a pioneering wave of women rodeo champs who were winning respect, fame, and, in some cases, more money than most men made in a year. Watching her stick to buckers in the ring, Alice and Marge were awestruck. "I used to watch her [on a bronc] and see how she done things, because I wanted to do it just like she did," Alice recalled. "She was my hero, all right."

Ben thrilled his girls by taking them behind the scenes to meet Fannie. The older woman was sweet and encouraging to them. Without even trying, she planted an image in Alice's and Marge's heads that would never leave them—that of a skilled, successful, and highly respected female rodeo star.

Neither Alice nor Marge graduated from high school. In fact, Vena, the eldest Greenough child, was the only one who did. The others would leave school after the eighth grade to work. Vena and Alice, for example, took over their father's mail route—another of Ben's many side jobs— in 1917, when Alice was about fifteen years old. For the next three winters and two summers, Alice completed a thirty-seven-mile route, on horseback or driving a wagon, to rural areas outside of Billings each day. In winter it was a frigid affair, and in any season it was a test of endurance.

By that time, America had entered World War I, creating a shortage of labor as men went off to fight. The Greenough kids, both the girls and the boys, stepped into some of the available jobs. Local farmers and ranchers hired them for cowboying, driving teams, and farm work such as plowing. If it involved horses, they knew the Greenoughs could do it.

If the Greenough brood worked hard, they also played hard. Competition on horseback was always part of their play. In addition to vying with one another, the Greenough kids held informal races, bucking-horse competitions, and other contests of horsemanship with neighborhood youngsters. When they were older, most of the Greenough siblings entered competitions at local rodeos. Both Alice and Marge were skilled enough to do just about anything—bronc busting, steer and bull riding, horse racing, trick riding, and more.

Of all the competitions they participated in, Alice and Marge especially loved racing on horseback. There were basically two kinds of horse racing at that time. "Flat" or "straight" races were the typical sort, in which a person rides one horse to the finish line. Those were fun, but even more exciting were relay races. In a relay, one rider rode three horses during the same race, going about half a mile on one before coming in at high speed to switch. A waiting cowboy held the next horse for the rider to mount. Most girls, including Marge and Alice, simply grabbed the next horse's saddle horn and "vaulted" from one saddle into the other. As soon as the rider touched the next horse, it was cut loose and set to running.

Riding a bronc, which both sisters excelled at, presented different challenges. Staying on a bucker took enormous abdominal and leg strength. The rider held the reins in one hand, while her other arm, stretched out, swung with the bucking of the horse and helped her keep her balance, like the rudder on a boat. She kept the reins short, pulling the horse's mouth close to its chest to prevent it from rearing. If she didn't hold them tightly enough, the horse might dive onto its front legs with its head down, pulling her arm right out of the socket or even "heading over"—that is, turning a somersault and landing on the rider. Horses tried a thousand strategies to shake riders off their backs. Skilled riders knew how to read a horse's body language to predict its actions. The key to staying on, or "sticking," was rhythm. If a rider became out of sync with the horse, she would soon be examining the ground up close.

Alice's first step into official public rodeos was in 1919, when she was seventeen. Friends at the Forsyth, Montana, rodeo urged her to test her mettle on a gray saddle bronc, and she stuck to the horse with ease. Marge's rodeo debut came in 1924, when she was sixteen. She won fifteen dollars at the Red Lodge rodeo, as a jockey in the half-mile cowgirl race. The girls would continue entering local competitions and winning. Despite that, neither sister considered competing on the national-level rodeo circuit.

The Greenough kids owed their athletic skills largely to their father's training. "He was a great teacher," Alice recalled. Her brother Turk remembered him as "a strict disciplinarian." In addition to riding, Ben taught all his children to ice skate. As a boy, he had been an excellent skater. In Billings, among his many jobs, Ben managed an ice rink, and the kids learned to skate there. Alice, in particular, did so well in figure-skating competitions that for a time she considered becoming a professional skater. In any case, the sport strengthened her legs—important for a rodeo rider.

As sisters, Alice and Marge were close, despite their difference in age and temperament. Alice was a tall brunette, outgoing and confident, with a big, radiant smile. Later, in glamorous photographs, that smile would help establish her as the "queen of rodeo." Redheaded Marge was soft-spoken and, in some ways, warmer than Alice. In spite of her shyness, Marge possessed, like all the Greenoughs, a will of iron and a bottomless capacity for competition and fun. Alice and Marge shared a bond of ambition and a passion for people, unique experiences, and good times.

In 1922, the Greenough family returned to Red Lodge, the town that had always held a special place in their hearts. They moved into a small house by the local ice rink, which, as in Billings, Ben had been hired to manage. By this time, Alice and the other older siblings were on their own; only the younger kids, including fourteen-year-old Marge, lived with their parents.

To support herself, Alice picked up various jobs. She had considered several careers—for example, being a forest ranger—but men returning from World War I had taken all those jobs. In 1922, the same year her family moved to Red Lodge, Alice, age twenty, got married. Her husband, Ray Cahill, was from Kansas City, but he had family in the Red Lodge area.

Ben and Myrtle moved again in 1924, but not far away. Vena had claimed a homestead in Rock Creek Canyon just south of Red Lodge. Ben built a house there for the family. This would be the Greenough clan's home base until Ben and Myrtle died in the 1950s.

In 1926, Turk became the first Greenough sibling to perform in a rodeo professionally, thanks to a chance encounter. On his twenty-first birthday, Turk attended a big Wild West show in Billings. As he was waiting for the show to start, an employee named Joe Orr—who would soon become a close friend of the whole Greenough family—approached him and asked if he could ride a bucker. The show's usual bronc rider had to drop out, Joe explained. Turk agreed to fill in, and he rode so well that he was offered a permanent job.

The job was an eye-opener for Turk. Life in a Wild West show was great. For doing one short ride a day, Turk could make at least fifty dollars, while at home, working at harder, less interesting jobs, he had earned perhaps thirty dollars in a month. With the show, he traveled widely, enjoying the company of fellow athletes and learning from them. While most performances in Wild West shows were staged, ensuring a thrill for paying audiences, the producers did sponsor a few rodeo-style contests in which the riders were allowed to truly compete, vying for cash prizes. Turk was so talented on a bronc, he often walked away with the money.

This first experience of being well paid to do what he loved was a turning point in Turk's life. He now knew that the skills he had taken for granted at home had serious value in the larger world. The following summer, he left the Wild West show and started entering every rodeo he could. Before long, Turk Greenough had become a famous name in the rodeo world.

Turk's success and happiness were not lost on Alice, Marge, and the other siblings. During this time Alice, with her husband, Ray, was moving around the West, living sometimes near Red Lodge but also in South Dakota and Wyoming. The couple had two sons, Thomas and E. Jay, but the marriage was troubled. Although Alice was not yet on the national rodeo circuit, she, like her siblings, enjoyed entering local competitions. This may have been hard for Ray to understand. Not only did he have little interest in rodeo, he also believed, as did many people at that time, that young mothers did not belong in a rodeo arena.

In the end, the marriage failed. Alice left Ray in 1928, and they divorced the following year. Ray returned to Kansas, where he raised the boys. Afterward, Alice had little contact with her children, though Ben, Myrtle, and Alice's siblings stayed in touch with them. For unknown reasons, she seldom mentioned them or the marriage.

In the winter of 1928–29, Alice, now twenty-seven, and Marge, twenty-one, were both waiting tables at a restaurant in Red Lodge when they stumbled on an intriguing opportunity. While idly thumbing through a magazine, one of the sisters spotted an advertisement from a Wild West show producer looking for "lady bronc riders" and showed it to the other. The two looked at each other with wide eyes. If Turk was succeeding as a professional rider, why couldn't they? They were just as good. They answered the ad, and soon a telegram arrived. "Come at once!" it said. In that instant, a new life opened up for Alice and Marge.

Only after they had packed their bags did the sisters inform their parents they were leaving. At first Myrtle and Ben were against it, but ultimately, Ben gave his daughters his blessing, telling them, "You got more nerve than you got brains anyway." As they were leaving he added, "Take Old Willy with you," reminding them to stay mentally strong.

To meet up with their new employer, the King Brothers Wild West Rodeo and Hippodrome Racing Unit, the Greenough sisters had to travel clear across the country to Alex City, Alabama, where the company had its winter headquarters. When everything was ready, the show hit the road.

As "lady bronc riders," Alice and Marge did all the things they were used to doing: riding broncs, trick riding, and other feats of horsemanship. But they also had to do things that struck them as silly, such as riding bison and performing in skits about the Old West. In one act, they had to wear old-timey dresses and run screaming out of a burning building. Nevertheless, Alice and Marge had discovered a world that suited them.

On tour, Alice, Marge, and the other performers led a gypsylike existence. They traveled with few possessions—just a bedroll, tent, washpan, bucket, and coffee pot—and usually camped beside their cars because hotels were too expensive. Most of the riders lived on "day money"—wages and winnings from that day alone—which tended to vanish quickly. If someone had extra money, Alice fondly remembered later, he or she shared it with the others. Money wasn't the main motivation for being in the show, anyway. Most of the riders worked more for the experience, the excitement, the travel, and the camaraderie than for the paycheck. After their first season, Alice and Marge's only profit was a can of tomato soup. They found themselves stuck in Des Moines, Iowa, waiting tables to earn enough money to get home.

Traveling and living together, the people in the show became a sort of family. Due to this closeness, sometimes romance bloomed among the performers. In fact, that is exactly what happened to Marge. She befriended another employee, a bronc rider and bulldogger named Charles "Heavy" Henson (bulldoggers leap from running horses onto the backs of steers and wrestle them to the ground). During one King Brothers show, Heavy broke his leg when a bronc fell on him. While he was in the hospital, the show moved on and left him, but Marge circled back to take care of her friend. The two fell in love, and the following year, in 1930, they married.

By that time, Marge, Heavy, and Alice had all left the King Brothers show and entered the professional rodeo circuit. During Alice's first season of competition in 1930, however, she broke her ankle when her foot got hung up in her stirrup. She had to spend the next nine months in a hospital in Texas, and for a while it looked like she might even lose her leg. Finally, doctors inserted ivory pegs into her ankle, and the injury healed. From then on, the press called Alice the "Girl with the Ivory Ankle."

Alice broke plenty of other bones during her career, including her ribs and her nose. Marge did not escape injury, either. Once, while she was mounting a squirrelly bronc in a chute, her wrist snapped. In the instant before the chute opened, Marge changed hands and completed the ride. Over the years, both sisters suffered various leg injuries. Later, as an old woman, Marge remarked humorously that both she and Alice had "legs that don't match," and that one of hers was permanently imprinted with the outline of a chute gate.

As Alice was getting back on her feet in Texas, Marge entered into a new venture: motherhood. In 1931, while on the road in Florida, she gave birth to her son, Charles Henson Junior, whom everyone called Chuck. Married life hadn't been a dramatic change for Marge, the way it had been for Alice. As a fellow athlete, Heavy understood, respected, and supported his wife. Now, even with a child, Marge carried on as she had before, taking baby Chuck with her on the rodeo circuit. His first crib was a pillow-stuffed fruit crate that Marge tied to her waist with a rope, dragging him behind her. Near the chutes, when it was time for Marge to mount her bronc, she simply handed the baby to a cowboy until her ride was over. When he got older, Chuck sometimes rode a pony in the shows. As an adult, he remembered watching his mother perform: "The harder a horse bucked, the better Mom liked it."

When Marge was expecting, she rode broncs until just a few months before her due date. Alice, too, had remained an active rider during her pregnancies. Later, Alice would write in a women's magazine that an expectant mother's vigorous physical activity did no harm to the fetus; in fact, strong muscles made giving birth easier. Alice's opinions seemed outlandish to most Americans at the time, but today we know she was right.

While Marge was enjoying her new life of rodeo and family, Alice was still in Texas with her ankle injury. To allow it to heal, she had to stay off broncs for nearly two years. She did not, however, stay off horses. In shows and rodeos, she participated in quadrilles, in which a rider leads her horse in a kind of dancing to music. One day in Texas in 1932, a show producer saw Alice perform and offered her an unusual gig: riding bulls in Europe. Alice accepted the job. First she trained in Mexico for two months before sailing across the Atlantic. In about thirty towns in Spain and a few in France and Portugal, Alice rode angry bulls. As they ran, the beasts would turn their heads and attempt to hook her with their horns. To protect herself, Alice sewed cushioned pads for her hips and elbows. Only once in her life did a bull ever succeed in bucking her off. When she landed, the animal trampled her and she passed out, but remarkably, she was okay.

By the time Alice and Marge came on the scene, the rodeo world was changing. Although professional rodeo had a tradition of women's competitive events stretching back before the time of Fannie Sperry Steele (the sisters' childhood idol), Americans eventually began to frown on the full participation of women in rodeo. After the death of a rodeo cowgirl during a competition in 1929, followed by a similar tragedy in 1933, women—or at least white, middle- and upper-class women—began to be seen as frail and in need of protection. While the public seemed to think it was okay for men to risk injury or death in the rodeo ring, the same choices were becoming unacceptable for women.

Despite the declining popularity of women's events, Alice and Marge were rising in their profession. The 1930s were hectic for both sisters as they crisscrossed the continent from Montana to Texas, Pennsylvania, and Wisconsin, and many big cities in between: Denver, Boston, Kansas City, and more. Sometimes separately and sometimes together, they traveled by automobile or train, occasionally hauling their own horses. Over the years, Marge won many bronc-riding contests and other events, while Alice, an even stronger rider, won still more. Both eventually performed in almost every state, and Alice would compete internationally.

Of all their skills, the Greenough sisters were best known for their bronc riding. In that sport, rodeo competitors drew numbers for which horses they would ride. Riders hoped for explosive broncs who would help them demonstrate their skills—and earn more points. The judges watched to see if a rider was sitting up straight during the bucking and keeping her head from jerking back and forth. She must not change hands on the reins and definitely mustn't hang on to the saddle, a no-no called "pulling leather." To have a chance at winning, a competitor had to stay on the horse for the required time, usually eight long seconds— during which period the horse bucked, on average, twenty times.

The most prestigious and best-paying venues were out east: Boston Garden and New York's Madison Square Garden. In Boston, a champion could win up to $40,000 in prize money, although prize amounts for women were usually less than for men. New York's prizes were nearly as amazing. Alice had competed at Madison Square Garden for the first time in 1930, though it was years before she won a championship there, and Marge never did.

Upon returning from her European bull-riding adventure in 1933, Alice went on to win the world championship in women's saddle-bronc riding at Boston Garden. Afterward she and her brother Turk, as two of America's top rodeo athletes, were chosen to compete at a rodeo in London. While there, Alice had tea with the Queen of England, who later sent her a pretty water pitcher as a present, just because Alice had admired it.

By this time Turk, a rising rodeo star, and brother Bill, also a rodeo athlete, were sometimes appearing with their sisters as the "Riding Greenoughs." Off and on through the years, the siblings performed together all over the country, with Frank sometimes joining in as well. Before long, the Greenoughs were the most famous family in rodeo.

The siblings continued their separate careers as well. Beginning in 1934, Alice competed in Australia most years, winning the international championship title the first year and again in 1939. Australians called bronc riding "buck-jumping," and rodeos were known as "cattlemen's picnics." Returning to Boston each year, Alice won two more championships, in 1935 and 1936. In the 1935 contest, Turk took the men's bronc-riding prize, so sister and brother proudly accepted their awards together.

Alice and Marge's career had its own kind of glamour. The sisters always dressed beautifully, both on and off their horses. Each rodeo season, they designed and sewed new cowgirl outfits, purchasing silk and other special fabrics in New York. Out east, in between rodeos, wealthy people would invite the renowned western duo to stay at their mansions. The Greenoughs played polo with millionaires and lunched with New York mayor Fiorello LaGuardia. They appeared on the covers of magazines. As celebrities, Marge and especially Alice, as well as Turk, increased their incomes by endorsing products, not only in the U.S. but in Australia too.

In the meantime Turk, like many other rodeo riders in those days, had made himself a second career in the movie industry. In the winter, when there were no rodeos, he went to California to do stunts and play small parts in motion pictures, especially westerns, a genre that had been popular since the early days of film. Hollywood recognized the rodeo world as a source of charismatic show people who could do just about anything on horseback.

After watching her brother for a few years, Alice decided to try acting herself. Hollywood had a tradition, after all, of featuring plucky cowgirl heroines in many westerns. In 1937 Alice got a part in the movie *The Californian*, for which the director made her bleach her dark hair blonde. When a reporter asked Alice what she thought of the new color, she responded, "It looks like hell." The whole experience convinced Alice that she wasn't really interested in becoming a movie actress. Still, working with horses in films fit well with her career in rodeo, especially during winter when the circuit was quiet, so she continued doing stunts and such on occasion. Other films Alice appeared in include *Cimarron* (1960) with Glenn Ford and several John Wayne pictures. Later, Marge, too, got in on the act. Both sisters would ride and drive teams in movies and on TV shows into their eighties.

The year 1939 was special for the Riding Greenoughs. Alice drove her father, Ben, who had never learned to drive a car, out east for the big rodeo at Madison Square Garden. In New York they met up with Marge, Turk, and Bill. Because he was returning to the city of his childhood, Ben received lots of newspaper coverage, which helped advertise the rodeo too. One day Ben even packed a horse and led it through the streets of downtown Manhattan. He also rode in the rodeo's parades and endorsed products along with his famous children. From New York, the family continued on to the Boston Garden rodeo.

The following year, 1940, Alice at last won the women's saddle-bronc championship at Madison Square Garden. She also entered into a very brief marriage with cowboy Pete Kerscher. Afterward, as with her first marriage, she almost never talked about it. She and Pete had no children.

The year after Alice's big win in New York, she and Marge both retired from the professional cowgirl circuit. Coincidentally, that was also the last year of the women's bronc-riding event at Madison Square Garden, marking the end of a golden era in rodeo, when women competed in the same events as men and the rodeo world encouraged and supported them.

Several factors influenced the increasingly restrictive view of women's role in rodeo. World War II had its effect. Wartime rationing and smaller audiences forced rodeo producers to make cuts, and the women's events were among the first things to be axed. Something similar had happened during World War I, but thanks to early Hollywood westerns, the image of the courageous and capable cowgirl remained popular— even beloved—in the American imagination. By the 1940s, however, conservative ideas about women, including rodeo women, were taking over. A cowgirl's looks were beginning to outweigh her skill on a horse. At many rodeos, women's events began to resemble beauty pageants on horseback.

Alice encountered these changes firsthand when she was hired in the mid-1940s to coach singer-turned-actress Dale Evans in riding. Pretty Evans was being groomed to become America's ideal western woman in movies, television, and song. But as Alice discovered when the lessons began, Evans had never even been on a horse before. Her horse and western gear were little more than props.

Marge experienced another change that discouraged new generations of women from participating widely in rodeo—bigger horses. For twelve years, between professional rodeos, Marge rode broncs in local shows produced by Leo Cremer, a stock supplier in Big Timber, Montana. Cremer bred regular horses with draft horses, creating large, tough-to-handle buckers. Marge was skilled enough to handle the big horses, but they "bucked her teeth out," as she put it, compared to the smaller horses used in most rodeos at the time. Eventually, these bigger horses became the standard throughout the sport, discouraging all but the strongest, most experienced riders—usually men—from competing. Luckily for Alice and Marge, they had made their mark during the heyday of women's rodeo, and by the time things changed, they were ready to retire.

Marge Greenough on Gold Bond, a Leo Cremer bronc, at the Colorado State Fair; date unknown
—Courtesy Carbon County Historical Society and Museum, Red Lodge, Montana

Although Alice stopped competing in national-level rodeos in 1941, she didn't stop working. That year, a new era in her life opened. She and longtime family friend Joe Orr—the man who'd first helped Turk get into professional rodeo—pooled their money to start their own rodeo company. Like Leo Cremer's outfit, the Greenough-Orr Rodeo Company provided horses and other animals for rodeo competitions across the western U.S. and Canada. Whenever they had the money, they would buy a new horse or steer to add to their herd. They also began producing rodeos. Alice managed the hiring, bookkeeping, and payroll while Joe ran the ring. Whenever she wanted, Alice hopped on a bronc herself, usually for exhibition, not competition. Often Marge,

Heavy, and other relatives and friends came out to perform too. The Greenough-Orr Rodeo Company was one of the first to feature a new women's event called barrel racing in its shows. Today, barrel racing is the main women's event at rodeos.

Both Alice and Marge competed now and then through the 1940s and '50s, but only in smaller, local rodeos and only for fun. During that time, Alice began spending time in Tucson, Arizona, mostly in the winter, returning to Montana each summer. In 1954 Alice, Marge, and Heavy all retired from rodeo riding, though Alice and Joe continued to operate their rodeo company. Heavy and Marge bought a ranch in Montana. By then, their son Chuck was grown and making his own career in rodeo.

As a young man, Chuck Henson rode in competitions, but eventually he became known as a top-notch rodeo clown. Rodeo clowns are not like circus clowns—their profession is extremely dangerous. Clowns keep contestants safe by distracting angry animals, especially bulls, away from riders when they jump or fall off their mounts.

Whenever Alice and Marge returned to their hometown, Red Lodge, they spent time with their father, who was old now. In his later years, Ben asked Alice to find a place where memorabilia from his long, eventful career could be displayed. A few years after his 1956 death, Alice was able to grant her father's wish, turning a building at an old fish hatchery at the south end of town into a Greenough family museum. During the summer, the museum stayed open from 6 am to 10 pm, and each night after closing, Alice slept in an adjacent cabin, armed with a shotgun to protect the contents. For two seasons she ran the display until it landed in more permanent (and secure) digs, ultimately becoming Red Lodge's Carbon County Historical Museum. The Greenough family artifacts remain a prized collection in the museum today.

In 1958, Alice and Joe sold their company. Shortly afterwards, Joe asked Alice, now fifty-six, to marry him. "Sounds like a good idea," she responded. "I've known you all my life. I know all your faults and you know mine." Later, she reflected, "We got along very good. No problem at all. We shared everything—our work and what little we saved. My friends were his friends and his friends were my friends. It wasn't a new life at all."

After tying the knot, Alice and Joe moved permanently to Tucson. Soon Marge and Heavy, tired of Montana winters, joined them in Arizona, moving in next door.

After Heavy Henson died in 1976, followed by Joe Orr two years later, Alice and Marge continued their life in Tucson, contentedly living side by side. It was never dull. In the 1980s both sisters did stunt work, driving wagons in the popular television series *Little House on the Prairie*. In 1987, Alice appeared in the TV movie *Poker Alice* with Elizabeth Taylor. For a time, harking back to their waitress days, the sisters ran a café at Tucson's livestock exchange.

Alice called her generation of rodeo performers the "Wild Bunch," and friends from that era, whenever they passed through Tucson, visited the sisters. "The men admire the women and vice versa and everyone's so happy to see each other," Alice said. "You can look on my back porch from 11 o'clock on and if there isn't five or six cowboys sitting there drinking coffee, something is wrong." Even the visitors' horses were given accommodations at the Greenough girls' place.

In the summer of 1992, Alice completed her annual ride in the Red Lodge Fourth of July parade for the last time. Three years later, she died at age ninety-three, only three months after the death of her brother Turk. Marge died in 2004 at ninety-five, outliving all her brothers and sisters.

In addition to the Greenough collection at the Carbon County Historical Museum, most other museums devoted to cowboys, cowgirls, or rodeo include displays about Alice and Marge's careers. The sisters have also been inducted into several Halls of Fame: the National Cowgirl Museum Hall of Fame in Fort Worth, Texas, inducted Alice in 1975 and Marge in 1978; in 1983, the National Cowboy Museum's Rodeo Hall of Fame in Oklahoma City inducted both sisters as well as Turk. The siblings' descendants continued the family tradition. Chuck Henson was inducted into the ProRodeo Hall of Fame in Colorado Springs in 1995, and Alice and Marge's nephew, Deb Greenough, was recognized by the same organization as a seven-time world champion bareback bronc rider. Younger generations of Greenoughs continue to compete in the "family business."

For many fans, Alice and Marge Greenough personify rodeo's best days, when male and female riders participated fully in all events. As Alice, in her later years, observed, "Rodeo was a different world when Margie and my brothers and I competed." These days, despite the decrease in women's events, cowgirls continue to compete in rodeos nationwide. Undoubtedly, the story of the hard-riding Greenough sisters are a source of inspiration for these young athletes.

Looking back and reminiscing, Alice and Marge invariably smiled. Marge said, "We did something we enjoyed," adding that she wished everyone could be so lucky. Every picture of her on a bronc looked "silly," she thought, "because I was grinning so." For her part, Alice summed up their careers well: "That rodeo life was a good old life."

9

MYRNA LOY

MORE THAN A MOVIE STAR

In 1938, when Adolf Hitler took over Czechoslovakia, that country's exiled foreign minister made a stirring radio speech. Lamenting his country's demolished democracy, he predicted a terrible world war. Upon hearing the speech in America, movie star Myrna Loy immediately telegrammed the Czech diplomat, expressing her sympathy and support. Word of the telegram spread internationally, even to Hitler's regime, which retaliated by banning Myrna's films in Germany. Myrna was pleased to have riled the Nazis: "Why should I be entertaining the Third Reich?" she later quipped. The fact that Hitler's Reich, at the height of its power, responded so forcefully to the telegram shows the influence that Myrna, a girl from Montana's Crow Creek Valley, wielded by the time she was thirty-three.

Beginning at age twenty, Myrna Loy appeared in 124 movies during a career that spanned six decades. In 1937, moviegoers voted her "Queen of the Movies." That year, she was also one of the highest-paid actors in the industry. She worked hard for the money. After her career took off, Myrna did not take a vacation for ten years.

Myrna Loy was beautiful, no doubt, but people loved her for more than just her looks. In films, she could be funny or elegant or both at the same time. Her timing was perfect and her performances subtle, making acting look easy. The famous director Sidney Lumet, who worked with

Publicity shot, Myrna Loy; date unknown —Courtesy Mary Ann Judy

Myrna on her last film, the 1980 comedy *Just Tell Me What You Want,* respected her for "what she held back" as an actor. Hollywood publicist John Springer described Myrna as "warm and cool all at once." In interviews in fan magazines, she sounded down-to-earth, like a regular person, not a big-screen idol.

———•••———

When Myrna Adele Williams, the future Myrna Loy, was born in 1905, filmmaking was in its infancy—short silent films were beginning to be shown in five-cent Nickelodeon theaters in big cities, and Hollywood still had dirt roads and open fields. As she was growing up, motion-picture technology was developing by leaps and bounds. When she was twenty-two, the first full-length "talkie," *The Jazz Singer,* premiered in New York City. Myrna was a working actress by then, and she actually appeared in *The Jazz Singer,* though just as a chorus girl. Yet she was already on her way to becoming a film-acting veteran, having appeared in more than twenty silent movies in the previous two years.

Myrna was born on August 2, 1905, in Helena, Montana. Her parents, David F. and Della Mae Williams, both grew up in Radersburg, a mining town about forty-five miles south of Helena. All four of Myrna's immigrant grandparents had moved to Radersburg in the 1860s and '70s.

Myrna's maternal grandmother, Isabel, immigrated to America from Scotland as a teenager. She married and had one son in Iowa before her husband died. Soon after, she joined a wagon train to Montana, her child in tow. In Radersburg, she met and married a Swedish immigrant carpenter and gold prospector named John Johnson, Myrna's grandfather. Myrna's mother, Della, was the youngest of the Johnsons' three children.

John Johnson died before Myrna was born, as did both of Myrna's other grandparents, David (Senior) and Ann Williams. Welsh immigrants, the Williamses lived first in Utah, then in Idaho, before moving to Radersburg to ranch in the Crow Creek Valley. Ann, pregnant at the time and accompanied by two small children and her blind mother, drove one of the wagons herself. As an actress, Myrna hankered to portray a strong western woman like her grandmothers someday, but such a role never came her way.

Myrna's mom was a strong woman as well. In 1905, when she was seven months pregnant with Myrna and her husband was away on business, Della joined some friends hiking up one of the highest peaks in the southern Rocky Mountains. At the top, one of the hikers snapped a picture of Della, the first woman known to have scaled the peak. The photograph later appeared on the cover of a national magazine, *Field and Stream*. When Myrna's dad saw the magazine, he "blew his stack," according to family lore. David had rigid beliefs about how women should behave in society. During their marriage, Della's free spirit often clashed with David's conservative values. Myrna loved them both, and in some ways, the two influences combined in her.

When Myrna's parents married in Helena, Montana's capital, in 1904, they had planned to stay in that city, but David's parents died shortly after the wedding, and out of duty the couple moved back to the Williams family's Crow Creek ranch. Here, little Myrna would spend her first five years. Her Scottish grandmother, Isabel, lived nearby. When Myrna was a baby, Isabel would push down on Myrna's snub nose to flatten it. It was good that it didn't work. That "tip-tilted" nose, as a reporter later described it, would become a trademark of Myrna's celebrated beauty.

Like most rural homes in those days, the Williamses' log cabin had no electricity or plumbing. Everyday life was challenging. The frigid winters could be fatal to livestock and even to humans. But Myrna's memories of the ranch were warm and positive. The red-haired, freckle-faced girl enjoyed poking around by herself in the foothills near her home, admiring the flowers, trees, and wildlife; riding the family's old workhorse, Dolly; chasing little lambs around the yard; and cuddling with her two kittens, Timothy and Alfalfa. Myrna's mother, who had studied at the American Conservatory of Music in Chicago, played piano and violin, and Myrna often fell asleep to Della's playing, frequently accompanied by Della's sister, Aunt Lou, and other musical friends and relatives.

Myrna's parents weren't happy on the ranch, however. David did not like ranching, and Della, stifled in the isolated valley, pined for culture.

The Williams family in Helena, 1910: Della, Myrna, and David Sr. Photo by J. Moriarty —Courtesy Montana Historical Society Research Center, Montana Historical Society, Helena, Montana

They both wanted to move back to Helena, but David would need a job. Before he was married, he had been a politician, serving as Montana's youngest state legislator, but he had no interest in returning to politics. Instead, he decided to try his hand at real estate and banking. In 1910 the family moved into a comfortable house on Fifth Avenue in Helena, not far from Central Elementary, where Myrna went to school. Myrna's beloved grandmother Isabel also moved to Helena from Crow Creek, so Myrna was able to spend a lot of time with her.

Helena was then a bustling community of twelve thousand, complete with streetcars, a public library, a hospital, and a zoo, not to mention the elegant state capitol. Best of all were the theaters and opera houses, where young Myrna would discover the magic of the stage. From the solitude of Crow Creek, Myrna now lived in a neighborhood full of other kids. Down the street lived Judge Cooper, whose son Frank attended the same elementary school as Myrna. Years later, after Frank Cooper had become actor Gary Cooper, Myrna would see her old neighbor in Hollywood, where they both appeared in the 1925 silent movie *Ben-Hur*. The two were not close, but as colleagues from the same hometown, they were always friendly.

In May 1911, when Myrna was not quite six, her brother, David Jr., was born. Not long after, Della became ill with pneumonia. Worried, her husband encouraged her to recuperate in the warm, sunny climate of southern California. For about seven months, Della and the two children lived in a rented house near San Diego. Sophisticated Della discovered she loved California, and little Myrna, who turned seven there, loved it, too, especially the beach, where she played in the ocean, hunted for eels, and collected seashells. Della tried to convince David to move to California, but he wanted to stay in Montana, and he insisted that his family come home. Della and the kids returned to Helena in time for Myrna to start school that fall.

California was not the only thing Myrna's parents disagreed on. Della was a Democrat and David was a Republican, which made for lively political talk over the dinner table. From the start, Myrna sympathized more with her mother's liberal views than with her father's more conservative leanings. In truth, however, Myrna's parents were not really so far apart; both were broad-minded and believed in social reforms. Not long after the Williamses returned to Helena, for example, a black family moved in across the street from them. Many of the white neighbors were hostile toward the family, but Myrna's mom encouraged the children to play together. Myrna's dad, as a legislator and afterward, was sympathetic to landless Montana Indians. In the 1910s, he helped Senator Joseph Dixon and Montana activist Frank Bird Linderman (the man who interviewed Pretty Shield; see chapter 3) establish Rocky Boy's Indian Reservation, near Havre, for the Chippewa tribe.

Because of her parents' political involvement, Myrna developed an avid interest in politics at a young age. In her family and in Montana in general, both women and men were active in political life. Myrna's Aunt Lou, for example, was elected county treasurer. Women in Montana gained the right to vote in 1914, six years before women's suffrage became national law, and the first woman elected to Congress, Jeannette Rankin, was from the Treasure State (see chapter 4, Jeannette Rankin).

As a young girl, Myrna was very independent and something of a tomboy, always climbing trees, skinning her knees, tearing her clothes, and getting herself dirty. This exasperated her mother, who dressed the children impeccably. Della was continually cleaning Myrna up, mending her clothing, and rebraiding her unruly red hair into neat pigtails.

In spite of her rambunctious side, Myrna did well in school. She enjoyed history, geography, and English, and she was especially good at art and music. After her grandmother took her to see some plays in town, Myrna became passionate about the theater, and she began putting on plays with her friends in the Williamses' basement.

In April 1916, when Myrna was ten, she suffered the loss of the grandmother she adored. Isabel's death left "a terrible void" in her life, she recalled. Later that year, Della learned that she needed an operation, and she decided to have it done in California, taking the children with her. This time they lived in Los Angeles, renting a little house with honeysuckle festooning the porch.

Myrna missed her father, but exploring the city thrilled her. One day she wandered onto a private beach where some movie stars in bathing suits were relaxing. Myrna sensed something different about them, something "really classy." After that, she and her friends would often go back to spy on the actors until someone chased them off. Later, Della took Myrna and little David on a tour of Universal Studios. Myrna held her breath as she watched the actors shooting scenes under blue lights.

More smitten with southern California than ever, Myrna's mom tried, once again, to convince her husband to move to the coast, but he wanted to stay in Montana. Again, before the year was out, David insisted that his family come home.

Back in Helena, Myrna enjoyed her first ballet lessons. Naturally, Della encouraged her daughter's passion for the performing arts. In 1917, when she was twelve, Myrna was invited to perform a dance at a talent show sponsored by her father's Elks Club. For the show, she choreographed her own version of *The Blue Bird*, a dance piece she had seen at the theater with her late grandmother. She made her own costume—a flowing blue silk dress embellished with blue ribbons. It was a big moment. Onstage that night, Myrna's shyness evaporated, replaced by grace and confidence.

The next day's newspaper praised her performance, but Myrna's joy was dampened by the fact that her father had not been there to see it. He had been out of town on a business trip, and Myrna knew deep down that he had stayed away on purpose. He was strongly opposed to her dancing in public. Up until the early twentieth century in America, women who danced professionally had a reputation for low morals. He feared Myrna would become, as he put it, a "chorus girl."

On April 6 of that year, 1917, the United States entered World War I. A year and a half later, in the fall of 1918, Myrna's father announced he was going to enlist in the army. Later, Myrna recognized that patriotism wasn't his only motivation. The friction between him and his wife, along with ongoing financial woes, had thrown him into a depression. Myrna, now thirteen, pleaded with him not to go, but he remained firm. Calling her his "little soldier," he asked her to promise that, if anything happened to him, she would take care of her mother and little brother.

But Myrna's father never went to war. Just a few weeks later, the Williams family came down with the flu. The great influenza epidemic of 1918–19 would kill millions of people worldwide. It was a terrible time. Doctors and nurses everywhere were overloaded, leaving many families to fend for themselves. At the Williams home, Della and David Junior were the first to get sick, followed by Myrna. Tenderly, Myrna's dad nursed his family through the illness. Then he came down with the virus himself, and within days he was dead. The sudden loss of her father tore Myrna's heart apart. Ironically, the day David was buried, World War I ended. As Helena and the rest of the nation celebrated the American victory, the Williams family quietly grieved.

Within a year after David's death, Della fulfilled her dream and moved the family to Los Angeles for good. With them came Aunt Lou, her daughter Laura Belle, and an elderly family friend from Radersburg, Mr. Sederburg. They arrived just as the population of Los Angeles was exploding. Over the next decade, the city would go from less than a hundred thousand residents to more than two million. Della bought a bungalow in a nice neighborhood. To support the household, she worked in a dress shop and gave piano lessons. Aunt Lou did most of the cooking and housekeeping.

For Myrna, now fourteen, the ocean, the warm weather, and the excitement and promise of the city soothed her grief. With a seriousness that actually worried her mother, precocious Myrna chose a life goal for herself: to become a professional dancer. Myrna particularly idolized the dancer and choreographer Ruth St. Denis. She loved to mimic St. Denis's style, dancing in the front yard and teaching moves to her friends.

Ruth St. Denis was among a wave of young dancers and choreographers who were reinventing dance for the new century and reclaiming it as an art form, not mere entertainment. Her dance school in Los Angeles, named Denishawn, trained dancers but also specialized in movement for movie actresses. St. Denis taught discipline and control of the body but rejected the artificiality and rigidity of ballet. Instead she encouraged natural, expressive movement rooted in spirituality. St. Denis's philosophy suited the free-spirited Myrna Williams to a tee. Later, when Myrna was hired in Hollywood, she would take some classes at Denishawn.

During her first two years in Los Angeles, Myrna attended Westlake School for Girls, a private high school where wealthy families sent their daughters. The school's focus was on social graces, not academics, but Della believed Myrna would get the best education there. Unlike most of the other Westlake parents, Della had to scrape the tuition together, but Myrna did not find her wealthy classmates intimidating. Her grace, good manners, and intelligence gave her the confidence to feel equal to anyone.

But eventually, Myrna discovered that the people at Westlake shared her father's attitude toward dance, viewing it as vulgar and immoral. Finally, she and her mother agreed that she should switch schools. "I decided that since I was already familiar with the correct fork to use, I really didn't need the school. I wanted more from life," Myrna recalled.

Myrna transferred to Venice Union Polytechnic High, a public school that valued and eagerly cultivated the arts. At her new school, Myrna focused on dance classes, auditions, and performances. Though her classmates liked and admired her, she spent little time with any but her closest girlfriends, and she hardly dated. This was partly because of her dedication to her dancing, but she was also busy with other activities. In addition to her regular classes and after-school dance education, she worked two part-time jobs to help support her family, giving dance lessons to children and processing movie film in a development lab.

Many of the teachers at Venice High were arts professionals. During Myrna's first year, one of the art teachers was sculpting a fountain for the school grounds. The design featured three human figures, and the teacher chose sixteen-year-old Myrna as the model for one of them. By this time, her beauty was blossoming, and she knew how to hold her body in dramatic yet elegant poses. When it was finished, the sculpture got much attention. The local newspaper called Myrna's statue "a Venus."

By then, however, Myrna was no longer at the school. She had dropped out early to take a full-time job. Myrna took the promise she had made to her father, to take care of her mother and brother, very seriously, but her part-time jobs brought little income. Even with Della working at the dress shop and giving piano lessons, it was hard for the family to make ends meet. Then in 1923, when Myrna was eighteen, she landed a job that not only paid well but also, marvelously, fit with her chosen career path: dancing in the chorus at a movie theater. In the early days of film, going to a movie was very special, not casual. Because the pictures were silent, they were usually accompanied by live music. The best theaters offered elaborate live performances with up to one hundred musicians and dancers as "prologues" before the film. Myrna auditioned and won a place as a dancer at Grauman's Egyptian Theatre, one of Hollywood's ritziest movie houses, for a substantial thirty-five dollars a week.

Over the course of the next year, the young dancer Myrna Williams transformed into actress Myrna Loy. It started with a photograph. After one of the prologues at the theater, a photographer chose a few dancers, including Myrna, to pose for some photos. The pictures were hanging in the photographer's studio when one of the biggest movie stars of the day, Rudolf Valentino, happened to come in. He stopped in front of a picture of Myrna. "Who's the girl?" he asked. Impressed with her photogenic beauty and grace, Valentino sensed that this young dancer might have a future in movies.

Soon afterward, Valentino brought Myrna to meet his wife, who was also in the movie business, and the couple arranged a screen test for her. (A screen test is a filmed audition that shows how an actor comes across on the screen.) Myrna had not been interested in film acting before, but now the idea intrigued her. To her chagrin, however, the screen test was awful. On film, she looked stiff and jerky. Learning that she did not get the part, Myrna cried for hours. She later found out that the film looked strange because someone had set it at the wrong speed.

Remarkably, Myrna's apparent failure did not discourage her from acting—on the contrary, it lit in her a desire to succeed as both an actress and a dancer. In Los Angeles, the best opportunities for performers were in the fast-growing movie industry. Revising her life goal to include acting, Myrna devoted herself to trying to break into motion pictures.

By 1925, Myrna had landed a few small roles, thanks in part to her dancing ability, which gave her an edge over other aspiring actors. That year, a publicity photo of Myrna, taken for a film called *What Price Beauty?*, appeared in a fan magazine with a short article about her, using, for the first time, the name Myrna Loy. Friends had advised her that the last name Williams was too plain. A friend suggested the name Loy, saying it came from a Chinese poem. The photo brought Myrna attention and, before long, a contract with Warner Brothers, her first studio. She was not yet twenty years old.

At Warner Brothers, Myrna was usually cast as an exotic temptress. Under wigs and makeup, she played women of various racial backgrounds, including Asian, Polynesian, Hispanic, Gypsy, and Native American. In those days of racial segregation, studios hired mostly white actors for all parts, including non-white characters. Even when Myrna appeared with her natural coloring, viewers could not tell that her hair was red since, in the early days, movies were filmed in black and white. It wasn't until 1949, when Myrna appeared in the Technicolor drama *The Red Pony*, that fans discovered Myrna's real hair color.

Hollywood tended to typecast actors, assigning them similar types of roles over and over. While some actors, many producers, and even the public welcomed typecasting, the practice also pushed actors into career ruts, limiting their opportunities to explore different characters and stretch artistically. Early in her career, Myrna began to feel boxed in by the roles she was given to play. She was making a good living, though, and was glad to be able to support her relatives. Even as she pursued her career in Hollywood, she stayed with her family, postponing marriage and a life of her own.

Throughout this time, Myrna was learning the ins and outs of moviemaking. Film acting was grueling. Actors worked long hours under hot lights that melted their makeup. Sometimes they waited hours just to say one line. At a moment's notice, they might be called upon to convincingly portray a moment of deep emotion, or the director might make them do a scene over and over until they got a certain line or a gesture just right.

Myrna's world, the world of movie making, was one of both camaraderie and competition. Actors were the most publicly visible members of a film's team, but behind the scenes an army of talented professionals built sets, styled hair, and designed and sewed costumes. On set, cinematographers and directors argued over shots, while lighting technicians and camera operators planned angles. At the top of the hierarchy were the studio executives, who watched over profits and public opinion like hawks and pressured everyone below them to stay in line. As her star rose, Myrna mingled with the most famous celebrities of her day, yet some of her dearest friends were people she had worked with behind the scenes.

In the late 1920s, Hollywood began making the transition from silent movies to "talkies," and Myrna, if her career was to survive, had to adjust. Since she was used to dancing and silent acting, speaking into a microphone made her nervous at first. Fortunately, her voice sounded pleasant, and she began getting speaking roles. Her first sound picture, *Midnight Taxi*, was produced in 1928. During these years, she worked almost constantly. Between 1926 and 1928, she appeared in thirty films, though most of the roles were small. Then things began to slow down. In 1930, Warner Brothers let Myrna go, saying they had no parts for her anymore. Undeterred, she signed on with an important talent agent and was soon getting better roles than before. Before long, Fox Film Corporation (later called 20th Century Fox) offered Myrna a contract, which she took, but she soon found herself being typecast again. Frustrated, she quit to freelance for a while.

Late in 1931, Metro Goldwyn Mayer (MGM), agreeing that Myrna could play many different types of parts, snapped her up and gave her a new contract. "They had me running from set to set," she later recalled in her autobiography, "making three pictures at once." MGM tried Myrna out in different roles including, interestingly, a gangster's moll, or girlfriend. As one such character in 1934's *Manhattan Melodrama*, Myrna Loy was one of the last movie stars that real-life gangster John Dillinger enjoyed on the screen before he exited Chicago's Biograph Theater and FBI agents gunned him down.

For all her success, Myrna was still hoping for a "breakthrough" role, one that would make her career soar. Her chance finally came in 1934. Up to that point, Myrna was known mostly for serious parts in dramatic movies. But Woody Van Dyke, who had directed her in *Manhattan Melodrama*, noticed how funny Myrna was in real life, sparking a hunch that she could play comedy. Van Dyke had also observed a special rapport between Myrna and one of her costars in that earlier picture, William Powell. The two of them seemed to bring out the best in each other's performance. He wanted to put Myrna and Bill Powell together again in his next comedy.

MGM balked at casting Myrna in a comic role, but Van Dyke did not give up. To convince company executives that Myrna could take a joke, he "auditioned" her by pushing her into a swimming pool at a Hollywood party. Apparently she came up laughing, passing the test. Van Dyke was now free to cast her as Nora Charles, the charming, game-for-anything wife of Powell's Nick Charles in the comedy-mystery *The Thin Man*.

The Thin Man was about a well-to-do husband and wife who solve a mystery together. Nick and Nora are a fun couple, teasing each other all the time and trading smart-aleck remarks. Along with their smart, cute fox terrier, Asta, they made a clever and hilarious team. The movie was not expected to be a big hit, but America immediately fell in love with Nick, Nora, and Asta, earning the film an Oscar nomination and prompting five *Thin Man* sequels over the years. *The Thin Man* made Myrna Loy a major star.

Myrna and Bill Powell became lifelong friends. They were never romantically involved, which many fans couldn't believe, since their chemistry onscreen was so amazing. But Bill was engaged to someone, and Myrna, after dating many stars and other interesting men, was in love with a Hollywood producer named Arthur Hornblow.

The popularity of the character Nora Charles gave Myrna new power. She knew she deserved a better contract and more pay—male actors in Hollywood made much more than the women—but the studio refused. When producers suddenly replaced Myrna in a film she was shooting— to punish her, she felt, for asking for more—she went on a one-woman strike. In 1935, she took a long-needed vacation, traveling for the first time to New York and later to Europe. It was good for her to get away because by this time, she was exhausted. In the ten years since she began her career, she had made almost a hundred movies with hardly a break.

When Myrna returned home several months later, she continued her game of hardball with MGM, refusing to come back until her demands were met. Finally the studio gave in, and Myrna went back to making movies. She worked at the same grueling pace as before, but with higher pay.

In 1936 Myrna and Arthur got married, quietly, in Mexico. She was thirty-one, considered old for a first-time bride in those days. Myrna's mother was not pleased. For years, Della had discouraged her daughter from marrying. As Myrna later put it, "She wanted to maintain her control."

The fall of 1937 was when Myrna heard the Czech foreign minister's radio speech and telegraphed her support. Few Americans at that point were very concerned about the ominous events in Europe, but Myrna recognized that Hitler was very dangerous. The diplomat's return telegram said simply, "Bless you." Myrna's studio bosses did not appreciate her outspokenness and insisted she keep quiet about political issues. They didn't like mixing business and politics. Myrna ignored them. In September 1939, Germany invaded Poland, and World War II was on in Europe. Myrna and many other Hollywood actors attended fundraisers to help the war-torn Europeans.

In 1940, Myrna had visited Montana with her mother. It was the first time she'd been back since she was fourteen. Myrna had the old homestead fixed up, and Della spent her summers there until she became too frail to stay; she would die in Los Angeles in 1966. Over the years, Myrna would visit her home state a few more times, but her busy schedule gave her little time for pleasure trips.

In December 1941, the Japanese bombed Pearl Harbor and America joined the fighting. Myrna and the others redoubled their fundraising efforts, putting on shows and promoting war bonds. At a naval base in California, Myrna worked the night shift handing out coffee and donuts to recruits. Later, in New York, she worked with the Red Cross, arranging shows to raise money for the troops and visiting wounded soldiers in hospitals.

In addition to giving her life a deeper sense of meaning, Myrna's war work was a distraction from unhappiness at home. Her marriage to Arthur Hornblow had started to unravel. "I loved him . . . but I couldn't live with him," she recalled in her autobiography. He had become a "tyrant." Worldly, educated in the East, Arthur tended to criticize Myrna and look down on her Montana roots. He also cared more about the things that come with wealth—the couple's beautiful Los Angeles home and all its luxurious furnishings—than happy-go-lucky, artistic Myrna did. Furthermore, their demanding careers left little time for intimacy, let alone working out their troubles. In 1942, after eight years of marriage, Myrna divorced Arthur. "It's the hardest thing I've ever had to do," she wrote.

Nora Charles in *The Thin Man* series, whom Myrna portrayed six times, was a good example of the type of modern female character that had begun to appear in movies in the 1930s and '40s—the ideal wife. Nora was smart, assertive, and witty, an even match for her husband, yet feminine, beautiful, and supportive. These women weren't necessarily shown caring for kids or doing housework, but when they were, they handled this work expertly, not as drudges. As Nora, Myrna embodied this wifely ideal. In a more subtle version of typecasting, she found herself playing more such women in subsequent films, and the press began calling her "the perfect wife." After her marriage with Arthur dissolved, Myrna found the title painfully ironic, and it would haunt her through three later divorces.

Through all her marriages, Myrna never had children. This was, according to her, her own choice. "It's hard enough trying to be a wife in this business without being a mother, too," she wrote. She was, however, very close to her stepson, Arthur's son Terry, and remained so long after the divorce.

Myrna was "a wreck" after the divorce, but a new friend had come into her life. John Hertz, Jr., a wealthy advertising executive, lost no time in romancing Myrna. Only six days after her divorce was final, Myrna impulsively married John in New York City. Myrna was now spending most of her time in New York while her mother and brother remained in Los Angeles, still supported by Myrna. John discouraged Myrna from working, and at first she didn't mind. She was glad to be away from Hollywood. Besides, with the war on, she was busy with her volunteer work.

Becoming more involved in politics, Myrna came to know important politicians and statesmen. She became particularly close friends with outspoken First Lady Eleanor Roosevelt. Eleanor and her husband, President Franklin Roosevelt, were personal heroes of Myrna's. Although she visited the White House many times, Myrna never met President Roosevelt, much to her disappointment. It was disappointing for him, too, because Myrna Loy was his favorite actress. But the raging war took precedence over hobnobbing with movie stars.

Meanwhile, Myrna's marriage to John Hertz was falling apart. John turned out to be a violent alcoholic, and after only two years of marriage, Myrna left him. In 1944, she returned to Hollywood after a three-year absence to star in the fifth *Thin Man* movie. Over the next several years, Myrna would star in some of the finest films of her career, including *The Best Years of Our Lives*, a serious and controversial movie about the difficulties faced by returning war veterans. It won the Oscar for Best Picture in 1946. That year, Myrna got married again, this time to Gene Markey, a handsome, charming screenwriter and navy officer who had been married to two other movie stars before Myrna. "I never knew one [woman] who could resist him. I certainly couldn't," she later wrote.

After the war, in 1945, the United Nations (UN) was founded in New York City. Its mission to promote international cooperation and peace stirred Myrna's imagination. Believing passionately in the organization's ideals—"no nation below or behind another," as she put it—she became a delegate. Working for the UN, specifically for UNESCO (United Nations Educational, Scientific, and Cultural Organization), Myrna made speeches all over the country and became the supporter, confidante, and advisor of important world figures, including President Truman. Her many years with the UN gave Myrna "a sense of commitment that my picture career had never inspired." She always credited her interest in world affairs to her Montana upbringing, recalling the constant discussion of current events at her family's dinner table.

Myrna's political involvement almost cost her her career. Right after the war and for about a decade afterward, a fear of communism gripped America. This period was known as the "Red Scare." At the time, ultra-conservative politicians as well as some moderates were convinced that communism was rampant in the United States and that American communists were trying to infiltrate the government and society, including the film industry. Early on, these politicians, especially members of the U.S. Congress, targeted Hollywood, convinced that communists were producing subversive movies with "un-American" messages. Among the accused were actors, directors, and producers who, like Myrna, were political liberals.

Actors Myrna Loy (left), Frederic March, and Lucille Ball broadcast a protest against House Un-American Activities Committee investigations, October 26, 1947. —Courtesy Associated Press

Myrna, in fact, was one of the first movie stars to be accused of communist sympathies. A Hollywood newspaper claimed that she and other stars had formed a communist conspiracy. Myrna did not sit still for this. She immediately threatened to sue the paper for libel (false reporting). In response, the paper published a retraction, pronouncing Myrna Loy "a patriotic American."

Others, however, were not so lucky. The House Un-American Activities Committee (HUAC), led by Senator Joseph McCarthy, ordered thousands of American citizens to Washington to be questioned. The nation, including Hollywood, soon became divided between supporters and opponents of the investigations. Afraid to take any chances, the studios began refusing to hire any director, actor, screenwriter, or other employee who had been accused of communism. This practice of shutting people out of work is known as "blacklisting."

Myrna was not blacklisted herself, but she battled hard against the practice, contributing money and speaking in defense of her exiled colleagues. To fight back, she and other film-industry liberals formed a group called the Committee for the First Amendment, but the group was soon accused of communism and discredited. Nevertheless, Myrna and others persevered. By the late 1950s, thanks to outspoken critics of McCarthy and his committee, the investigations had fallen out of public favor. By then, however, hundreds of careers in Hollywood and in Washington, D.C., had been ruined.

While all this was going on, Myrna divorced her husband, Gene Markey, who had been unfaithful, in 1950. When she was appointed to a three-year position with the UN, she was excited to buy a home and become a resident of Washington, D.C. Her work brought her into frequent contact with government officials, among them Howland Sargeant, a State Department officer involved with UNESCO. Howland and Myrna became friends, then fell in love, and in 1951, they were married.

For Myrna, marriage to Howland brought an unexpected—and frustrating—twist. As the wife of a State Department official, she was not allowed to express political opinions in public. Myrna was glad when Howland left his job in 1953 and she could be vocal again. Unfortunately, it became apparent that Howland did not like taking a backseat to his wife. The couple divorced in 1960. Discouraged by the failure of her fourth attempt at matrimony, Myrna never married again.

Settling permanently in New York City, Myrna continued her work with UNESCO. She also managed to do a few movies. By 1960, her status as a top movie star had faded, but she refused to take roles she did not like just to maintain her visibility. She did want to keep working, though. To keep her career going, she began making television appearances and took a few smaller, supporting roles in movies. Then, in 1961, she tackled a new challenge—live acting on stage.

Stage acting is quite different from movie acting, and Myrna had no training or background in it, so she was afraid she couldn't do it.

In fact, the first time she read for a part in a play, it didn't go well. The understated style she was known for in film did not play well on the stage, which requires bigger, bolder, louder performances. About a year later, however, her friends persuaded her to try again, and she won the female lead in a comedy, *The Marriage-Go-Round*. To help her master certain stage techniques, such as voice projection, Myrna hired a drama coach and worked with other theater professionals. Her first few performances may have been less than perfect, but "around the third or fourth performance," as she recalled, "I hit it." The play was a success.

Whenever she was in Hollywood, it was easy for Myrna to feel like a "has-been," but in New York City she felt at home—that city's energy fit the person she had become. She grew increasingly immersed in the Big Apple's vibrant theater community. In 1963, she helped found the American Place Theatre, which over the years has become a New York landmark, famous for nurturing some of America's best playwrights. In 1964 Myrna gave her most successful stage performance yet. Appearing in the Neil Simon comedy *Barefoot in the Park*, she received rave reviews as well as an acting award.

In addition to continuing her acting career, Myrna remained politically involved through the 1960s and beyond. In 1960 she helped get John F. Kennedy elected; later, he appointed her as co-leader of the National Committee Against Discrimination in Housing. It's not surprising that, during the 1960s, Myrna supported civil rights, since almost thirty years earlier she had asked MGM executives, "Why does every black person in the movies have to play a servant? How about a black person walking up the steps of a courthouse carrying a briefcase?" Myrna also protested the war in Vietnam.

As energetic as ever, Myrna kept acting in movies, plays, and television into the early 1980s, in spite of two surgeries for breast cancer in the 1970s. She took her last film role, in the comedy *Just Tell Me What You Want*, at age seventy-five. In 1987, eighty-two-year-old Myrna worked with a writer friend, James Kotsilibas-Davis, to publish a memoir, *Myrna Loy: Being and Becoming*. As part of the process, the two spent a week in Montana. "That trip gave me more of a sense of Myrna than anything," Kotsilibas-Davis said. "That feeling of vastness and cleanliness and integrity."

In her personal life, aside from a few "escorts and beaus," Myrna mostly focused on her surrogate family, composed of close friends and their children, her several godchildren, and especially stepson Terry Hornblow and his family. There were many things about "Aunt Myrna" that young people found inspiring. For one girl, the daughter of friends, it was Myrna's air of "female independence" and her aristocratic posture, "like a tree rooted in the earth—nothing was going to blow her over."

In her later years, Myrna was showered with tributes and awards, including the prestigious Kennedy Center Lifetime Achievement Award in 1988 in Washington, D.C. After the award ceremony, at a reception at the White House, President Ronald Reagan (whose election Myrna had opposed) praised her as "lovely and mysterious," a master who acted with "great ease and comfort, as though she were possessed of answers to questions you hadn't even thought of asking." Three years later, the Myrna Loy Center for the Performing Arts, named in honor of this Montana native daughter, opened in Helena. Also in 1991, Myrna received an honorary Academy Award for her lifetime achievement in film. By then Myrna was suffering from several serious illnesses and was too frail to travel to Los Angeles to accept her Oscar in person. Instead, she sent her thanks via satellite from her New York home.

On December 14, 1993, Myrna Loy died in a New York hospital. She was eighty-eight. Her ashes were interred in the Forestvale Cemetery in Helena, beside her parents. In 2012, a star with Myrna's name was placed on the Hollywood Walk of Fame, an eighteen-block-long monument to the movie industry's greatest stars.

As a teen, Myrna Williams devoted herself to the arts and to high ideals. Although life had many surprises in store, Myrna held fast to her principles as she navigated a challenging career in Hollywood and a rocky personal life. Later, in her civic-service and political work, she was able to work directly for her ideal of a just world. Myrna's fans could sense her deep integrity, and perhaps that—more than her talent, charm, or beauty—is why they loved her.

Alma Smith Jacobs, circa 1964 —Courtesy Ken Robison

10

ALMA SMITH JACOBS

THE POWER OF BOOKS

From her spacious executive office on the third floor of the just-built Great Falls Public Library, Alma Jacobs, head librarian, had a wonderful view of the city she had grown up in and knew so well. Through her fine, large windows, she could see the top of the Rainbow Hotel, where her late father had worked for decades. Over the rooftops rose the elegant dome of the Cascade County Courthouse, a reminder of justice, an ideal that Alma had been fighting for since her childhood as a black girl in a white-dominated world. At the core of her efforts was her belief in libraries. From books would come knowledge, from knowledge would come understanding, and from understanding would come justice, including racial justice.

The new library, which cost over a million dollars, was breathtaking. The red brick structure was three stories high, with ten white pillars gracing the entrance, which was concave, as if welcoming people in. Inside was sixty thousand square feet of space—six times the size of the old library—providing enough room, Alma told a reporter, "for every activity." It was the first modernized library to be built in Montana, or in any of its surrounding states, in fifty years.

At the library's dedication ceremony on November 12, 1967, Alma was lauded as a local hero. She had been, without question, the driving force behind the library's creation. It had taken her six years of tireless advocacy to pass the bond issue that raised the money for it. Now her hard-fought dream was a reality. "I have to go by there every day and make sure it's still there," Alma gushed. "I just can't believe it yet."

Little did she know, as she savored her victory in 1967, that her biggest achievement was still to come. In 1973, she would be named Montana's first African American state librarian. Through her passionate commitment to making information available to absolutely everyone, Alma Smith Jacobs strengthened and modernized libraries throughout the state. She also ushered in a new, more enlightened attitude toward minority citizens and created a more compassionate Montana. Her remarkable career and unshakable spirit are still honored today.

———•••———

Alma Victoria Smith was born on November 21, 1916, in Lewistown, Montana. At the time, her father, Martin Luther Smith, worked as a cook, mainly for the Milwaukee Railroad. Her mother, Emma Louise Riley Smith, often did housekeeping for white families in addition to caring for her own home and family. Eventually, that family would include five children, including Alma's older sister, Madeline, her younger sister, Lucille, and her two younger brothers, Martin and Morris.

Emma, born in Arkansas, had met Martin, a native of Missouri, in Butte around 1914. By 1915, the two were married with one daughter, Madeline. Shortly afterward, the Smiths moved to Lewistown, where Alma came into the world. About six years later and after two more kids were born, the family moved to Great Falls, where Martin had transferred to the Great Northern Railroad. Alma's youngest sibling, Morris, was born shortly after the move, in 1923.

When they moved to Great Falls, the Smiths were one of only a few hundred African American families in the whole state, but they were not isolated. In fact, Montana had more black residents than any of its neighboring states, and its bigger cities—such as Helena, Butte, Missoula, and Great Falls—had significant African American communities. Black Montanans endured segregation and prejudice, but in general, Montana

Young Alma Smith with her mom, Emma, and sisters at Spring Creek near Lewistown, circa 1920. Left to right: Madeline, Emma, Lucille, Alma. —Courtesy Montana Historical Society Research Center, Montana Historical Society, Helena, Montana

offered them more freedom and better opportunities than they could find in most other places in the country.

Indeed, the African American community that welcomed the Smiths to Great Falls was a strong one. Many of the men worked for the railroad, like Martin, while others worked as laborers or in local hotels and restaurants. A few had their own businesses, and at least one family ranched. A lot of the community's women worked, too. Emma quickly found a job cooking for a white family.

Before she met and married Martin, Emma had led an unusual life. Her past would become a source of fascinating stories—and great pride—to Alma, the rest of the family, and the entire African American community in Great Falls. It gave her a unique perspective that shaped her children as well.

Born in Forrest City, Arkansas, in 1881, Emma lived in that state until about age fourteen, when her family moved to Liberia, in western Africa. Liberia was founded in 1822 as a haven for former slaves and other free black Americans, initiating a movement called "Back to Africa." Facing intolerable bigotry and violence in the U.S., some African Americans believed the best thing to do was to return to the land from which they'd been kidnapped, and immigration to Liberia began. By 1847 Liberia was an independent nation. After the Civil War, conditions gradually became worse for black Americans, and the Back to Africa movement gained renewed popularity in the 1880s and into the early twentieth century.

Emma's great-grandfather had always supported the idea of returning to Africa. His grandson, Emma's father, finally turned the idea into action in 1885, moving with his wife and their two children, Emma and her brother, to Liberia. There, Emma attended a missionary school. Emma's sister, Thelma, was born shortly after the family arrived. For the next fifteen years, the Rileys farmed rice, ginger, potatoes, and coffee in their adopted country.

When Emma was about twenty-nine, both of her parents and her brother became sick and died. Emma decided to take Thelma back to Arkansas to go to school in America. Emma didn't plan to stay in the United States for very long, but she could not go back to Liberia right away. In the meantime, she tried to readjust to life in Arkansas.

Being in the South again turned out to be harder than Emma thought it would be. After living in a nation where black people were the majority and ran the country, and where black women moved about without fear, owned businesses, and were treated with respect, Emma could not stand Arkansas. Throughout the South in those days, racial segregation was the law, racism was intense, and African Americans had few opportunities to pull themselves out of poverty. Worst of all, they faced the constant threat of harassment and even physical harm from white racists, with small hope of justice afterward.

After a few years, Emma had had enough of Arkansas. As she later recalled in an interview, she told herself, "There are better places to live, and I'm going to find them." She traveled west to visit a friend in Cheyenne, Wyoming, where she heard that there were plentiful jobs in Butte, Montana. She decided to head north. "After I got settled in Montana," Emma said, "I wouldn't like to exchange places with no state that I have visited. I think I'll stay here until the end, God willing." Sure enough, Emma ended up marrying Martin, then moving to Lewistown, and from there, to Great Falls to stay and raise her family.

In Great Falls, Alma and her siblings grew up on the lower south side, where many black families lived. At the center of the neighborhood was Union Bethel African Methodist Episcopal Church, founded in 1891. The Smith family was deeply involved with this church, particularly Alma's mom, who organized many social and fund-raising events and served for decades as board secretary.

Emma was also active in several key community organizations run by African American women. One was the Dunbar Art and Study Club (named after African American poet Paul Laurence Dunbar), which was committed to the improvement of its members and the community. Among other activities, Emma and the other Dunbar Club women raised funds for churches, schools, libraries, and community centers to aid poor people of all colors. The Dunbar Club was part of the Montana Federation of Colored Women's Clubs, a statewide group founded in 1921. When Alma grew up, she too would work for change through these respected organizations, as both a member and a leader.

Thanks to Emma's outgoing personality, the Smith house was a hub for neighborhood kids. Emma's fresh-baked cookies, dramatic recital of poems from memory, and amazing stories of life in Africa drew young people in. A devoted reader, she often read aloud to her five children, and when they were old enough, she sent them off on their own to explore the Great Falls Library. In her spare time, Emma preferred fishing to almost anything else, and she slipped off to fish whenever she could— with friends, with the kids, or by herself.

In contrast to the dynamic Emma, Martin Luther Smith was quiet and gentle. In the summer, his favorite spot was beside the radio in the living room, listening to baseball. He also worked in Emma's large vegetable garden behind the house. Come fall, he would go hunting. Around 1930, after years with the railroads, Martin took a job as a porter at the Rainbow Hotel, a job he would keep for the rest of his life.

All the kids in Alma's neighborhood were tight. In some ways, they were like one big family, constantly in and out of one another's houses and doing things together. None of them had bicycles—they were too expensive for most black families—so the kids went on long rambles together on foot in the hills south of town. Alma usually joined them, though as a child, she tended to be quiet and serious, like her father.

Alma's neighborhood friends were black, but her friends at school were white. Schools in Montana were not racially segregated after 1895 (though Boy Scout and Girl Scout troops remained segregated), but there were so few black children in Great Falls that Alma was the only African American in her class. The white kids mostly accepted her, but she did experience prejudice and discrimination. For example, according to a story she told years later, when she was around ten years old, a school friend invited her to a swimming party at the YMCA. As she and her friends, all of whom were white, waited excitedly at the entrance to the facility, an adult singled Alma out and told her she could not go in. "Negroes" weren't allowed in the pool.

All black kids knew, from accompanying their parents around town, that certain restaurants and other businesses in Great Falls refused to serve people of color, but the pool incident was still a shock to Alma. While racism in Montana was generally not as pervasive or as dangerous for people of color as it was in the South, it could still be ugly and painful. Alma's sister Lucille remembered white kids chanting:

> God made the n----r
> Made 'em in the night
> Made 'em in a hurry
> Forgot to paint 'em white.

The black kids had a chant of their own, firing back:

God made the white trash
Made 'em in a shack
Made 'em in a hurry
Forgot to paint 'em black.

Sensitive to the difficulties of growing up African American in a predominantly white town, Alma enjoyed spending time with younger black kids, in part to give them extra support and attention. She even planned activities for them, most of which involved learning and reading, hoping to bolster their self-esteem. As an adult, Alma would continue to make special efforts to reach children, especially needy ones.

Of course, the adults in Alma's neighborhood were very much aware of the racism in Great Falls. Determined to meet that negative force with strength, they did all they could to create a close community of love and support, not just for their own children, but for all the local black kids. Despite varying incomes, occupations, and personalities, Great Falls's African American families gathered often for community baseball games, picnics, and special dinners where the men cooked and the women relaxed.

Alongside the encouragement and support, the city's black parents raised their children with strict standards of behavior. In the Smith family, for example, Alma's sister Lucille remembered that she and her siblings were not allowed to leave the yard unless their hair was combed and their faces washed. Emma believed that, in a way, every black person represented the entire African American community, so it was important that her family looked respectable and acted honorably in order to counter negative images of black people.

Boosted by the strength of her family and community, Alma did well in high school. In addition to getting good grades, she belonged to the Mathematics Club, the Art Club, and the Young Authors Club, among other groups. She also worked for one period a day in the school library. Alma's achievements came to the attention of the school principal, whose brother worked at a small, prestigious all-black private college in

Alabama, Talladega College. The principal encouraged Alma to apply. She did, and when she graduated from high school in 1934, she received a four-year scholarship to Talladega. Lucille also went to school there, as did Morris, later.

Alma's mother had prepared her for the rampant bigotry in the South. Racial segregation was enforced by a series of "Jim Crow" laws, which restricted black people from opportunities in housing, education, employment, recreational facilities, and social organizations. In spite of this, Alma adapted well to Alabama and thrived at Talledega. She majored in sociology and minored in psychology, thinking she might like to become a social worker. She also took a part-time job in the college library, where she was ultimately promoted to library assistant.

At the library, Alma did her job well, and when she graduated from Talladega in 1938, the college asked her to stay on there. Alma decided that she liked library work so much that she wanted to make it her profession. Over the next several summers, she studied library science on a scholarship at Columbia University in New York, returning to her job at Talladega during the school year. Later, Alma would laugh remembering how, when she was young, she thought librarians were supposed to read every book in the library. Of course that was impossible, but she still seemed to try. Alma read voraciously, developing a pattern of reading early in the morning and late at night, sleeping only a few hours.

During her time at the library, Alma ran the bookmobile, an old truck the college had converted into a library on wheels. In it, Alma trundled out to the countryside around Talladega so that poor rural black people, especially kids, could borrow books. Through the bookmobile, the college was trying to spread education in underprivileged African American communities, because in the South, schooling for black children tended to be terrible. Unlike the schools for white children, African American schools received little funding or resources.

Alma's colleague on the bookmobile was an older black man in his eighties. He was there not just to help drive, but also for safety—personal security was something that black people, especially women, could not count on. Later in life, Alma told a friend a story from her bookmobile days that shows what daily life was like for black folks in the South. One day, the bookmobile ran out of gas. While the old man stayed with the vehicle, Alma walked to the nearest gas station. She could pay for the fuel, but she didn't have a gas can to carry it in. The white woman at the station would not lend her one, insisting that they bring the truck there to fill the tank. Alma and her elderly companion had no choice but to push the hulking vehicle full of books to the gas station.

In spite of the difficulties, running the bookmobile was a very positive experience for Alma. She witnessed firsthand the huge difference her work made in the lives of the rural residents. The children, especially, were ravenous for knowledge. Reading aloud to them, she was amazed at the way they drank the stories in, and she saw how quickly they could progress with a little help.

While at Talladega, Alma had another life-changing experience—she fell in love. The object of her affection was a classmate named Marcus Jacobs. He felt the same, but in 1942 he joined the military to fight in World War II. That same year, Alma received her library science degree from Columbia and returned to her job at the Talladega library.

In 1946, Alma decided to move back to Great Falls. Before she left, some of her bookmobile patrons threw her a going-away party at one of the local schools. The children showered her with gifts—sometimes just a potato or a few homegrown peanuts in a paper sack. Alma never forgot their generosity, or their suffering.

Alma, who had reunited with Marcus after the war ended in 1945, returned to Great Falls as Mrs. Marcus Jacobs, with her new husband in tow. She was hired at the Great Falls Public Library—the same library she and her siblings had used as kids—as a catalog librarian, and Marcus ended up working for the post office. The couple built a house, starting with the basement, which they lived in until the rest was complete. Their home was stuffed with books. Although Alma and Marcus would stay together many years, they had no children.

As catalog librarian, Alma's main task was deciding how to categorize the new books that came in and how to describe them accurately, in writing, for the public. She loved her job and worked well with her coworkers and the public. A friend remembered her "wonderful, deep laugh." In 1954, eight years after Alma started at the library, her boss, the head librarian, stepped down, and Alma was appointed to replace her, temporarily at least. Although Alma's work was excellent, the library was cautious about having an African American in such a high position. How would it be for the mostly white employees to work under a black boss? Would the predominantly white community of Great Falls have trouble accepting a black head librarian?

A few months went by, and no one complained. In July 1954, at a time when many American libraries wouldn't even admit black people through their doors, Alma Jacobs was officially made head librarian of the Great Falls Public Library, a position she held for the next nineteen years.

In her new position, Alma focused less on directly helping the public and more on problems facing the institution as a whole. At that time, the biggest problem was space. When the library was built in 1903, it housed ten thousand books. Now, more than fifty years later, the small brick building was bursting with sixty thousand items. Bookshelves reached the ceiling and covered the windows, and patrons could barely move through the cramped aisles.

Immediately, Alma set the goal of building a brand-new, bigger library for Great Falls. It would require a lot of work and money. The new library needed to be six times bigger than the old one, with modern features. The estimated cost was a million dollars. To raise that money, voters would have to pass what is known as a "bond issue" to tax themselves more, at least temporarily. Paying more taxes is seldom popular, so Alma knew she would have some convincing to do. The vote on the library bond issue was scheduled for 1959, and Alma immediately got to work to persuade the people of Great Falls to support it. Mainly, she met with leaders in the community, figuring that if she could convince them to support a new library, they would in turn convince the citizens.

In the meantime, Alma had other goals, too, as head librarian. Concerned that people in the rural areas of central Montana had no easy access to the library, she started a bookmobile service in rural Cascade County in 1956. Like the one in Alabama, the Montana bookmobile was a success.

Alma also made other efforts to reach rural Montanans. As an active member of the Montana Library Association, Alma, along with Montana's state librarian at the time, Ruth Longworth, traveled to small community libraries around the state, helping them improve their collections. Patricia McNamer, president of the library board in tiny Conrad, Montana, in the 1950s, remembered Alma and Ruth coming to the Conrad library to overhaul its "little, old, bad collection of books." Together they sorted through the collection, removing many outdated books and replacing them with fresh ones from the state library. "Ruth and Alma, I think, were in every small library in Montana," McNamer said.

Sometimes, staff members at the Great Falls Library accompanied Alma on these trips. One of them remembered that they always carried a picnic with them in case restaurants along the way refused to serve Alma because of her race. Alma and her staff also traveled outside the state on library business, sometimes in the South, where Alma had to sit at the back of public buses. Unwilling to follow this bigoted rule, her white coworkers sat with her. Alma's attitude toward such treatment inspired them. She refused to let it bother her, knowing that she was bigger than racism and that better days would come.

When it came to prejudice, Great Falls was not much better than other American towns in the mid-twentieth century. During World War II, when the Great Falls Army Air Base, now called Malmstrom Air Force Base, opened, the black airmen stationed there, as well as their families, faced discrimination. Mistrustful of the growing black population, some white-run businesses and institutions closed their doors even harder against African Americans. Among them was the USO (United Service Organization) Club in town, which provided entertainment and services to military members. When Great Falls's black citizens learned that the USO refused to admit "colored" servicemen, they organized another USO just for them. Around the same time, the Dunbar Club, to which Emma Smith belonged, protested discrimination against black figure skaters at the Great Falls Skating Club.

Race relations in Great Falls did not improve after the war, when Alma arrived home from the South. Many businesses still refused service to

African Americans, and they could still be denied housing because of their color—city laws allowed it. In addition, many unions didn't accept black members, shutting those workers out of union jobs and limiting their hopes for better wages and working conditions.

In 1953, the year she was temporarily made head librarian, Alma and other concerned citizens formed a group, the Great Falls Interracial Council, to address racial injustice in the city. Over the next two decades, Alma would do everything she could to remove barriers faced by the black citizens of Great Falls. Time after time, quietly yet forcefully, she sat down with city leaders and business owners to hash out solutions. Because she had grown up in Great Falls, Alma knew many local people and how to talk to them. Her appeals for making their city a fairer place carried weight.

In addition, Alma was gradually opening hearts and minds in Great Falls just by being who she was. Her opinions about civic affairs, along with her picture, appeared frequently in local newspapers. In 1957 she helped found the Montana Advisory Committee to the U.S. Civil Rights Commission. Eventually, white residents grew used to the fact that one of their town leaders was a black woman, and she was doing an excellent job. "There's nobody in Great Falls more responsible than Alma for the integration of the city," a friend and colleague on the Interracial Council, Dorothy Bohn, reflected later. "It was due to her that people mellowed here in Great Falls. They met her day by day as they went into the library . . . and it had an effect."

Despite the constant, sometimes disheartening work of trying to improve local race relations, Alma was happy in her job and embraced it with verve and creativity. To promote reading, for example, she gave oral book reviews to audiences at the library that reportedly rendered them spellbound; afterward, they rushed to check out the book. At Christmastime, Alma traveled to small Montana libraries to recite Dylan Thomas's long and magical poem, "A Child's Christmas in Wales." Ever since she was young, Alma had loved working with children. "She was a children's librarian at heart," a former coworker remembered. In fact, another of Alma's many goals was to improve the library's children's section and introduce fun activities to encourage kids to read. As another colleague once remarked, "Alma is happiest when schoolchildren are using the library."

As a librarian, Alma also battled against censorship. During the 1950s, especially, libraries were often criticized for making controversial materials available to the public. Some people were offended by sexual content, while others were concerned about "anti-American" material. During the "Red Scare" of the early to mid-1950s, when officials tried to purge American culture of communist and socialist ideas, both Alma and Ruth Longworth were labeled communists for keeping "subversive" materials in Montana libraries. (Fortunately, the accusations went nowhere.) No matter what the risk, Alma stood against censorship of any kind. She believed that people were capable of making their own choices about what to read, so everyone should have access to all kinds of information.

A friend of hers once told a story about Alma's resolve to defend free speech. One day, a woman stormed into the Great Falls Library demanding that a certain book be taken off the shelves. After checking the book out, the woman had marked with a pencil every passage she found offensive. When she showed her handiwork to Alma, the librarian handed her an eraser and told her to erase every mark she had made. Stunned, the woman obeyed.

By the late 1950s, Alma was starting to get noticed for her dedication to the library, to the community of Great Falls, and to social justice. In 1957 she became the first Montanan to be elected president of the Northwest Library Association. That same year, the Business and Professional Women's Club of Great Falls named her Woman of the Year.

Even amid this whirl of activity, Alma never lost sight of her goal to build a new library. When the library bond issue appeared on the ballot in 1959, however, the people of Great Falls, unwilling to raise their own taxes, voted against it. Alma was disappointed but not defeated—not even close. She redoubled her efforts to get the bond issue passed the next time, which would be in 1963. Meanwhile, Alma's list of achievements kept growing. In 1960 she became the first African

American president of the Montana Library Association. Two years later, Montana State University awarded her an honorary doctorate degree.

The library bond issue came around again in 1963, and again, Great Falls citizens voted against it. Crushed, Alma vowed to triple her efforts to get the bond passed, making sure it would appear on the ballot again in 1965. Over the next two years, she spent most of her free time at dinners and meetings, talking up the need for a new library. That was not a hard task for Alma, since she was passionate about the importance of libraries. She called them "the people's university," believing that "self-education is the key to living in this world of daily advances."

At last, in 1965, Alma's message got through to the people of Great Falls: they voted yes for the new library. Pausing only to mourn the death of her dear father, Martin, in September, Alma dove into the challenge of getting the new library built. She had already been working with architects on the plans. The new building would be constructed on the site of the old one. With those plans under way, the next step was to move all the library's materials, some to a temporary location and the rest into storage, all while ensuring that library services remained uninterrupted. Alma worked closely with contractors as the old building came down and the new one rose. Finally, it was finished, and Alma supervised as all of the library's holdings were moved in.

At the November 12, 1967, dedication for the new library, Boy Scouts raised the American flag over the courtyard for the very first time, and a band struck up the "Stars and Stripes Forever." Among those present were representatives from the American Library Association in Chicago, which three years before had honored Alma by naming her to its executive board, and Lew Callaway, publisher of *Newsweek* magazine and a Great Falls native. In a speech, Callaway remarked, "Alma Jacobs's goals have a way of turning into achievements."

Alma's hard work and devotion continued to bring her recognition. In 1968 the Montana Library Association named Alma "Librarian of the Year." The same year, she received her second honorary doctorate, this one from Mount Holyoke College, the oldest women's college in

Head librarian Alma Jacobs surveys the brand new Great Falls Public Library, October 1967. Photo by Ray Ozmon. —Courtesy The History Museum, Great Falls, Montana

the United States. In presenting the degree, a college official told Alma, "Your courage has brought great honor to all librarians."

When, around the same time, Alma was nominated for a Golden Apple award from the Montana Education Association (MEA), both the mayor of Great Falls and U.S. Senator Mike Mansfield wrote letters endorsing her, as did many others. One supporter praised her "abundance of courage, humor, and . . . clear sense of purpose." Another called her "untiring in service" and "willing to do for all." The award, honoring "an individual outside the teaching profession who displays a dedicated service to youth," was presented to Alma in 1971. She was chosen, according the MEA, for her "unusual perception of community and state needs" and for her "civic, educational, and professional contributions to the state's young people."

In her personal life, Alma adored reading of course, but she was no recluse. She entertained frequently, often hosting civil rights groups and youth organizations in her home. She also spent a lot of time with her mother, who remained active into her old age. Still involved with Union Bethel Church, Emma was also a master quilter—in fact, some of Emma Smith's quilts are registered with the Montana Historic Quilt Project. Maintaining her connection with Africa, Emma sometimes housed young Africans going to school in Great Falls. She also taught her grandchildren words of Kru, her language in Liberia. In the late 1960s, when Emma was in her eighties, Alma took her on a very special trip back to Liberia. While there, they even ran into people who remembered Emma and her family. The visit was moving for both mother and daughter.

Alma remained close to her siblings and loved visiting with her nieces and nephews. Only her brother Martin, a mechanic at Malmstrom Air Force Base, lived in Great Falls, but Alma traveled to see the rest of the family often. Whenever her relatives visited her, they inevitably ended up at the library.

Madeline, the eldest Smith sibling, and Morris, the youngest, both lived in California. Madeline was a secretary for a state legislator, and Morris worked in social services. Morris's daughter, Maisha, remembered that her Aunt Alma always sent her a special book for her birthday: that year's Caldecott Award winner. Later, Maisha became a professor and wrote a book about literacy, using a photograph of Alma and her Talladega bookmobile for the cover.

Alma's sister Lucille, also a librarian, lived much closer, in Bozeman, where she moved after splitting from her husband in 1963. For a while, as Lucille adjusted to her job at the Montana State University library, her sons, Alan and Jamie, lived with Emma and Alma in Great Falls.

Alma's affection for them was mutual. Alan later remembered "How [Alma] always carried herself to overcome challenges was what inspired me. She was a model." In 1970, Alma and Lucille collaborated on an important reference work. Called *The Negro in Montana: 1800–1945*, it was a twenty-three-page listing of books, articles, and documents related to African American Montanans.

In 1973, when Alma was sixty-seven, the state of Montana named her state librarian. She was the first African American to hold that position. Her barrier-breaking appointment was big news. The story was featured in *Jet*, a popular African American magazine, as well as in local newspapers. To take the job, Alma had to leave her hometown and move to Montana's capital, Helena. Marcus went with her, as did Emma, but not long after the move, Marcus and Alma decided to divorce, and Marcus moved back to Alabama. Emma would live in Helena until her death in 1979, at age ninety-seven.

As state librarian, Alma oversaw twenty-six employees. Together they worked to improve the quality and efficiency of public and school libraries across Montana. For the second time in her career, Alma oversaw a major relocation of books when the state library's holdings, which had been scattered around Helena, were consolidated into one place. She told a reporter, "Moving a library is probably one of the most horrendous jobs in existence." On Alma's watch, Montana's library systems were increasingly computerized. Another part of her job was lobbying the state legislature for funding to support libraries across Montana.

Sadly, in 1981, Alma began showing the symptoms of Alzheimer's disease. Now she had to let go of the career that she had built, was so good at, and loved. Retiring from her job as state librarian, Alma moved to Bozeman to be close to Lucille and her family. She spent the last years of her life in a Bozeman nursing home, but even there, she enriched other people's lives by reading books aloud to her fellow residents. Alma Smith Jacobs passed away on December 15, 1997, at age eighty-one. She was buried beside her family members in Highland Cemetery in Great Falls.

Alma continued to be honored after her death. In 1999, the *Great Falls Tribune* named her one of the Top Montanans of the Twentieth Century. Eleven years later, the same paper included her among Montana's Top 125 Newsmakers.

In 2009, a special project was completed at the Great Falls Public Library. To enhance the "House that Alma Built," as the library was known locally, and to commemorate the woman responsible for it, an outdoor plaza was created at the front entrance. A plaque identifies the space as the Alma Jacobs Memorial Plaza, "honoring an exceptional librarian and community leader." At the plaza's dedication ceremony on June 20, Mayor Dona Stebbins proclaimed July 16 through 22, 2009, "Alma Jacobs Week" in Great Falls.

The focal point of the plaza is a fountain, a large arch made of local sandstone. A former library staff member, Joy Hamlett, said, "Every time I see that fountain bubbling in front of the library, and it's so tall and substantial and so steady, I always think it is symbolic of Alma Jacobs."

The following year, 2010, a group of civic-minded Alma admirers in Montana founded the Alma Smith Jacobs Foundation to address "social and economic issues in Great Falls." Among other things, it awards scholarships to Montana colleges and helps maintain the historical Union Bethel AME Church, still at the heart of African American life in Great Falls. At the library each year during Black History Month, the foundation presents a Black Heritage program, including a tribute to Alma.

In 2016, two local artists painted a mural of Alma's portrait on the south-facing outside wall at the Great Falls library. Alma "was very well known and respected in this community, very inspiring," noted the library's director. The vice president of the Great Falls Public Library Foundation, which funded the mural, said, "We think this project will create a positive awareness of the library. And it will serve as a testament . . . to Alma's lasting legacy—the library."

Most recently, in 2017, Alma was honored as Outstanding Montanan, placing her name in the Gallery of ans Outstanding Montanans at the state capitol.

When Alma was a child, her mother made sure that the Smith children were always neat in appearance and courteous in behavior, so they would represent African Americans in a positive light. Clearly, Alma took Emma's philosophy to heart. In a speech she gave at the Montana Federation of Colored Women's Clubs' fiftieth anniversary celebration in 1971, Alma said that black women in Montana could best counter prejudice "not by noisy protestations of what we are not, but by a dignified showing of what we are and hope to become." No one made a more dignified showing of who she was—and what she hoped others could become—than Alma Smith Jacobs.

Society does not usually equate being a librarian with big, exciting action. Yet through passionate commitment to ideals, including making information available to everyone, Alma helped enact sweeping changes in her town, state, region, and nation. When she died, she left behind a lifetime of achievement.

Elouise Cobell at a celebration in Browning, Montana, January 2011
—Courtesy *Great Falls Tribune*

11

ELOUISE PEPION COBELL

ACCOUNTING FOR JUSTICE

Elouise Cobell, age forty, stood at the Lincoln Memorial, one of the most famous monuments in Washington, D.C., and looked out over the skyline. It was June 1996. She knew this city well by now. She'd been traveling to Washington frequently in recent years from her home in northwestern Montana. The view included so many massive, impressive buildings. It was America's capital, after all, the center of the world's most powerful nation.

That's when Elouise felt goosebumps of fear. That very day, she planned to sue the United States government, specifically the Departments of the Treasury and the Interior, in court. She, a woman who grew up poor on an Indian reservation, was about to challenge the might and wealth that all those big buildings represented. Elouise knew her case was just, and the government was wrong—very wrong. But was it possible to fight the U.S. government and win? Anxiety seized her again. She hurried back to her hotel and picked up the phone to call a friend. After listening to Elouise's misgivings, her friend said, "If you don't do this, Elouise, who will?"

Elouise calmed down. She knew her friend was right. It was almost as if she, Elouise Pepion Cobell, had been preparing for this battle her whole life.

———•••———

Elouise Pepion was born on the Blackfeet Indian Reservation, located just east of Glacier National Park, at the reservation hospital on November 5, 1945. Her Blackfeet, or Pikuni, name was Yellow Bird Woman. Her parents, Polite (pronounced "Pleet") Pepion and Catherine DuBray Pepion, had a cattle ranch in an area called Birch Creek, about twenty-five miles southeast of Browning, near the reservation's southern border. In addition to ranching, Polite worked as a tribal stock inspector—an important job in ranch country—and served on the tribal council. Both roles made him a leader in the Blackfeet community, as his father had been before him.

Elouise's parents, Catherine and Polite Pepion, in an undated family photo. —Courtesy Cobell family

Catherine and Polite had nine children. In order, they were Shirley, Dale, Faye, Thelma, Julene, Ernie, Elouise, Joy, and Karen—seven girls and two boys. Elouise never knew Shirley, who died of pneumonia at age two. When Elouise was nine, she lost two more sisters when Faye and Thelma, in high school by then, were killed in a car accident.

The ranch house the large family lived in, along with Elouise's grandfather and several other relatives, was small. Until Elouise was twelve, there was no electricity, central heating, television, or even running water. But the Pepions were no different from other Blackfeet families. Most people on the reservation were poor. A strong woman and devoted mother, Catherine taught her children never to pity themselves, and that the most important thing they had in life was one another.

In the rolling hills of the reservation, below Glacier's forbidding peaks, ranches seemed far apart and isolated, yet neighboring families knew each other and their kids played together. Elouise's best friend, Zita Bremner, distantly related to Elouise through their grandparents, was one of her closest neighbors. Often, Zita rode a horse over to Elouise's house, or Elouise hopped on the bare back of the Pepions' family horse, called simply "the Buckskin Mare," and rode to Zita's. The girls spent hours exploring the area around their homes together on horseback. One of their favorite destinations was the home of an elderly couple they knew as Uncle George and Aunt Rosie, who lived up a secluded draw. George and Rosie always enjoyed seeing the girls, often serving them tea and cake.

When Elouise and Zita were older, if they felt too lazy to leave the house, they wrote notes to each other in their own secret language and sent their younger siblings to deliver them. During the summer, when tourists visited the Rocky Mountains, Elouise and Zita practiced their business skills. At the Birch Creek campground near their homes, they traded rides on their horses for treats such as cookies or grapes. They also sold lemonade at stands at the Birch Creek Rodeo and along the highway. One day, Elouise vowed, she and Zita would travel that same highway themselves in a pink Cadillac and a pink travel trailer.

Before Elouise was old enough to start school, many Native American children, including most of her older sisters and brothers, had to leave home if they wanted a good education. The government-run Indian boarding schools were set up, in part, to make Native American children conform to mainstream American ways, as opposed to following their own tribal customs. In many cases, for example, they were allowed to speak only English, and if they said anything in their tribal language, they could be punished. Removing children from their homes and families made it easier for the schools to change the students' ideas and behavior. From the first to eighth grades, the older Pepion kids attended an Indian boarding school nearly fifty miles away in Cutbank, Montana. For high school, they had to go even farther, to a school in Flandreau, South Dakota.

By the time Elouise was ready for first grade, though, U.S. government policies regarding Indian education had changed. Not only were Indian children now allowed to attend regular public schools, but tribes were allowed to establish their own local schools on the reservations. Elouise's parents and neighbors worked hard to get an elementary school built in the Birch Creek area, and Elouise attended that one-room school, called Grandview, which was only a mile from her house. Her parents also started a 4-H chapter, where local kids, including Elouise, learned agricultural and domestic skills. Elouise's mom taught sewing.

Elouise was a good student at Grandview. When her teacher shared newspapers and magazines with the class, the girl devoured every word. She was curious about the world and wanted to learn everything about it.

When the Pepion kids weren't in school, both the boys and the girls had many chores around the ranch, such as feeding the livestock. In winter, the cattle's water froze over, and holes had to be chopped into it constantly so the animals could drink. The girls, particularly Elouise, also helped their mother in the house. For example, when Elouise got home from school, she had to peel the potatoes for supper before she relaxed or did her homework.

Catherine and Polite made sure their children learned and appreciated the history of their family and of the Blackfeet people. Elouise was proud to be the great-granddaughter of respected Blackfeet leader Mountain Chief. In 1870 the U.S. Army, trying to gain dominance over the Indians during a time of hostilities, chased Mountain Chief and his band through northwestern Montana, planning to attack them. Under Mountain Chief's leadership, the band eluded the soldiers, but during the pursuit, the army came upon another Blackfeet band and its leader, Heavy Runner. Even though the soldiers knew Heavy Runner had signed a peace agreement with the U.S., they attacked anyway, killing some two hundred men, women, and children. It was a story of senseless cruelty that Elouise, like many Blackfeet, would never forget.

History surrounded Elouise as she was growing up. Every time the family drove to Browning, they passed Badger Creek, where the old Blackfeet agency stood from 1880 to 1894. From there, the highway gradually climbed and crossed a long ridge that people called Ghost Ridge. During the harsh winter of 1883–84, hundreds of Blackfeet families were camped there, near the agency, on which they depended for food since the buffalo were gone. But the supplies of food that came to the agency were seriously inadequate. More than five hundred people died from hunger and cold that winter, which became known as the Starvation Winter. The dead were buried in mass graves. Later, Elouise would say that it was for them that she fought "the same government that tried to get rid of this entire race of people."

Because Elouise's father was a tribal leader, neighbors frequently came to him when they had a problem. Often, the problem was money. There were times when a family member was desperately ill, for example, or a child did not have enough clothes for school, but the family could not pay for what they needed. Yet it was clear to Elouise that they weren't asking her father for charity or even a loan. These people owned land on the reservation and had their own money that the government kept for them, like a bank. But somehow, when they needed their money, they had trouble getting it out, and too often on the reservation, loved ones died without medical care and children had to do without. There was little her father could do to help, it seemed. Why couldn't Blackfeet families get their own money? Elouise wondered. When she was older, she would find out.

When it was time for high school, kids in Birch Creek had the choice of going to the nearest public school, which was in the town of Valier, off the reservation, or going all the way, every day, to the high school in Browning. Elouise chose Valier while Zita chose Browning, but the girls still saw each other at home and at school events such as basketball games. Once, after convincing their parents to take them to a dance in Browning, Elouise and Zita dressed in matching poodle skirts, considered the height of fashion in the 1950s.

Starting as a teenager, Elouise adored Elvis Presley, and it was one of the thrills of her life when, in the late 1950s, the singer passed through Browning on a train. When the train stopped, he stepped out and waved. Elouise waved back madly from the crowd. Even as an adult, she never lost her passion for Elvis. Zita, on the other hand, turned up her nose at "the King," becoming a Beatles fan instead.

Petite and pretty, with horn-rimmed glasses, Elouise was very active in high school. She wrote for the school newspaper, was in the chorus and pep club, and served on the yearbook staff. In the summer she competed in the Birch Creek rodeo and, when she was a high school junior, was crowned Miss Bucking Horse Queen. Around the same time, Elouise had her first taste of a big city. Her grandparents took her and Zita on a train to Seattle for the World's Fair. They went up in the Space Needle and swam in the ocean. Sometime after this, Elouise bought her first car—a Volkswagen Beetle.

After high school graduation in 1963, Elouise enrolled in a business college in Great Falls. She was especially good at accounting, which involves recording, monitoring, and evaluating the financial transactions of individuals and organizations. Examples of accounting include preparing yearly tax returns and examining monthly bank statements, which show customers exactly how much money they have in their bank accounts. If a bank or fund manager makes any mistakes, a good accountant will find them.

After finishing her classes in Great Falls, Elouise continued studying business at Montana State University in Bozeman, but in 1968 she dropped out and hurried home when her mother became ill with cancer. Only two weeks after Elouise's return, Catherine Pepion died. Grieving her mother's death, Elouise didn't return to school. Instead, she and Zita took summer jobs at Glacier National Park, working for the National Park Service as secretaries. Part of Elouise's job was helping with accounting.

When the summer was over, the friends decided to hit the road together, though it wouldn't be in a pink Cadillac. By then, Elouise, who loved cars, had bought a bright red Mustang convertible. Their plan was to drive to Seattle and find jobs there. Before leaving, Elouise went to the Bureau of Indian Affairs (BIA) office in Browning to get some money. Her mother had left her funds in what was called an Individual Indian Money account, or IIM. The BIA, part of the U.S. Department of the Interior, managed IIM accounts for Native Americans all over the country.

Withdrawing money from IIMs was never straightforward, the way it is at a regular bank. To withdraw their own money, account holders had to tell BIA officials what they wanted to use the money for and get government approval. Sometimes, instead of just giving a person cash— for example, to buy furniture—the official would take the person's money and go buy the furniture for them, even though the person might not like what the official picked out. It was a crazy and unfair system, but it had always been that way, and the account holders didn't know what to do about it.

At the BIA office, Elouise asked an official for a statement of her account, to see how much money was in it. He told her he couldn't give her a statement—and even if he could, he said, she wouldn't know how to read it. Elouise was deeply insulted. She was an educated young woman. She had even studied and worked in accounting. How dare this man assume she couldn't read a bank statement! His attitude seemed like pure prejudice against Indians. As Elouise would discover later, it was also an intimidation tactic, to keep account holders from asking more questions. Remembering how, when she was little, people would talk about their difficulties getting money from their accounts, Elouise experienced the problem firsthand now, and it made her angry.

Since the early 1800s, the federal (national) government had handled money for individual tribal members and for tribes. At the time, it was believed that Indians, unused to the American system of money, were incapable of managing their own finances. The government put all the Indians' money into large accounts called "trusts." The account holders could not draw their money from these trust accounts without permission. Unjust to begin with, this system was now outdated as well as unjust, yet it was unclear how it might be reformed.

Where did the Indians' money come from in the first place? Not all the account holders had paying jobs or money of their own, but they did have land. In 1887 the government passed a law to divide up the land on many reservations. Until then, reservation land belonged to the tribes, not to individuals. But under the new law, the land was broken into private lots and the ownership was transferred to individual tribal members.

Regardless of who the owner was, however, the BIA still controlled what was done with the land. For example, the bureau rented out land to farmers to graze cattle or grow crops, or to companies to drill for oil, dig for coal, or harvest timber. The money produced from these activities, called royalties, went into a landowner's IIM account. Now, many decades later, this system was still in place. Most adults on the reservation had IIMs, including, after Catherine died, Elouise and her siblings.

At this point in her life, it didn't matter to Elouise whether the BIA gave her money or not. Either way, she was going to Seattle. So, for the time being, she let the matter drop and went on with her plans.

In Seattle, Elouise and Zita moved in with Zita's aunt, and Elouise landed a job in accounting at the city's KING-TV station. Zita and Elouise enjoyed life in Seattle, surrounded by other young Blackfeet friends and relatives who also lived and worked in the city. Among them was Alvin "Turk" Cobell, whom Elouise had dated a bit during high school. Turk worked as a commercial fisherman, which took him back and forth between Seattle and Alaska. Elouise and Turk began dating again, and their relationship grew serious. They married in Seattle in 1969. Before long, they had a son. They named him Turk, after his father.

Meanwhile, Polite Pepion retired from ranching, and he needed someone to take over the place. Happy to return to Montana, Elouise, Turk, and little Turk moved back to Birch Creek, into the old Pepion ranch house, in 1971. In addition to raising livestock, Turk and Elouise still held outside jobs. For a while, Elouise drove fifty miles to Conrad, Montana, to work. The U.S. military had constructed a system of missiles in the Conrad area, and Elouise worked for a company that helped construct and maintain the system. During summers, Turk, still working as a commercial fisherman, was often gone.

Shortly after the Cobells returned to the ranch, Elouise's brother Ernie was in a terrible car wreck that left him a quadriplegic (paralyzed below the neck), with only partial use of one hand. After he got out of the hospital, Ernie moved in with Elouise and Turk at the ranch. While recovering, he learned to paint using a brace for his arm and hand. No one predicted that he would become known throughout the country and even around the world for his art. Loving and generous, Ernie was the mainstay of the family, encouraging everyone in their pursuits—especially Elouise.

In 1976, when she was thirty, Elouise was asked to become the Blackfeet tribal treasurer. She agreed to take the job, which was in Browning. Her official responsibilities involved handling the tribe's money, and one of the first things she did was transfer old financial records onto computers. Less officially, Elouise spent a lot of time advising tribal members, especially elders, on their money problems. She had become, just like her father, a person they came to for help. In her kitchen over tea or coffee, she would help them prepare their taxes, chatting while they completed the forms.

Through helping her fellow Blackfeet and transferring the tribal records, Elouise learned much about tribal members' financial situations. There was no doubt in her mind, after doing the calculations, that the payments of money that tribal landowners received each year from the government were much smaller than they should have been. A landowner might have five oil wells pumping on his or her land or a farmer growing lush crops on it, yet the royalty payments were next to nothing. Something was very wrong.

On top of all this was the question that had first crossed Elouise's mind when she was small. Why couldn't people get to their own money? Now, as treasurer, Elouise was able to gain access to some BIA account information and dig in, searching for answers.

The tribal members' IIM accounts, it turned out, were a mess. Even Elouise, an experienced accountant, couldn't make sense of them. For help in understanding, she telephoned the BIA. The bureau officials told her to put her questions in writing, so she wrote them formal letters. They didn't reply. As Elouise would later find out, several different government agencies had examined the BIA accounts over the years and issued reports calling for major improvements, but every time, the BIA had ignored the recommendations.

As part of her job, Elouise traveled frequently to business meetings and conferences around the country, where she met other tribal treasurers.

She found out that they had had the same experiences with their land-holders' accounts and the BIA. Eventually Elouise came to the conclusion that the problem wasn't just government incompetence and confusion, it was also government corruption. Keeping sloppy records of Indian money made it easy to steal Indian money. The more Elouise learned, the more it looked like the U.S. government and its officials had been doing just that for a long, long time—and covering it up.

While Elouise was uncovering this truth, her life at home went on. No matter how busy she was with work or travel, she always attended her son Turk's sports events. She was very close to her son. She taught him that the world is full of opportunity. "You can do what you want," she said, "but you've got to do it." In other words, you can't just dream, you have to act. Elouise was also very involved with her siblings and her extended family, who supported and relied on one other, so there was always someone available to help or something to celebrate.

In addition to her full-time job, Elouise had the ranch to tend to. Arriving home from work, Elouise might discover that the cattle had gotten out. She'd have to drive them back in, then search for the hole in the fence and fix it. During calving season, she helped the cows give birth. In cold weather, she was known to take the weaker newborn calves into the house for a warm shower, drying them off with her blowdryer.

No matter what Elouise was doing, the Indian accounts mess was never far from her mind. On Fridays after work in Browning, she would gather with Zita and other girlfriends to talk and relax. They heard her vow, on several occasions, that she would stop the wrong being done to Native Americans and would make the government pay.

Elouise served as the Blackfeet tribal treasurer for thirteen years. During her term, the reservation, which had always been poor, faced a true crisis in 1983, when Browning's only bank closed due to bad management. Several years passed, and the reservation still had no bank. Residents had to drive for miles in all kinds of weather just to make a deposit or cash a check. Local companies had nowhere safe to deposit money at the end of the business day.

With no banking services, it was hard for companies to keep doing business on the reservation, and the closing of stores and services, Elouise knew, would cause further distress in the community. Urgently, she traveled the state, begging different banks to move their operations to Browning. All of the bankers she talked to said the same thing: they did not want to do business on an Indian reservation—a fact that Elouise said made her blood boil.

Since no bank would come to the Blackfeet, Elouise decided that the only solution was for the tribe to start a bank of its own. Establishing a bank would not be easy. It would involve investing a lot of tribal money as well as finding other investors and assembling the voluminous amount of paperwork that was needed. Even so, when Elouise proposed the idea at a tribal meeting, the members voted to go forward.

In order to be entrusted with people's money, a would-be bank must prove to the U.S. government that it can meet stringent standards for keeping that money safe. Considering what Elouise learned about how badly the government itself was mismanaging Indian money, the fact that it had super-strict rules for banks was ironic. Nevertheless, Elouise and the tribe completed all the necessary forms to apply for a charter, a document that allows a bank to operate. When they were done with the paperwork, the result was hundreds of thousands of pages long! Finally, in 1987, the Blackfeet National Bank (BNB)—the first national bank owned by an Indian tribe—opened its doors. Later, other tribes bought into the bank so that, in 2001, it became the Native American Bank, headquartered in Denver—with a branch, of course, in Browning.

Meanwhile, in the mid-1980s, after more wrangling with the BIA over the IIM accounts, Elouise and some of her colleagues from other tribes began contacting members of the U.S. Congress, explaining this serious problem and asking them to take action for reform. Although many in Congress brushed them off, they finally found a supporter in Mike Synar, a representative from Oklahoma who had many Native American constituents. Synar took up the cause and, with the help of testimony from Elouise and others, he got a congressional investigation going in 1989.

The two-year investigation revealed that, for more than a hundred years, the BIA had been collecting Native American funds without a sound accounting system in place. When royalties came in from oil companies and other sources, bureau officials, in violation of the law, simply diverted the money into a general fund account, claiming they had no way of knowing to whom the money belonged. Placed in the general fund, the money could then be used for just about anything, whether it benefitted Indian people or not. For example, it is suspected that in the 1970s, the federal government used Indian money to save small American banks during a financial crisis. This system—or lack of one—also made it easy for officials at various levels of government to skim cash for their own pockets. Elouise's suspicions had proved to be correct: the government was essentially stealing money that belonged to Native American tribes and individuals.

Of course, the officials were careful to keep all this a secret. One year, in Montana, a BIA employee discovered that his agency had deposited between $7.5 and $11 million more than it had distributed to Indian landowners. When he reported his discovery, he was fired.

In 1992 Congress published its findings in a scathing report entitled "Misplaced Trust: Bureau of Indian Affairs Mismanagement of the Indian Trust Fund." Two years later, Congress passed a law, the American Indian Trust Fund Management Reform Act of 1994, to fix the problem. Among other things, the law required that BIA officials give a full report of the bureau's finances, including the details of accounts going back to the "earliest possible date."

After the report came out in 1992, Elouise found a sympathetic BIA official, who was Native American himself, to advise her on what to do next. He was about to leave office, but to help her, he set up a meeting for her with some influential government officials and banking experts. Dennis Gingold, one of the best banking lawyers in the country, happened to be at the meeting. When he heard about the state of American Indians' money, he was flabbergasted. He told Elouise that she should sue the U.S. government. But a lawsuit like that would cost a huge amount of money—money that the tribes did not have. Elouise hoped it wouldn't come to that.

After Congress passed the reform act, President Bill Clinton appointed a special trustee, Paul Homan, whose office (Office of the Special Trustee for American Indians, or OST) was assigned to make sure the BIA complied with the new law and to help sort out and manage the tribal accounts, including the IIMs. Indian people across the country were pleased—at first. But a year went by, then two. Amazingly, Native Americans were still not getting their money. Paul Homan was doing his best, but in defiance of the new law, the BIA was not cooperating with him.

By 1996, Elouise had run out of patience. Even if the BIA would not produce the records, it was clear the government owed the Indians money, and the money needed to be paid. As a colleague of Elouise's later put it, "If they can't show it, they owe it." Thinking of the elders and other vulnerable people at home and on other reservations who were still waiting for relief, Elouise kept pushing.

One day at a conference, Elouise was excited to meet the highest-ranking lawyer in the land, U.S. Attorney General Janet Reno. It was a dream come true for Elouise. During her long years of fighting with government officials, she had often wished she could meet the president or some other high-level official. Surely if she could explain to someone in a position of great authority about the egregious wrongs done to Indian people and their money, that person would step in and help. Now Elouise had her chance. After she told Reno about the problems with the BIA, the attorney general invited Elouise to meet with her in Washington, promising to take a personal interest in the case. Elouise was excited.

When Elouise arrived in Washington for the meeting, however, she was told that Reno was unavailable and a deputy attorney would meet with her instead. The deputy basically told Elouise not to get her hopes up. Elouise was furious. She also felt foolish for believing that Reno really cared. Later, she called herself a "Pollyanna" (someone who sees only goodness and hope, despite evidence to the contrary) for having thought that talking with an important government official would make a difference.

Around the same time, Elouise also met with a group of officials from the three federal agencies involved with handling Indian money: the Department of the Interior, which oversees the BIA; the Treasury, in charge of the government's money and accounting; and the Department of Justice, which deals with laws and crime. At the meeting, when Elouise expressed her frustration at the government's lack of response, one man snidely replied, "Why don't you just sue us?" This was the last straw for Elouise. "All right," she said, "I will."

Suing the government had been Elouise's last resort. "No one should have to sue for access to their own money," Elouise later fumed in a speech. But now she knew that, no matter what the cost, she had to do it. She asked her lawyer acquaintance, Dennis Gingold, to take the case. It would be a long, hard battle, he cautioned, but he agreed to do it. The Native American Rights Fund, a group in Colorado, prepared and filed the suit against the U.S. Department of the Interior and the Department of the Treasury. Elouise was the lead plaintiff (the person suing) along with over 300,000 other individual Indian account holders in what is called a "class-action" (group) lawsuit.

So in June 1996, Elouise Cobell found herself on the steps of the Lincoln Memorial. Later, after talking to her friend and recovering from her panic, she proceeded to the federal court building and filed the suit. It was done. The wheels were in motion.

Elouise estimated that the amount the government owed Indian account holders, accumulated over the one hundred-plus years since the trusts had been set up, came to about $47 billion, though some accountants put the figure as high as $176 billion. The plaintiffs did not specify an amount in the original lawsuit, however. They only demanded that the BIA give a full accounting of its funds and that a new accounting system be put in place. After that, they reasoned, they could determine how much money to ask for.

To raise money for the suit, Elouise traveled incessantly, talking about the case to supportive groups and asking them to donate to the cause.

She had good success. One foundation awarded her a $75,000 grant and a $60,000 loan. Another pledged $4 million to help pay for the case. And in 1997 Elouise was thrilled to learn she would receive a $300,000 grant (popularly called a "genius grant") from the MacArthur Foundation.

Elouise estimated that the lawsuit would take three years to settle. It ended up taking sixteen. First, the government tried to prove that its departments were not banks, so they didn't have to follow banking laws. But the court sided with Elouise and the other plaintiffs, ruling that the government had violated its legal responsibilities. The government appealed the decision, that is, it requested another trial, hoping for a different result. At one point, the federal government had over a hundred lawyers working on the case. Every time the government lost, its lawyers appealed. These constant appeals and other legal maneuvers delayed the case again and again, costing Elouise and her side more and more money and energy. Through it all, the government remained like a brick wall. It did not want to admit any wrongdoing or pay a single dollar. Comparing herself to a wolverine—a small but fierce animal that bites and never lets go—Elouise didn't give up.

Over the years, the case took astounding twists and turns. Early on, the judge charged the secretaries of the Interior and the Treasury with contempt of court after they failed to produce the records they had been ordered to provide. For this violation, the government had to pay a large fine. Later, it came out that the government had knowingly destroyed hundreds of boxes of paper records from the BIA. Over the decades, many other papers had been lost or damaged due to careless storage. Elouise's team found BIA records stashed in leaky warehouses across the country. In one case in Oklahoma, records had been stored in an old barn; whenever the barn got full, BIA officials had simply thrown older papers away to make room for new ones.

Elouise and her lawyers also found serious security flaws in the government's computer system. The court allowed her team to prove it by bringing in computer hackers to hack into the system, create fake accounts, and move money around—just to show the judge how easy it was.

Exposing wrongdoing can be exhausting. It can even be dangerous. Over the course of the suit, Elouise received death threats—letters and anonymous phone calls suggesting that the case wasn't good for her or her family. After one of the plaintiffs included in the suit died mysteriously, Elouise's family asked tribal leaders to hold a special ceremony for Elouise in Browning. The place overflowed with supporters as the Blackfeet leaders called for spiritual protection to keep Elouise safe.

At one point, the government stopped sending account holders any money at all and blamed it on the case, trying to turn Indian people against Elouise. Sometimes it worked, which may have been the hardest thing for Elouise—the fact that there were Native Americans, even some Blackfeet, who were against what she was doing. The reasons were complicated. When Elouise brought suit in 1996, she had to choose whether to sue on behalf of tribes, whose accounts were also a mess, or on behalf of individual landowners. Elouise chose to sue on behalf of individuals, knowing that tribes might have the resources to sue on their own, later, but so many individual landowners she knew—poor people she had grown up with on the Blackfeet Reservation and had met in countless locales across the nation—would never be able to sue on their own. But Elouise's choice upset some people. Others simply thought the suit was a waste of time and money. At certain points in the case, some believed Elouise should accept what was offered and stop fighting. Others cynically said Elouise was in it for herself, hoping to get a big payment.

Elouise responded to these criticisms by redoubling her efforts to communicate with the tribes. She and her legal team traveled frequently to remote reservations around the country to explain to everyone involved with the case what was happening and why.

In the meantime, during the 1990s and early 2000s, Elouise never stopped working to improve life on the Blackfeet reservation. In 1996, she helped found and ran the Native American Community Development Corporation (NACDC), a not-for-profit arm of the Native American Bank. The NACDC helped and advised Native American business owners. It also assisted reservation farmers in getting the money they needed to farm their own land. Elouise was especially fond of an NACDC program that taught kids "financial literacy" by setting up "mini banks" in schools. Students pooled their dollars and took turns role-playing banker and customer. The NACDC also set up a recycling program on the Blackfeet reservation.

Another of Elouise's favorite projects was the Blackfeet Indian Land Trust (BILT) that she, with major state conservation groups, helped found in 2001. It was the first land trust ever established on an Indian reservation. Land trusts preserve wild land by restricting building and other development. The BILT consisted of about one thousand acres just west of Browning.

In 2002 the Blackfeet acknowledged Elouise's dedication to her people by naming her a warrior of the tribe, a rare honor for a woman. Her battles were not the violent kind, yet they still required exceptional courage. In the ceremony, Elouise was presented with an eagle feather, a symbol of warrior status.

Meanwhile, the lawsuit dragged on. Over the years, Elouise made many personal sacrifices as she pursued justice in the courts. Just about any money she received went toward paying the costs of the suit. In addition, the government harassed Elouise by auditing her taxes—a lengthy headache of a process—four years in a row. Elouise also felt bad that, because she was constantly traveling in connection with the suit, her husband, Turk, was often left to run the ranch alone.

Dealing with the lawsuit and the government's bullying was hard on Elouise, but she was determined not to let those pressures ruin her life. She visited her son, who lived in Las Vegas, as often as she could. In 2003 Turk Junior got married, and before long, Elouise had two granddaughters. As a doting grandma, Elouise tried to spend at least a few days each month with her son's family. She went on some special trips as well—for example, she took Turk Senior to the Kentucky Derby horse race, where she wore a big, fancy hat in the Derby tradition. Occasionally Elouise and Turk got away from it all at their cabin near Glacier National Park.

Unfortunately, Turk Senior, who suffered from diabetes, eventually developed kidney disease. In 2004 the doctors told the Cobells that Turk needed a new kidney. Elouise learned that she was medically eligible to donate one of her kidneys to her husband, and she did not hesitate to do so, saving his life. A year after this ordeal, Elouise's brother Ernie died—a huge loss for the family and the art world.

Returning to the IIM accounts battle, in 2009 Elouise and the other plaintiffs finally started negotiating a final cash settlement with the government. They had to come up with a compromise figure that would bring the case to a close. The first offer the government made was such a small fraction of what was owed that Elouise said no. She wanted to make sure that the settlement figure was high enough to give each of the more than 300,000 individual Native Americans represented in the suit a reasonable amount of money.

In the end, after 220 days in court and eighty court decisions, Elouise and the other plaintiffs settled the case for $3.4 billion, the largest amount of money any class-action suit had ever won from the U.S. government. Elouise and the others knew it was much less than the government really owed, but the suit had been going on for thirteen years, and many of the plaintiffs who were sick or old had already died without seeing any money. This way, people could at least start getting some money. According to the settlement, each plaintiff would receive at least $1,000, and some would receive more.

In addition to the money paid to the individual accounts, part of the settlement would be used to establish a "buyback" program for Indian landowners, where they could sell their portions of reservation land to their tribe for cash. In effect, the government would pay individual Indians for their land and award that land back to the tribes. The plaintiffs also received about $60 million to create a scholarship fund for Native American college students. Elouise called the settlement a "bittersweet victory."

After the agreement was reached, the plaintiffs still had to wait for congressional approval and a presidential signature before it was final. A year later, in December 2010, President Barack Obama signed the settlement agreement. Elouise, now sixty-five years old, traveled to Washington,

Drawing of Elouise Cobell by fifth-grader Alysa LaPlante, printed in the Glacier Reporter, *June 2014* —Courtesy John McGill

D.C., for the ceremony. The president praised Elouise's courage and determination, saying, "It's finally time to make things right."

Elouise said that winning the lawsuit was like riding into the U.S. Cavalry and coming out alive. She looked forward to getting back to a normal life on the ranch. She planned to retire from most of her projects so she could spend more time with her family. There was one project she intended to continue working on, though—the land trust near Browning. She wanted to see it through to its ultimate success. As for the settlement money, Elouise had plans for that too. Over the years, she and her husband had never had the money or time to fix up their house—the house Elouise had grown up in. With her share of the lawsuit settlement, Elouise thought she might buy a brand-new house. She also wanted to travel to France, where the first Pepion had come from long ago.

Sadly, Elouise never got to do those things because she never got her payment. Only a few months after the signing ceremony, Elouise learned that, like her mother and one of her sisters, she had ovarian cancer. On October 16, 2011, a few weeks before her sixty-sixth birthday, Elouise Pepion Cobell, Yellow Bird Woman, died in a Great Falls hospital, surrounded by family and close friends.

News of Elouise's death caused a wave of grief across the nation. Even though the federal government had fought her, flags at the Department of the Interior and the BIA flew at half-mast in her honor. Fellow tribal members, Montanans, and government officials, including President Obama, publicly expressed their admiration for this strong and courageous woman and their sorrow at her passing. The *New York Times*, the *Washington Post*, and the *Los Angeles Times*, as well as many smaller newspapers, carried her obituary. The *Great Falls Tribune* said, "We've lost a hero."

On October 22, hundreds of people gathered in the Browning gym to say goodbye to Elouise and celebrate her life. From across the country came colleagues and admirers from other tribes and even some of the government officials she had battled. All day, a local radio station played Elvis Presley songs in Elouise's honor. After the memorial ceremony, a long line of cars moved slowly down the highway from Browning to the ranch, where she was to be buried. On the way, the hearse carrying her body blew a tire, so her casket was transferred to the bed of a pickup. Some thought Elouise would have found that amusing—and might even have preferred the pickup ride.

Before Elouise died, a judge had approved the method of distribution of money to account holders so payments could begin. However, that decision, too, was appealed, causing another delay. Indian account holders finally began receiving their first payments shortly after Elouise's death. The second payment checks began arriving in the fall of 2014.

Everywhere across the country, people called the payments "Cobell checks." In Browning, after the first payout arrived, signs appeared in shop windows: "Thank you, Elouise!" Soon, outside Browning's Native American Bank, a little tree donated in gratitude to Elouise by the United South and Eastern Tribes was covered with ribbons and thank-you notes.

The government's reservation land buyback program and the Indian scholarship fund continue today, as do most of the organizations and projects that Elouise started. The Native American Bank she established still operates in Browning. This bank, along with the Native American Community Development Corporation, has helped support many Indian-owned businesses on the Blackfeet reservation.

Although Elouise had her share of critics during her life, her supporters far outnumbered them. The list of her honors and awards is long and impressive. Highlights include an award from the International Women's Forum in 2002; one from the National Center for American Indian Enterprise Development in 2004; and three honorary degrees, from Montana State University (which she attended in the 1960s) in 2003, Rollins College in Florida in 2007, and the prestigious Dartmouth College in 2011. In 2010 the National Congress of American Indians honored her with the Indian Country Leadership Award.

In Montana, Elouise was especially revered. In 2011, shortly before her death, the Montana Trial Lawyers Association named her "Montana Citizen of the Year." The new federal courthouse in Billings, built in 2012, features the Elouise Cobell Hall and Jury Assembly Room. On the reservation, the Blackfeet Indian Land Trust Reserve, dedicated in 2013, was named Yellow Bird Woman Sanctuary in honor of Elouise. The town of Browning named its city park after her, too. At the University of Montana in Missoula is the Elouise Cobell Land and Culture Institute, dedicated in 2014. And in 2015, Governor Steve Bullock declared Elouise's birthday, November 5, Elouise Cobell Day.

A documentary about Elouise and the lawsuit, *100 Years: One Woman's Fight for Justice*, by filmmaker Melinda Janko, was released in 2016. Later that year, President Obama honored Elouise's memory with the Presidential Medal of Freedom, the nation's highest civilian honor. Her son Turk said, "I know this day would have brought a wonderful smile to her face and a sparkle to her eyes."

By standing her ground, remaining as immovable as the high mountains bordering her home, Elouise Cobell, Yellow Bird Woman, became, in the words of Montana senator Jon Tester, an American hero. Tester continued, in his tribute:

> Elouise Cobell was a star—truly a guiding light that will always lead the way for all Americans who fight for justice and fairness. Elouise's tireless leadership set this nation on a new course, and what she accomplished reminds us that any person in any part of this country has the power to stand up and right a wrong, no matter how difficult it may be. . . . Future generations will learn about Elouise Cobell's legacy and they will be inspired to follow her lead.

Sites to Visit

Below are sites associated with the bold women in this book. Some are physical places where certain scenes from their lives took place. Others are online, where you can see pictures and sometimes videos of these women. Also check out the excellent recent Montana Historical Society website, "Women's History Matters": http://montanawomenshistory.org.

RUNNING EAGLE (PITAMAKIN)

Running Eagle/Pitamakin Falls is in the Two Medicine area of Glacier National Park. Easily accessible. (406) 888-7800. Website, https://www.nps.gov/glac/index.htm.

Marias Pass (Running Eagle Pass or Bear Pass), on US 2, is west of the town of East Glacier. The pass is marked with an obelisk and a statue of an explorer.

Some of Running Eagle's descendants still live on the **Blackfeet Reservation**. Blackfeet Nation, PO Box 850, All Chiefs Square, Browning, MT 59417; (406) 338-7521. Official website, www.blackfeetnation.com.

Also in Browning is the **Museum of the Plains Indian**, 19 Museum Loop; (406) 338-2230. Website, http://www.browningmontana.com/museum.html.

ANNIE MORGAN

The Morgan-Case Homestead, Rock Creek Rd. (FS Rd. 102), is thirty miles south of I-90. Call USDA Forest Service, Lolo National Forest, (406) 329-3814, for information or cabin rental. Learn more about Annie Morgan's cabin on the "Friends of Upper Rock Creek Historic District" Facebook page. The May 25, 2011, post contains photos of the artifacts from her cabin doorway.

Philipsburg, where Annie lived for a while, is a wonderful historic town. At the Philipsburg Cemetery (at the far north end of Pearl Street) is Annie's tombstone, a small white column with a cross on top, south of the road that divides the cemetery.

PRETTY SHIELD

The Crow Reservation includes many historical and cultural sites. Guides are available for hire; inquire at the tribal offices. Crow Nation, PO Box 159, Bacheeitche Avenue, Crow Agency, MT 59022; (406) 638-3708. Official website, http://www.crow-nsn.gov/.

On the Crow Reservation north of Lodge Grass and south of Crow Agency is **Benteen**. Between mile markers 6 and 7 on Highway 451, looking west, stood the house where Pretty Shield raised Alma, on Nest Creek, across the Little Bighorn River.

Also on the reservation is **Chief Plenty Coups State Park**, 1 Edgar Road, Pryor, Montana; (406) 252-1289. The visitor center includes exhibits on Crow history and culture. Website, http://stateparks.mt.gov/chief-plenty-coups/.

Another site on the reservation is **Little Bighorn Battlefield National Monument**, 756 Battlefield Tour Road, Crow Agency, MT; (406) 638-2621. Pretty Shield and Goes Ahead's joint grave is in the Custer National Cemetery, front row of Section A. Her name is on the back of the marker.

In Fort Smith, the area where Alma and Bill retired, is the **Big Horn Baptist Church**, 500 First St., Fort Smith, MT; (406) 666-2294. Alma's and Bill's graves are in the church cemetery.

The **Pretty Shield Foundation** continues Pretty Shield's and Alma's legacy of caring for community. 3122 Brayton St., Billings, MT 59102; (406) 256-4040. Website, http://prettyshieldfoundation.org/.

JEANNETTE RANKIN

In **Missoula**, Montana, are several sites related to Jeannette. Up Grant Creek Road, the **Rankin ranch** was about 2.5 miles north of I-90, west of the road; it is now private property. Downtown is the unmarked site of the Rankin house, south of Broadway on Madison Street, north of the river. Jeannette attended the **University of Montana** from 1898 to 1902. The original university library, which currently houses offices and classrooms, is now called Jeannette Rankin Hall. Last but not least is the **Jeannette Rankin Peace Center**, 519 S. Higgins Ave.; (406) 543-3955. Website, https://jrpc.org/.

A bronze **statue** of Jeannette can be seen in the rotunda of the **Montana State Capitol** in Helena, 1301 E. 6th Ave. The original statue is in the Congressional Hall of Statuary at the **U.S. Capitol** in Washington, D.C.

Two miles northwest of **Watkinsville, Georgia**, on Mars Hill Road near the intersection with GA 53, is a historical marker commemorating Jeannette Rankin and the home she built nearby.

The **Jeannette Rankin Foundation** in **Athens, Georgia**, was created to help "mature, unemployed women workers" return to school. 1 Huntington Rd., Suite 701, Athens, GA, 30606; (706) 208-1211. Website, http://www.rankinfoundation.org/.

You can hear Jeannette's voice—very faintly—in this **recording** of the US House of Representatives declaration of war vote, December 8, 1941, part of an exclusive report by Walter Cronkite, in the archives of NPR's "All Things Considered." Link at http://www.npr.org/programs/atc/features/2001/dec/cronkite/011207.cronkite. html.

See and hear elderly Jeannette in this **video**: "Jeannette Rankin: First Lady of Peace," WGTV, Athens, GA, 1972.

WOMEN'S PROTECTIVE UNION

The **Butte-Silver Bow Public Archives** has WPU documents, pictures, and artifacts. 17 W. Quartz St., Butte, MT, 59701; (406) 782-3280. Website, https://buttearchives.org/.

The **Granite Mountain-Speculator Fire Memorial** on Alexander Street in Butte includes the story of the Women's Protective Union. (406) 782-3280. Website, http://www.minememorial.org/.

Also in Butte are several locations where the WPU met at one time or another. Various labor unions still meet at the **Carpenters Union Hall** building, 156 W. Granite. **Pioneer Hall**, 21 S. Montana St., is now a liquor store. The **Miners Union Hall**, on North Main near Quartz Street, was set on fire in 1914; a small historical monument marks the spot.

While you're in Butte, check out the **World Museum of Mining** at 155 Museum Way; (406) 723-7211. Website, http://miningmuseum.org/.

More WPU info and materials can be found at the **Montana Historical Society**, 225 N. Roberts, Helena, MT, 59620; (406) 444-2694. Website, https://mhs.mt.gov/.

Richard I. Gibson, author of *Lost Butte, Montana*, maintains a **website** with blogs and stories about Butte women and the city's history. http://buttehistory.blogspot.com/.

FREIDA FLIGELMAN AND
BELLE FLIGELMAN WINESTINE

In Helena, the **New York Block building**, which housed the New York Dry Goods Store (later called Fligelman's), 46 N. Last Chance Gulch, is now a mixed-use building. Look for the tailor and seamstress gargoyles and the shields of medieval textile guilds on the building front.

Also in Helena is the former **Temple Emanu-El**, now the Helena Catholic Diocese building, at 515 N. Ewing in Helena. The two onion domes are missing, but you can still see the cornerstone inscribed "5651" (the Jewish-calendar equivalent of 1890).

Today's **Helena YWCA**, at 501 North Park Avenue, is two blocks north of the site of the **Electric Building** (later known as the Electric Block) at North Park Avenue and 6th Street, where the Helena YWCA first operated and where Frieda worked; it is now a parking lot.

Frieda and Belle are buried with other family members in Helena's **Home of Peace Jewish Cemetery**, on an unmarked road behind Capital High School.

Based in Helena, the **Montana Historical Society** has some materials related to the Fligelman family, including a quilt that Minnie Fligelman made from Herman's cloth samples. The MHS is at 225 N. Roberts, Helena, MT, 59620; (406) 444-2694. Website, https://mhs.mt.gov/.

For more info on Fligelman's store, Temple Emanu-El, the YWCA, the Home of Peace Cemetery, and more, visit the "Helena as She Was" **website**, http://www.helenahistory.org/.

ISABELLE JOHNSON

The **Museum of the Beartooths**, at 440 E. 5th Ave. N., Columbus, Montana, has displays about Isabelle Johnson and her family, including ranch and studio artifacts and even some ranch buildings. The museum's archives contain Johnson family documents and photographs. (406) 322-4588. Website, http://museumofthebeartooths.com/.

Explore the landscape around Isabelle's hometown of **Absarokee**, Montana. Isabelle painted the countryside and mountains throughout the area.

In Absarokee is the **Immanuel Lutheran Church**, 301 S. Montana Ave.; (406) 328-4671. Website, http://www.immanuellutheranmt.org. Isabelle's father helped build this church, and Isabelle was a lifelong member.

Isabelle's grave is in the Johnson family plot in **Rosebud Cemetery**, on Rosebud Cemetery Road south of Absarokee.

The former **Johnson ranch** is now part of the **Tippet Rise Art Center**, 96 S. Grove Creek Rd., Fishtail, MT, 59028. No phone number. Reservations are required and can be made on the website, http://tippetrise.org/.

Isabelle left most of her work to the **Yellowstone Art Museum** in Billings. If it's not on display, call to make an appointment to see it. It's located at 401 N. 27th St., Billings, MT, 59101; (406) 256-6804. Website, http://www.artmuseum.org/.

ALICE GREENOUGH ORR AND
MARGE GREENOUGH HENSON

The **Carbon County Historical Society Museum** in Red Lodge displays the saddle Alice Greenough won in Boston in 1935 and much more. The archives contain Greenough family papers and photographs. It's located at 224 N. Broadway, Red Lodge, MT, 59068; (406) 446-3667. Website, http://www.carboncountyhistory.com/.

Fox, Montana, is now basically a grain elevator at mile marker 96 on US Route 212, north of Red Lodge. If you turn east at the elevator on East Bench Road and cross Rock Creek, then go left at the T for .2 miles and look left, you can see the site of the Greenough family's homestead, where Alice was born.

The later **Greenough ranch**, where the family lived upon their return from Billings in 1922, was south of Red Lodge on US Route 212. It's now private property, but you can drive by the place. From Route 212, turn east on East Side Road and cross the creek; it's immediately on your left, below Mt. Maurice.

Beartooth Lake, along the Beartooth Highway off US Route 212, is in the Shoshone National Forest near Cody, Wyoming. Website, http://www.fs.usda.gov/recarea/shoshone/recreation/camping-cabins/recarea/?recid=35819&actid=29.

To watch some of the **movies** Alice and Marge worked in, buy or rent the dvd or try TCM.com or your favorite online movie service. Selections include *The Californian* (1937); *Cimarron* (1960); and *Poker Alice* (1987), a made-for-televison movie.

MYRNA LOY

The **Myrna Loy Center for the Performing and Media Arts** in Helena displays the star's photos and memorabilia in the lobby. It's at 15 North Ewing St., Helena, MT, 59601; (406) 443-0287. Website, http://myrnaloycenter.com/.

Also in Helena are Myrna's grade school, **Central Elementary School**, 402 N. Warren St., and gravesite, in **Forestvale Cemetery**, 490 Forestvale Rd. (Myrna is buried in the "Valley View" section with her parents, Della and David Williams).

Radersburg, Montana, and the Crow Creek Valley, where Myrna grew up, are southeast of Helena. To get to Radersburg from Helena, take US-287 south for 44 miles to MT Route 285 (Totson exit), then follow MT-285 about 9 miles to Main Street in Radersburg.

A bronze re-creation of **Myrna Loy's statue**, the original of which was created in 1922 as part of a fountain with two other figures, stands in front of **Venice High School in Los Angeles**. The fountain had deteriorated and had to be removed in the early 2000s. The school is located at 13000 Venice Blvd., Los Angeles, CA, 90066; (310) 577-4200.

To watch some of Myrna Loy's **movies**, buy or rent the dvd or try TCM.com or your favorite online movie service. Among her best-known films are *The Thin Man* (1934) and its sequels; *The Best Years of Our Lives* (1946); *The Bachelor and the Bobby-Soxer* (1947); and *Mr. Blandings Builds His Dream House* (1948).

ALMA SMITH JACOBS

Alma's proudest achievement, the **Great Falls Public Library**, is located at 301 2nd Ave. N., Great Falls, MT, 59401; (406) 453-0349. Tributes to Alma can be found both in the library and all around **Alma Jacobs Memorial Plaza**, including the dedication plaque with Alma's name, the fountain, and the mural of her face. Inside, on the third floor near the elevator, is a small Alma Jacobs exhibit. Website, http://greatfallslibrary.org/.

The **Alma Smith Jacobs Foundation** is a not-for-profit organization that awards scholarships, supports cultural preservation, and hosts educational events. Contact the Great Falls Public Library (above) for information.

Union Bethel African Methodist Episcopal Church is at 916 5th Ave. S., Great Falls, MT, 59405; (406) 727-7998. Look for the stained-glass window commemorating the Smith family. Visitors are welcome at services, but at other times, the door may be locked, so call ahead.

In Helena is the **Montana State Library**, at 1515 E. 6th Ave., where Alma served as the state librarian; (406) 444-3115. While in Helena, stop by the **Montana**

Historical Society, at 225 N. Roberts, which has artifacts related to the Smith family, including ribbons awarded to Alma by the Montana Federation of Women's Clubs and four quilts made by Emma Smith, Alma's mother (contact the society for appointment). Phone (406) 444-2694; website, https://mhs.mt.gov/.

ELOUISE PEPION COBELL

On the **Blackfeet Reservation**, Elouise grew up in the Blacktail Creek area, a few miles north of the reservation's southern border, west of US Route 89 (on the day of her funeral, cars lined US Route 89). Elouise's elementary school, Grandview, is closed, but the red brick building still stands. Elouise spent much time in **Browning**, the reservation's main town. Contact Blackfeet Nation, PO Box 850, All Chiefs Square, Browning, MT 59417; (406) 338-7521. Official website, www. blackfeetnation.com.

While you're in Browning, check out the **Native American Bank** Elouise helped establish, with Elouise's **commemorative tree** out front: 125 N. Public Square, Browning, MT, 59417; (406) 338-7000. Website, http://www.nabna.com/.

Also on the Blackfeet Reservation is **Yellow Bird Woman Sanctuary**, the land trust Elouise helped found. It's about seven miles west of Browning on US Route 89, south of the highway. Before you visit, contact a Blackfeet Land Trust board member: Terry Tatsey, Blackfeet Community College, (406) 338-5441, ext. 2210; or Mark Magee, Blackfeet Land Department, (406) 338-2667.

The **Elouise Cobell Land and Culture Institute**, at the University of Montana in Missoula, is in the basement of the Payne Family Native American Center. Elouise Cobell Land and Culture Institute, Payne Family Native American Center, Missoula, MT, 59812; (406) 243-5831. Website, http://hs.umt.edu/cobell/.

Selected Sources

RUNNING EAGLE (PITAMAKAN)

Carbaugh, Donal, and Lisa Rudnick. "Which Place, What Story? Cultural Discourses at the Border of the Blackfeet Reservation and Glacier National Park." *Great Plains Quarterly* 26 (Summer 2006).

Ewers, John C. "Deadlier than the Male." *American Heritage*, June 1965.

Hungry Wolf, Adolf. *The Blackfoot Papers.* Vols 1-4. Skookumchuck, Canada: Good Medicine Cultural Foundation, 2006.

Hungry Wolf, Beverly. *The Ways of My Grandmothers.* New York: Quill, 1982.

National Park Service. "The Story of Running Eagle." Interpretive sign at Pitamakan Falls, Glacier National Park, Montana.

Robison, Ken. "The Saga of Pitamakan, the Pikuni Blackfeet Joan of Arc." Website, Historical Fort Benton, 2011. http://fortbenton.blogspot.com/2011/04/saga-of-pitamakan-pikuni-blackfeet-joan.html.

Schultz, James Willard. *Running Eagle, the Warrior Girl.* Memphis: General Books, 2012.

Personal communications: Dona Rutherford, February 28, 2014; Darnell and Robert Rides-at-the-Door, March 24 to April 5, 2014.

ANNIE MORGAN

Anderson, Jeffrey E. *Hoodoo, Voodoo, and Conjure.* Westport, CT: Greenwood Folklore Handbooks, Greenwood Press, 2008.

Auge, C. Riley. "Ritual Belief at the 19th-Century Morgan-Case Homestead." Paper presented at the Montana Archaeological Society meeting, Kalispell, Mont., April 2009.

Hagen, Delia, and Janene Caywood. National Register of Historic Places Registration and Nomination. US Department of the Interior, National Park Service, July 2004.

Olson, Darlene. *Up the Creek: History of Early Settlers on Rock Creek, Bonita, and Quigley.* Clinton, MT: Valley Publishing, 1990.

Philipsburg Mail. "Was With Custer: Cook of Late General Dies at Lower Rock Creek Home." April 10, 1914.

Stalcup, Cindy. Blog post. http://milescity.com/forums/posts/view/106923/. Posted September 19, 2009.

Taylor, Quintard, and Shirley Ann Wilson Moore, eds. *African-American Women Confront the West, 1600-2000.* Norman: University of Oklahoma Press, 2003.

Personal communications: Janene Caywood, August 4, 2011 to December 22, 2015.

PRETTY SHIELD

Hogan, Lillian Bullshows. *The Woman Who Loved Mankind: The Life of a Twentieth-Century Crow Elder.* Lincoln: University of Nebraska Press, 2012.

Linderman, Frank B. *Pretty-Shield: Medicine Woman of the Crows.* Lincoln: University of Nebraska Press, 1972.

Snell, Alma Hogan. *Grandmother's Grandchild: My Crow Indian Life.* Lincoln: University of Nebraska Press, 2000.

———. *A Taste of Heritage: Crow Indian Recipes and Herbal Medicines.* Lincoln: University of Nebraska Press, 2006.

Personal communications: Tim McCleary, January 1, 2014; Bill and Karen Snell, September 19 and 20, 2014.

JEANNETTE RANKIN

Chall, Malca, and Hannah Josephson. *Suffragists' Oral History Project.* Bancroft Library, Berkeley, California.

Hoff-Wilson, Joan. "'Peace Is a Woman's Job': Jeannette Rankin and American Foreign Policy: The Origins of Her Pacifism." *Montana: The Magazine of Western History,* Winter 1980.

———. "Remarks." In *Acceptance and Dedication of the Statue of Jeannette Rankin, Presented by the State of Montana, Proceedings in the Rotunda, United States Capitol, May 1, 1985.* 99th Congress, 2d Session, Sen. Doc. 99–32. Washington, DC: Government Printing Office, 1987.

Jeannette Rankin Peace Center. Scrapbooks, vols. 1–3. Missoula, Montana.

Josephson, Hannah. *Jeannette Rankin: First Lady in Congress.* Indianapolis and New York: Bobbs-Merrill Co., 1974.

Lopach, James, and Jean A. Luckowski. *Jeannette Rankin: A Political Woman.* Boulder: University Press of Colorado, 2005.

Smith, Norma. *Jeannette Rankin: America's Conscience.* Helena: Montana Historical Society, 2002.

WOMEN'S PROTECTIVE UNION

Case, Bridgette Dawn. "The Women's Protective Union: Women Union Activists in a Union Town, 1890–1929." MA Thesis, Montana State University, 2004.

Finn, Janet, and Ellen Crain, eds. *Motherlode: Legacies of Womens' Lives and Labors in Butte, Montana.* Livingston, Mont.: Clark City Press, 2005.

Murphy, Mary. *Interview with Blanche Averett Copenhaver.* February 21, 1980. Butte Oral History Project, Missoula. Oral History Collection, University of Montana, Missoula.

Murphy, Mary. *Interview with Valentine Catherine Kenney Webster, Butte, Montana.* February 24, 1980. Butte Oral History Project, Missoula. Oral History Collection, University of Montana, Missoula.

Sundberg, Yvonne. "Bridget (Murphy) Shea: A Short Biography." No date. Butte-Silver Bow Archives, Butte, Mont. p

Personal communications: Bill Antonioli, November 18, 2013; Carol Barber, July 22, 2016; Marilyn Ross, November 5, 2013; Whitney Willliams, September 13, 2013.

FRIEDA FLIGELMAN AND
BELLE FLIGELMAN WINESTINE

Abrams, Jeanne E. *Jewish Women Pioneering the Frontier Trail.* New York: New York University Press, 2006.

Fligelman, Frieda. Frieda Fligelman Papers, 1927–84. Archives & Special Collections, Mansfield Library, University of Montana, Missoula.

———. *Notes for a Novel: The Selected Poems of Frieda Fligelman.* Edited by Alexandra Swaney and Rick Newby. Helena, MT: Drumlummon Institute, 2008.

Hanshew, Annie. *Border to Border: Historic Quilts and Quiltmakers of Montana.* Helena: Montana Historical Society Press, 2009.

"Helena as She Was." Website. http://www.helenahistory.org/.

Leaphart, Susan, ed. "Frieda and Belle Fligelman: A Frontier-City Girlhood in the 1890s." *Montana: The Magazine of Western History* 32, no. 3 (Summer 1982).

Winestine, Belle Fligelman. "Mother Was Shocked." In *Montana: The Magazine of Western History*, Summer 1974.

Personal communications: Ellen Baumler, June 6, 2014; Susan Leaphart, May 4, 2014; Arnie Malina, April 19, 2012; Alex Swaney, April 21, 2014.

ISABELLE JOHNSON

Annin, Jim. *They Gazed on the Beartooths.* Vol. 1. Billings, MT: Reporter Printing and Supply Co., 1964.

Johnson, Isabelle. *Isabelle Johnson: 1901–1992.* Videotape and transcripts. Yellowstone Art Center, Billings, Mont.

———. Isabelle Johnson Collection. Museum of the Beartooths Archives, Absarokee, Mont.

McConnell, Gordon. *Making Connections.* Billings, MT: Yellowstone Art Museum, 2005.

Yellowstone Art Museum. *A Lonely Business: Isabelle Johnson's Montana.* Billings, MT: Yellowstone Art Museum, 2015.

Personal communications: Dan Aadland, September 1, 2016; Donna Forbes, September 17, 2013; Joe and Johanna Kern, September 17, 2013.

ALICE GREENOUGH ORR AND MARGIE GREENOUGH HENSON

Greenough Collection. Carbon County Museum Archives, Red Lodge, MT.

Jordan, Teresa. *Cowgirls: Women of the American West.* Lincoln: University of Nebraska Press, 1992.

LeCompte, Mary Lou. *Cowgirls of the Rodeo: Pioneer Professional Athletes.* Urbana and Chicago: University of Illinois Press, 1993.

Loeser, Doris. *I'll Ride That Horse! Montana Women Bronc Riders.* Videotape. KBYU and Rattatosk Films, 1994.

The Ridin' Greenoughs. Videotape. Rodeo Video Inc., 1989.

Ringley, Tom. *When the Whistle Blows: The Turk Greenough Story.* Greybull, WY: Pronghorn Press, 2008.

MYRNA LOY

Kotsilibas-Davis, James, and Myrna Loy. *Myrna Loy: Being and Becoming.* New York: Alfred A. Knopf, 1987.

Leider, Emily W. *Myrna Loy: The Only Good Girl in Hollywood.* Berkeley: University of California Press, 2011.

ALMA SMITH JACOBS

African Americans in Montana Heritage Resources Project. Website, Montana Historical Society, http://svcalt.mt.gov/research/AfricanAmerican/African AmericanInMT.asp.

Riley, Peggy. "Women of the Great Falls African Methodist Episcopal Church, 1870–1910." In *African American Women Confront the West, 1600-2000.* Quintard Taylor and Shirley Ann Wilson Moore, eds. Norman: University of Oklahoma Press, 2003.

Robison, Ken. "Alma Jacobs Memorial Plaza." Blog post. Historical Black Americans in Northern Montana. http://blackamericansmt.blogspot.com/2009/05/alma-jacobs-memorial-plaza.html.

———. "Everyone's Welcome at the Ozark Club: Great Falls, Montana's African American Nightclub." *Montana, the Magazine of Western History,* Summer 2012.

———. "'She is gentle, good, and virtuous': Exceptional Librarian & Community Leader Alma Smith Jacobs." In *The Best of Great Falls* 4, no. 4 (Winter 2012). Pdf. http://www.bestofgreatfalls.com/UserFiles/File/Best%20of%20Great%20 Falls%20Winter%202012.pdf.

Stix, Amy. "Lifting as She Climbed: The Libraries that Ms. Jacobs Built." *Montana Quarterly* 8, no 3 (Fall 2012).

Personal communications: Darlene Staffeldt, October 5, 2012; Ruth Parker McClendon, August 30, 2012; Patricia McNamer, October 26, 2012; Alan Thompson, various dates, June 2012 to November 2016.

ELOUISE PEPION COBELL

Cobell, Elouise. "The Power of Generations: Pursuing Social Justice through Sacred Relationships." Keynote speech, National Network of Grantmakers Conference, October 8 to 11, 2005. https://www.youtube.com/watch?v=HkEYFwrtlBw.

Kennedy, J. Michael. "Truth and Consequences on the Reservation." *Los Angeles Times,* July 7, 2002.

Ratledge, Mark. "The Burial of Elouise Cobell." *High Country News,* November 28, 2011.

Whitty, Julia. "Elouise Cobell's Accounting Coup." *Mother Jones,* September 1, 2005.

Women's International News Gathering Service. Interview with Elouise Cobell. "In Other Words" radio show, December 30, 2008. KUFM, University of Montana, Missoula.

Personal communications: Zita Bremner, November 9, 2014; Turk Cobell, November 12, 2014; Julene Kennerly, January 4, 2015.

Index

Note: Unless otherwise specified, towns listed are in Montana. *Italics* indicate graphics, pictures, or captions.

—Photo by Libby Langston/Christof Bango

Beth Judy grew up near Chicago and currently lives in Missoula. After receiving a BA from Harvard University, she moved to Atlanta, Georgia, where she worked in public health, the arts, and later, writing and publication services. In 1992, she moved to Missoula and earned an MFA in creative writing at the University of Montana. From 1994 to 2014, she was a producer at Montana Public Radio, where she was known for her medicinal-plants program, "The Plant Detective." As a freelance writer, Beth has written for "Prairie Home Companion" and *Montana Magazine*, among other publications. She loves history, traveling, nature, and her home in Montana.